THE ETERNAL WARRIOR'S SMILE

THE CANDID GUIDE TO A GREAT LIFE

Rhett Ogston

Printed in Australia

First Printing: Sept 2020
Shawline Publishing Group
www.shawlinepublishing.com.au

ISBN-13

9780648733591 Paperback

9780648827610 Ebook

ABOUT THE AUTHOR

Rhett Ogston has been providing life-changing experiences for individuals all over the world for over twenty years. Some were so inspired that they nominated Rhett for Australian of the Year multiple times, first in 2015. Having years of experience in the field of healing as a doctor of Chinese medicine, life coach, remedial therapist, Reiki master, and the world's first Advanced BodyTalk™ Practitioner, Rhett is positioned to offer you the most relevant, up-to-date, no-nonsense information to support you in your thriving process.

Rhett is the founder of Qi Health Clinic Pty Ltd, and has developed various 'innate healing systems' under the umbrella of Rhett Ogston Applications (ROAs). Rhett's signature ROAs are FlameTree: *the personal development & healing system*, and his lifestyle and exercise program 409 Degrees – *Just hold it.*

Rhett is committed to serving people and has the knowledge, insight, understanding, skill, and heart to reach out to people. He is a student of life, always continuing to deepen and expand his understanding, knowledge, and awareness of life. Throughout his career, Rhett has successfully assisted people to resolve their symptoms and dis-eases, while simultaneously helping them to find true health and enhancing the quality of their life expression and experiences. He is continually seeking to expand his own knowledge and demonstrates an unusually high level of commitment to his clients.

Rhett is passionate about helping people who suffer from symptoms and dis-eases to find their optimal self through *Being* in alignment, synergy, authenticity, and synergism so that they can live their life of purpose. He has an openness for possibility and an uncanny ability to help people see the constraints holding them back in life. Rhett is committed to making a difference and transforming people's lives all over the world, having practised in Australia, America, Holland, China, Thailand, Fiji, and Canada.

Rhett's mother was the victim of a careless driver in her youth. As a result of the accident, she was left with a damaged spine, which caused all sorts of pain for her. From a very young age, Rhett began alleviating his mother's pain and suffering. From this experience, he realised he wanted to heal people — and he had a gift for it! As soon as he could afford it, he enrolled in every short course on massage available to him at the time. Although he always knew he wanted to heal people, it was around the age of fourteen that people started telling him, 'You really need to think about what you want to do in life.' So, this got him pondering the future, and initially, he thought he wanted to become a doctor of Western medicine. However, in the end, his love for science won. He spent five years and completed his bachelor of science (Honours) at Melbourne

University, learning all there was to know about every possible science, ranging from anatomy to physics.

During his final year, he was invited to become involved in an Honours project, which investigated the immunomodulatory properties of Chinese herbs — in short, using the science knowledge he had gained to scientifically prove an ancient healing method. It can be said that completing his Honours degree and proving scientifically the beneficial effects of an age-old medicinal system, as well as adding to the collective body of knowledge of science, was a great attainment for him.

After a short stint in the United States, he returned and completed a degree encompassing Chinese medicine and human biology at RMIT. Rhett was a self-funded student and worked many varied jobs such as fresh-produce manager, night fill manager, bakery attendant, labourer, landscaper, barman, gaming-machine attendant, bouncer, waiter, writer, presenter and scientist, to name a few. The three most valuable things he learned from this experience were:

- He did not wish to work for bosses driven only by dollars (therefore he needed to be self-employed).
- Working in these jobs made him realise his true passion lay in helping people.
- He wanted to make sufficient money to lead a happy life.

Therefore, he became a healer, using any technique that he found that has the ability to heal people. From these experiences evolved Rhett Ogston Applications (ROAs) and he has now extended this healing principle into writing books to help more people worldwide and achieve his goal of rapidly and dynamically transforming the world! Rhett's belief is best stated by Socrates, who once said:

I know you won't believe me, but the highest form of human excellence is to question one's self and others.[1]

His life has been one of continuous striving, an unremitting sadhana (dedication to learning something), a relentless search for truth — not abstract or metaphysical truth, but the truth that can be realised in human relations. All that he has learned is presented to you in all of his books and ROAs with the intent that it may help you in your life as much as it has helped him and his clients.

Information is knowledge, but applied knowledge is wisdom. Wisdom changes your life, so please apply the information in this book to your life and benefit from the power of wisdom. Some of the concepts presented are not easy to understand, but Rhett has made every effort to ensure the information is presented in an easy-to-understand format. In saying this, we might look to Socrates's student Plato, who criticises the written transmission of knowledge as faulty, favouring instead the spoken logos: *He who has knowledge of the just and the good and beautiful ... will not, when in earnest, write them in ink, sowing them through a pen with words which cannot defend themselves by argument and cannot teach the truth effectually.*[2]

The same argument is repeated in Plato's Seventh Letter:

Every serious man, in dealing with really serious subjects, carefully avoids writing ... I can certainly declare concerning all these writers who claim to know the subjects which I seriously study ... there does not exist, nor will there ever exist, any treatise of mine dealing therewith. [Such secrecy is necessary in order not] to expose them to unseemly and degrading treatment.[3]

Rhett also agrees with the Socratic paradox of 'I know that I know nothing'.[4] It is hoped that you will enjoy, learn and apply the wisdom he shares with you so that you can strive to be at your highest form of human excellence and live your life of purpose to achieve the ROA motto... Live optimally, Live purposely.

Imagination is everything,
It is a preview of life's coming attractions.
(Albert Einstein, 1879–1955)

Whatever the mind can conceive and believe, it can achieve.
(Napoleon Hill, 1883–1970)

Disclaimer

Rhett Ogston

This book is dedicated to Carmen Maré (6 January 1923 – 17 February 2017)

Rhett Ogston

INTRODUCTION

The potential of humankind starts with you, especially you!
Rhett Ogston

What does 'The potential of humankind starts with you, especially you!' mean? It means that you must eternally strive in life to be a warrior and not a worrier. You may achieve this by knowing the introductory elements (discussed below) to the awakening process and following the various strategies from the 'The Eternal Warriors Smile' (this book). By applying these strategies, you may overcome your self-imposed limiting beliefs, or as what I refer to them, as 'eternal worrier beliefs', so that you are 'Being' (discussed below) the eternal warrior. The question you need to ask yourself now is: Are you authentically *Being* the eternal warrior, or are you, in fact, the eternal worrier of your life? You may have romanticised being a warrior as seen in the movies, and you would most likely want to identify yourself as being the warrior because society perceives the warrior as strong, gallant and so on, yet a closer investigation of your life as it is unfolding before your eyes may reveal that you are not *really Being* the eternal warrior of your life, let alone the warrior who can assist humankind to reach its potential. Before you can authentically answer the question above, what you need to firstly consider is that 'eternal' refers to *always* actively *Being* the warrior, where you are consistently, every single day, training and fulfilling your essential needs while living life optimally and purposefully. Secondly, if you are not constantly actively *Being* the eternal warrior, you are functioning sub-optimally. The outcome of functioning sub-optimally is that what you don't use, you lose, and this will transform any warrior into a worrier!

Now that you are beginning to understand the meaning of *Being* an eternal warrior, chances are that your answer to the above question is that you are more than likely currently being a worrier, that is worrying about:

- your savings/financial future, financial obligations/credit card debts, paying your bills and making your rent or mortgage repayments
- job security, meeting work targets or goals
- your ageing appearance/physique, generally getting old, your health and dietary intake, your lack of exercise
- your relationships (whether you find the right partner/whether your current partner is right for you/whether your partner still loves you/a friend or family member you have fallen out with or who may be ill/whether you are a good parent/raising your children right and so on)
- leaving your house open or having someone steal something from your home, car or work and this list goes on!

Despite wanting to be a warrior, if any of the above is true for you, then your current reality is that you are a *worrier!*

If you are still uncertain whether you may be a worrier, I suggest that you rate the six issues below (if you have not already done so on the ROA website) to discover whether you are.

The test: Are you a worrier or warrior?

Rate each of the following issues from 1 to 5, where 1 reflects no concern and 5 reflects greatest concern:

1. Not having an income (security of money)
   1 2 3 4 5
2. Not having a place to live (security of shelter)
   1 2 3 4 5
3. Not having a plan to follow for a specific activity (security of knowing)
   1 2 3 4 5

4. Plans fail to go the way you expected (self-esteem)

1 2 3 4 5

5. Having to face an illness, such as cancer (fear of
death)

1 2 3 4 5

6. Growing old/finding yourself alone (fear of
incapacity/loneliness)

1 2 3 4 5

Add each of your ratings together so that you achieve a total end score. If your score is 6, you are a warrior! You have a choice to continue reading or to stop now, but by making the choice to continue, you will learn the art of *Being* an inspired, authentic warrior, living life optimally and purposefully, as explained later in this book (unless, that is, you are already doing so). If your score is between 7 and 18, you are a mild worrier, and if it is 19 and above, you are an intense worrier. The good news for any worrier is that, by reading this book, you will learn that creating change from being a worrier to *Being* a warrior is possible. If, after rating the questions above, you discover that you are classified as a warrior, then this book will still assist you to further enhance your warrior abilities. Either way, you will have a win by reading this book.

Now that you have established your worrier/warrior status, why is this book essential reading for you, regardless of your status? Because when I was growing up, I cannot recall being taught by my family, school or university how to be the eternal warrior of my life to live optimally and purposefully! I do recall being told that I had the potential to be 'anything I wanted to be', but instead of being taught the skills of an eternal warrior, as this book does, I was instead immersed in a world full of people who were eternal worriers — from observing my parents worrying about work, paying bills, looking good, having manners, not being late, to students worrying about results at school and not upsetting their teachers, completing their homework on time, passing exams to continue on with their education, or not being accepted for who they are in their life by those around them. This is certainly not the environment that creates eternal warriors!

I certainly don't remember seeing 'Being a successful eternal warrior in life 101' on the syllabus at school or university! If it was there, I would have enrolled in it, as I'm certain you would have, given the amount of worry and distress currently occurring in the world. I also recall that, when the worriers in my life were informing me that I had the potential to be anything I wanted to be, it was often associated with a glass ceiling. Said another way, 'You can be anything you want, but don't dream *too* big', which may be another worry associated with the 'tall poppy syndrome' as referred to in Australia, or the worry about disappointment if you don't reach your dreams. The popular story of a flea in a jar springs to mind. Although I have not tested it personally and cannot find any results of a test, I use it here because it is a useful illustration of my key message about how this book may assist you.

If you haven't heard the flea story, it goes something like this. If you place a flea in glass jar, it can at any time jump straight out of the jar (fleas are well known for their jumping prowess). If you want to stop the flea from escaping its glass prison, you just pop a lid on the jar.

After several attempts of jumping into the lid, the flea quickly learns that jumping optimally causes pain (i.e. smacking into the lid). The flea, having established the belief that every time it jumps to its optimal potential, pain is felt, adapts its behaviour, and will jump sub-optimally to avoid the pain of crashing into the lid.

The height the flea now jumps to becomes its self-imposed limiting belief. Even after the lid is removed, the flea will continue jumping sub-optimally to a height just below the now absent lid to avoid reproducing the pain! The flea is now contained within the glass jar even without the lid, and its self-imposed limiting belief will prevent it from ever reaching its optimal potential and life purpose as a free-roaming flea. It is trapped, and will continue being trapped because of its adapted self-imposed limiting behaviour until:

- it spontaneously jumps optimally again and rediscovers that its optimal jumping potential does not cause pain (given that there is no lid)
- new fleas are introduced into the glass jar that don't have this self-imposed belief and the conditioned flea observes the unconditioned fleas jumping out of the jar
- the flea makes a conscious choice to change its current self-imposed limiting belief, allowing it to jump optimally again, despite the past physical and emotional pain.

How does this story of a flea in a jar (an analogy for life) relate to you? Firstly, you may have been told the 'you have the potential to be anything you want to be' story, and essentially, as a newborn/toddler, you were *Being* the optimal you, living your life at your full potential. But the analogy here is that you, like the flea, were conditioned by your environment (e.g. your family, society and culture) as you were developing into a child/teenager/adult, and as such, you have accepted various limitations (the glass ceiling) that may have occurred because of, for example, emotional, physical or mental pain created by expressing yourself optimally, but not in the way that was accepted by your environment. This has then prevented you (the self-imposed limiting beliefs) from listening to your innate wisdom (discussed later in this book) and from living your life optimally and purposefully. This has occurred without you even realising it! It is more than likely that these self-imposed limiting belief systems (the glass ceiling) are occurring unconsciously for you, which will also be explained in more detail later in this book.

You may, however, have already noticed this glass ceiling limitation, but not have associated it with how you are feeling through your emotional reactions to life events — you are being a worrier without realising that this is what you are doing. If you read this book from cover to cover, I may assist you with your understanding of how this might occur by raising your consciousness to accept that you are a worrier with self-imposed limiting beliefs that prevent you from reaching your optimal potential and life purpose, and then empowering you with the knowledge and tools that might enable you to remove, or crash through, your self-imposed glass ceiling/limiting belief so that you may begin to transform from being a worrier to Being a warrior.

Throughout this book, I discuss with you how you can best achieve your optimal potential and live your life's purpose. The information contained within this book is invaluable, provided that you are coachable. If you are coachable, then through this book, I will be your personal coach, coaching you on how to learn about the Law of Creation and who you are Being (which are discussed in more detail in chapter 8), and how the two may integrate in order to better explain the world you currently live in, and how this might assist you to create change in your life so that you may transform from a worrier to a warrior in order to live optimally and purposefully. I emphasise here that, when you focus yourself with the eternally Being aspect of life, what you may very soon realise is, not only your own optimal potential and life's purpose, but also your potential to play an important role in assisting humankind in reaching our potential.

The two quotes that you read above by Einstein and Hill were not randomly placed there to take up space or for mere motivation. They were specifically selected to illustrate the point that great minds, such as Einstein and Hill, already had an understanding that your imagination and mind shape your life's reality. This is true, but when you understand and are focused on what I refer to as eternally 'Being', integrated with my understanding of the Law of Creation, you have the potential to achieve anything you put your mind to, provided that, as mentioned before, you are coachable and you are also able to accept (discussed below as the first element of the awakening process) the fact that you are a worrier with self-imposed limiting belief systems at work preventing you from reaching your optimal potential and life's purpose, and by knowing this, you are willing to make the choice to remove these self-imposed limitations (or the glass lid, as told in the story of the flea in a jar above).

Prior to discussing further where these self-imposed limiting belief systems may arise from, it is important to understand my meaning above that you need to understand and focus on *Being*. Unlike the accepted dictionary definition of being, *Being* involves four elements — alignment, synergy, authenticity and synergism — and is defined as '***actively existing***' in a reality where all possibilities are achievable and available to you, where everything in your life flows with the energies of the universe (the Uni-code — discussed more in chapter 7), harmoniously and peacefully'. An emphasis is placed on ***actively existing***, because you need to be actively doing something, like the warrior, to create the necessary changes in your life for living optimally and purposefully. You will also note that *Being* involves both synergy and synergism. Although you could argue these are the same thing, they are not in this regard. Synergy refers to trusting that the Uni-code will be expressed through your bio-electric code and guide you in life. Said another way, it is *Being* on the right path at the right time, where your life occurs with ease and flow. Synergism, however, refers to all the interactions or cooperation between two or more bio-electric and chemical signals and cues, organisations, substances and other agents to produce a combined effect greater than the sum of their separate parts.

I found the need to redefine 'being' based on interactions with a diverse number of people from all over the world who are not actively participating in their life and who are not in alignment, synergy, authenticity or synergism (*Being*), yet they are expecting changes to occur! These people are examples of eternal worriers who have been conditioned with the self-imposed limiting belief of what I refer to as the 'something for nothing disease', and are passively being!

Due to this observation, I generalise that humanity (which includes you) is currently facing a pandemic of worriers who suffer the 'something for nothing disease'. The point that needs to be emphasised here is that, when you repeatedly do ***nothing*** (suffering the 'something for nothing disease'), this insidiously leads you down the slippery slope of *dis*-ease, *dis*-harmony and sub-optimal living! When doing nothing is allowed to continue because you think it is easier and more comfortable than doing something (anything), you are, without realising it, leading yourself down the pathway to trouble. You won't change this direction because of your self-imposed limiting belief system that doing nothing will not harm you. On the contrary, the long-term consequence for doing nothing is high, and paradoxically becomes very uncomfortable! I emphasis here that this is not a judgement on you (or humanity), and the cause for this 'something for nothing disease' pandemic is very different to what Brian Tracey refers to in his book *Something for nothing*, where he suggests that we are just inherently wired this way![1] Although it is also suggested by Stein et al. that the worrier with 'something for nothing disease', who is passively being is a behavioural phenotype that reflects the action of multiple different genes[2], you will learn in chapter 4 that you are not a victim of your genes! On the contrary, by reading this book, you will learn the skills that not only assist you personally but will contribute to you becoming part of the global solution to this pandemic. It is therefore essential that you make a mental note of this *Being* definition, because whenever you see the word *Being* written this way, it indicates exactly what I have redefined, as opposed to the dictionary definition of the word 'being'.

Now that you have appointed me as your coach, and you have begun to grasp the idea of *Being*, had the pandemic facing you (and humanity) — the 'something for nothing disease' brought to your attention — and have also accepted that you are possibly this worrier with self-imposed limiting beliefs, hopefully this has not only got you thinking, but seeking the answer to where your self-imposed limitations came from and how can you change this situation.

Let's first start with answering how self-imposed belief systems occur. This is multi-factorial; that is, your limitations come from your society, parents, teachers, friends, partners, children, the news, in fact, from everywhere within your environment!

Limiting beliefs can only become self-limiting if you choose to accept them as true, and as a newborn/toddler developing into a child/teenager/adult, you had no choice but to accept the limiting beliefs taught to you within your environment as your truth, as explained with the story of the flea in the jar.

It stands to reason that the easiest way to avoid being conditioned to limiting beliefs would be to stop accepting them as true and remove all the factors that caused them in the first place! This may appear to be impossible for you to achieve, and would result in solitary confinement with no stimuli! An easier, more practical method is to remove your conditioning and brainwashing from you so that all your self-imposed limiting beliefs and messages just don't register — in a way, you become immune to them. The method for removing your conditioning and brainwashing may at first seem unusual or implausible to you, but this may change as you continue reading this book, because I will coach you through each of the steps, elements, components and processes that might assist you to create this change so that you can then be open to the possibility of reaching your optimal potential and living your life purposefully.

The first element in this process of overcoming your self-imposed limiting beliefs is to realise and accept that you have been conned, you have been duped, and you have been lied to by almost everyone in your life, and this is the direct cause of your self-imposed limiting beliefs and you being the eternal worrier! Yes, everyone! Parents, partners, siblings, family, friends, employees, governments, multinational companies, the media — the list goes on! Yes, this is a big statement to make, and may, and as it did for me, come as a shock to you. But your first step to accepting this reality is to allow me as your coach to help you unpack this statement in more detail so that you are better able to process and understand this first element. By making this choice, you too may begin your transformation from being an eternal worrier to *Being* an eternal warrior, who is immune to the 'something for nothing disease', and is actively *Being* and is living life optimally and purposefully.

Once you get over the shock of realising that you have been lied to and that you have been living your life as the eternal worrier with self-imposed limiting beliefs, as I did, you are now ready to move onto the second element of the awakening process, which is feeling angry, or at least mad. Yes, I am saying that the second element is making the choice to right now feel angry or mad! Let's face it, nothing in your life ever changes until you say, 'That is it. I've had it up to here and I will not stand for it anymore!' This is one of the main functions of the emotion of anger, which rarely gets acknowledged as a healthy emotional response — it provides you with enough emotional and mental energy to force a change in your life by breaking through your glass ceiling. This book is all about change, so if you feel anger, then embrace it, the caveat here being to use your feeling of anger as it is naturally intended — as a dynamic force to bring about a healthy change in your life and crash through your glass ceiling, not something destructive or abusive. Unfortunately, anger is poorly stereotyped in society, and as a result, it is poorly expressed by most of us (e.g. reactively yelling at someone, physically abusing someone or objects). When used destructively, the healthy force of anger is inherently wasted!

I would ask you to consider for a moment this second element in the awakening process of using anger for the emotional and mental energy to make a change in your life. Think back to that exact point in your life when you thought, 'It's really too hard to change, I am not even angry about it and I choose to not try?' So instead of choosing to feel angry enough to create change, you chose to give up and not fight any more. Can you recall it? If you can't recall it, you are not alone! Most people cannot recall the specific moment when this occurred. Why? Because there is no one single event! The acceptance of self-imposed limiting beliefs is in fact insidious in nature, and comes on so slowly that you do not actually realise that this process of sub-optimal conditioning (just like the flea in the jar) is happening! Some people vehemently deny it has happened to them, but the reality is we are or have been at a time a victim of this! Even when people realise the blatant truth that they have indeed 'quit' their life of Being the warrior, living optimally, living purposefully, this is still not enough of a trigger to inspire them to instigate an immediate change in their life to crash through their glass ceiling! This may come as another shock to you, but it shouldn't! There are two main reasons why a lack of healthy anger occurs, even when you realise that you are living sub-optimally with these self-imposed limiting belief systems (i.e. when you are living your life as the worrier): (1) you do not want to take responsibility, and (2) you have fear.

This is where I introduce to you what I refer to as the 'river and canoe' analogy for life. You see, there are, in my opinion, two types of people who get in a canoe: those who do paddle (they are Being the eternal warrior who is immune to the 'something for nothing disease', actively Being the inspired go-getter paddler who takes responsibility, living their life optimally and with purpose), and those who do not paddle (they are being the worrier, 'something for nothing disease' sufferer, passively being the lazy drifter who has no life's purpose and blames everyone and everything else for their life). Although I assume that you have a clearer picture of the warrior and worrier, let's look at one last example that is aimed at offering you a further explanation of what I mean by these two types of people who get into a canoe.

Let's say, for example, five people get into a canoe and are all given paddles. At first, everyone is excited and paddles, but eventually, once all the excitement is over (or sometime sooner), you will see the true colour/character of these people. Some (the worriers) get bored easily and then rely on the other, more enthusiastic paddlers (the warriors), who take responsibility to do the work for them by paddling. If you don't have a canoe and river handy and would like to know the character of a person, then here is a hint. I recommend you play a game with them for an afternoon! Game-playing may also reveal a person's true character, and if someone gives up easily or quits the game, you can bet that this will be their reaction to the game of life.

Now let's return to the 'river and canoe' analogy for life. If you see behaviour such as the worrier, then you can almost guarantee what kind of person they are in life. Can you guess? This is the type of person who, when in the canoe alone, will believe they have no control over where they end up; that is, they may appear to make the choice to paddle, but if they do, it is short-lived, and they are, in fact, glad for the currents of the river to do the work for them, carrying them along to wherever the river takes them, hence why they are referred to as drifters. This means they now get to blame the river when they get washed up on the shore, tipped over, stuck in dead water, or end up in part of the river where they didn't want to be. Even if the river did lead them to a place, they thought was good, they then blame it on fate or destiny that they ended up somewhere they believed was a good place to end up! In other words, irrespective of where the river current took them (a good or bad place), it was not their fault for getting there. After all, it was the river or fate that took them there, not them! They get to blame the river or something else for wherever they end up!

A question to ask yourself now: would you want a worrier ('something for nothing disease' sufferer, passively being the lazy drifter who has no life's purpose and blames everyone and everything else for their life) in your canoe or in your life? As revealed to you at the beginning of this book, **you** are a little like that! This is not to offend you, but to awaken you! Stop now for a moment and ponder the question: Do you think the worrier would ever start *really* paddling again? Well, they do sometimes, but only for quite significant reasons — that is, it's a life changing reason, such as an emotional shock, that forces them to paddle, shocking them back into action! However, this shock is again out of their control — they are still being the worrier! For example, this type of person may change their actions due to the unexpected shock of a partner leaving them, by being fired from their job, or by a near-death experience, because they were not focused on what they were doing in the first place, that is, they were not *Being* the warrior who is immune to the 'something for nothing disease', actively *Being* the inspired go-getter paddler who takes responsibility for their life, living their life optimally and with purpose!

When was the last time you experienced a life crisis that made you question how you saw your life, even if only for a split second? Did you start paddling again, that is, did you change your actions, albeit for a short period? If you did, how long did it take for you to stop paddling again, to go back to your previous behaviour and actions? The probability of this occurring very quickly is high, because unless that reason for change (a life crisis) comes along, then you are still being the worrier! You have not changed your actions to enable you to successfully transform from being the eternal worrier to Being the eternal warrior.

To further illustrate this point made by the 'river and canoe' analogy for life, I will share with you a real-life story about my old gym buddy. Now, this gym buddy really wanted to work for a supermarket that he had an interest in, but he was working in the family business. The buddy felt that he had no choice but to continue working in the family business that he disliked immensely, exacerbated by the very poor pay and long working hours. This buddy never discussed his feelings about the low hourly rate with his boss (his dad) because he just accepted that this choice was made for him and he had no control over it, although he complained endlessly about the long hours, the low rate of pay and the actual work itself. For me, it didn't make sense that my buddy believed that he wanted to work for a supermarket in a job he had tried and enjoyed, yet he stayed in a job that he complained about constantly! I spent many an hour coaching my gym buddy around what he really wanted to do in his life, but he continually reinforced his position of wanting to work in a supermarket because it was something he had tried and immensely enjoyed, but the decision was already made to stay in the family business. Whenever he showed his anger towards the family business, despite being prompted to re-evaluate his life choices, he would default to his standard answer of, 'I work in the family business. Oh well, nothing I can do about it now!' The translation of this response, now that you understand the point of the 'river and canoe' analogy for life above is: 'The river (my family business job) is in control of my canoe (my life)'. My gym buddy was being the worrier ('something for nothing disease' sufferer, passively being the lazy drifter who blamed everyone and everything else for his life situation!).

The flip side to this 'river and canoe' analogy for life is the other type of person in the canoe. Yes, that's right — the person who gets in that canoe and paddles passionately. This type of person is Being the warrior (immune to the 'something for nothing disease', actively Being the inspired go-getter paddler who takes responsibility, living their life optimally and with purpose) and is dedicated to getting the job done. They like to be challenged and they may want to race people in another canoe to the next bend in the river or to reach the next bank. They are prepared to do the paddling for the entire canoe of worriers if they must, so that they can get to where they are going, despite the risk of being blamed by the worriers for wherever their destination ends up being. Nothing stops this person paddling because they are 'in the zone', that is, they are *Being* (in alignment, synergy, authenticity and synergism). Those *Being* the eternal warrior enjoy the buzz they feel while in the zone and the feeling of knowing their purpose, and as such, they are actively in control of where they and their canoe are going and are inspired do whatever it takes to get there.

Are you actively participating in your life with a clear purpose, and inspired to maintain your focus so that you achieve your goals? This is what *Being* the eternal warrior of your life is all about, and what you — and every other person — most probably desires to be. The question that inevitably arises is: How do you stop being the worrier? Understanding and applying the next two elements in the awakening process allows you to change and overcome your self-imposed limiting beliefs. The third element of awakening to *Being* an eternal warrior is knowing your purpose. Using the 'river and canoe' analogy for life, no river is going to control where the warrior goes, unlike the worrier. The decision that you must now make is — who do you want to be like? Do you want to be the warrior or worrier? Before you consider your answer, you need to know the fourth element to awakening and *Being* the eternal warrior, and that element is flexibility.

You need to be flexible with your self-imposed limiting belief systems and your thinking. Being flexible is something that you most likely associate with your physical body, and while it is an asset in relation to physical fitness, it may also influence your thinking. Although it is important that you know where you are going (purpose), and have the power (inspiration) to get there, *Being* flexible about where you are going will aid you more than being rigid about it. This reinforces the saying, 'it's better to bend than to break'. Using the 'river and canoe' analogy for life to illustrate the meaning of *Being* flexible, let's say that you made the choice of *Being* a warrior and you decided that you were going to race another person across the river. In this scenario, you are in your own individual canoes, and both you and your opponent strike out hard. As you both reach the dead centre of the river, you are level, but suddenly you both encounter a strong current in the water. Now at this point in the race, you both have the same two choices: either paddle harder against the current in order to reach the bank, and as a consequence become completely physically exhausted and potentially not reach the goal, or make the choice to let the strong current push you away from your goal temporarily, where you are able to relax and go with the flow until that time when the strong current has lessened so the choice of paddling hard again is possible. This choice of action prevents you from becoming physical exhausted and leaves you energy for resuming the paddling to complete your goal of reaching the opposite bank, albeit slightly downstream.

I propose this question to you: Why would you exhaust yourself if you know your life's purpose and where you are going? If you know your purpose, you innately have the inspiration, drive and power to achieve your goals, and if you know who you are Being, that is you are Being the warrior of your life, then nothing is going to stop you! Provided you know who you are Being, follow the Law of Creation and actively listen (discussed more in chapter 8), does making a choice that saves you energy and may show you a different part of the river (as per the example above) really make any difference to you living your life optimally and purposefully? No! Why? Because you are still making the choice to be flexible. Based on the scenario above, the eternal warrior would be choosing to chill out waiting until the strong current was calmer, while making the choice to enjoy the scenery and then resume paddling, knowing that they had never once stopped taking their focus off reaching their goal.

This begs the question, why do people *not* choose to be flexible in their life? Simple. As explained above with worrier behaviour, you still get to *blame* someone or something in your life for maybe how crummy, unhappy, unfulfilling or even happy it is, and so on. Stop for a moment and reflect on this question: Who do *you* blame in your life?

There is no judgement attached to this question, it's simply for the purpose of raising your consciousness that blame is actually a part of your life without you consciously realising it. The reality here is that people continually blame. Listen for it and you will hear it everywhere, for example:

> '*I would have done more with my life, but I had children.*'
>
> '*I would have got that promotion if *insert name* didn't get hired.*'
>
> '*I would have gone overseas but I had to work.*'
>
> '*I feel happy when the sun is out and the weather is warm.*'
>
> '*Winter makes me feel depressed and makes my joint pains worse*'.
>
> '*You make me feel loved and appreciated.*'

This list could go on and on. Blame is everywhere!

Blaming someone or something **may** help you sleep better at night or make you feel better about yourself and your life, but the cost of blaming is huge. Every time you blame someone or something, you are relinquishing control of your own life. You make yourself a slave to circumstance, and you lose power to change the situation. In doing so, you obstruct the Law of Creation and you stop *Being* the warrior, by default being the worrier. At this point in the book, I am aware that, given the reality of blame and the potential reluctance to take ownership of what's occurring in your life, there must be a payoff to keep blaming — but what is the payoff? The reality of blaming is that you automatically remove the responsibility from yourself and place it on someone or something else, and in so doing you receive one or more of the following payoffs:

1. being able to avoid responsibility or consequence
2. being able to avoid success or failure
3. being able to avoid failure, but can claim success (the coat-tail rider).

These three payoff reasons for blaming are discussed in more detail below so that you can see that, not only is the logic of blaming flawed, but blaming comes at a heavy cost to the person whose self-imposed limiting belief system justifies blame as a viable option to choose in their life.

Payoff reason 1 – being able to avoid responsibility or consequence

How can you really avoid responsibility or consequence? It has been part of your life for so long you probably don't even know it's there! Let's give you an example that supports this assertion. Recall back at school, if you didn't complete your homework tasks on time, you would have been held accountable for it; not do it again, and you may have received detention. What are the consequences if you are not responsible in paying your rent or home loan repayments? What would occur if you didn't turn up to work? So realistically, you live in a world of responsibility and consequence, but by being the worrier, there is a false sense of reality that you get to avoid responsibilities and consequences — you don't!

Payoff reason 2 – being able to avoid success or failure

Essentially, everything you do will have an associated self-imposed limiting belief system relating to either a success or failure. For example, once you enter a venture and you have tasks that you are responsible for, there are ultimately only two outcomes that can occur: success or failure.

No one likes failure, and by blaming others for things going wrong, you get to avoid failure. Why do you make failing feel so bad? Because you mistakenly take the failure personally, believing that you have failed (which is discussed in more detail in chapter 1), and having this belief doesn't feel so good!

As strange as it sounds, most people also fear success. You may say that you want to be successful, but what happens when you **are** successful? People notice you!

Traditionally, the fear of public speaking (people listening to you) ranks higher than the fear of death in surveys. This may indicate that people would rather die than be noticed (being successful). Either way, blaming someone or something else gives you a false sense of security that you may avoid success or failure.

Payoff reason 3 – being able to avoid failure but can claim success (the coat-tail rider) Although this may appear like payoff reason 2, it is different. This is usually associated with you taking the backseat role in something, where someone else is responsible for the outcomes. In this scenario, there are two possible outcomes:

- You don't have to be responsible for being the leader whose name is 'on the line' when you let someone else lead and they take responsibility. If the leader pulls the team through, then you obtain the recognition of being on the successful team, which means you achieved success, without being noticed. The only catch here is that, by not being actively involved as the leader, you didn't play *big*; therefore, you will never win *big*. Simple, isn't it? If you play small, you can only win small.
- You avoid being responsible and being the leader (the person who is responsible for the task succeeding or failing). The payoff here is that, if the task fails, the person leading would ultimately bear the responsibility for this failure. This means that you, yet again, get to 'avoid' the consequences of being responsible. In addition to this, you are also in the position to sit back and say, 'Told you so!' For example, 'I told you this task would not work.'

This means that you get to live a life of 'being right' based on the faulty belief that you need to avoid being wrong at all costs! Living life in this way means that you never get to be the person who tries and makes it, and you will also never be the person who tried and didn't make it, as will be discussed further in chapter 1. This is based on trying to avoid fear, for example, fear of failing. Instead of *Being* the warrior, you are being the worrier, and all you will ever be is the person everyone eventually dislikes because they know if they try and they don't make it, you will be there waiting to say, 'Told you so', and if they do make it, you are there accepting recognition from their success! Eventually, this behaviour results in no one wanting you on their team because you are perceived as too negative! Subconsciously, you may also be wanting the person who is *Being* the warrior to fail (and you are probably unconsciously sabotaging their efforts, even if it is as simple as not performing as well as you could), just so you get to say, 'I told you so'. The question I want you to think about here for a moment goes like this: Is it really that important for you to be right? When you read through chapter 1, your answer will become clear.

Once you begin to understand and see that the above three payoffs are prevalent in your life because you are being the worrier, and once you realise that you have been conned, duped and lied to about life, which reinforces the worrier reality, then this should make you feel angry, as discussed above! Why? Because possibly for the first time in your life you may have realised that you *have* been the person holding yourself back from finding your optimal potential and living your life of purpose, because of your self-imposed belief systems. Once you have made this realisation, I encourage you to use the healthy expression of anger (as discussed above) to fire yourself up so that you can finish reading this book in order to begin making healthy and lasting changes from being the eternal worrier to *Being* the eternal warrior, immune to the 'something for nothing disease', actively *Being* the inspired go-getter paddler who takes responsibility for their life, living their life optimally and with purpose and flexibility. It's tempting, however, to fall into automatic reactionary behaviours where you rant and rave about being wronged and so on, and then immediately fall back into either settling or quitting. Either way, nothing changes in your life! Why? Because your perceived expectation of reality (which is explained in more detail in chapter 9) is currently set to believe it is easier to stay as you are than seek out the alternative, that is, to change. The payoff here is that you do not have to face responsibility and fear — there is less responsibility and fear when nothing changes!

By reading this book, you will soon realise that you can moan and complain for as much or as long as you choose, but this does not actually change anything. You are being the eternal worrier! You will also realise that being the worrier comes at a cost, and the reality that you have not yet consciously accepted is that the cost of moaning and complaining is extremely high! How much value do you place on living your life optimally and purposefully? Well, if nothing changes now, then this is what you are saying no to! The alternative, of course, is change. Yes, that scary 'c' word, which usually causes fear, because if something changes, then your whole inflexible view on life changes, which means anything can change! This is where taking responsibility and the fear of the unknown possibly paralyses you, because you are taking responsibility for something and no one can know what it will be and what it will cost when these changes occur. As a human, you were taught to fear what you don't know. You were also taught to fear taking responsibility for change because it usually places you outside of your comfort zone.

I want to make you aware that I purposely refer to you as having been 'taught' to fear. Why? Because when you observe a toddler, they are naturally inquisitive. Unlike most adults, toddlers rarely fear what they do not know. Toddlers dive straight in because they are inquisitive by nature, like other mammals (especially dolphins and apes), and have no fear of new things or change. That's not to say they fear nothing. We are all (including toddlers) innately fearful of things that will hurt us or cause us damage of any kind. In our current modernised urban society, even though we don't usually have to fear bears mauling us or cougar attacks, fear consumes us! Why is that? Let us take a closer look at our 'friend' fear in chapter 1.

The take-home message — your transformation from eternal _worrier_ to eternal _warrior_

The _eternal worrier smiles_ because they avoid responsibility and they get to blame someone or something else when things don't work out in their life. They are not aware of the four elements of the awakening process or Being and as such, they live in fear and suffer the 'something for nothing disease', passively being the lazy drifter who has no life purpose, blames everyone and everything else for their life, and is inflexible.

They continually allow the river to take them on their journey because of the payoffs of avoiding responsibility and consequence, avoiding failure and success, and they get to ride on the coat-tails of success and get to blame the river for where they end up.

The _eternal warrior smiles_ because they welcome responsibility and face their fears readily, with toddler-like enthusiasm. They know and accept the four elements of the awakening process and Being and are awake. They are prepared to make choices and know what they want in their life (purpose) and where they are heading. They are aware of the Law of Creation, understand the meaning of eternally Being, and are immune to the 'something for nothing disease', actively *Being* the inspired go-getter paddler who is living life optimally and flexibly. They work with the river, striking out willingly for what they want while *Being* flexible, so wherever they end up, they made the choice and took the responsibility for being there.

CHAPTER 1

Fear and laziness

When you change something, it means that you must be both 'listening' and prepared to take responsibility for making the desired change. *Being* the eternal warrior, who is immune to the 'something for nothing disease', actively *Being* the inspired adaptable go-getter paddler who takes responsibility for their life, living their life optimally with purpose, can allow you to implement these changes.

The eternal warrior actively listens to their innate wisdom, innately knows without question when a change is required, and implements the Law of Creation to create this change (which is discussed in more detail in chapter 8). The eternal worrier, however, does not listen to their innate wisdom! Why? Because they are emotionally reactive to life and therefore fail to listen! Instead, they are consumed by the 'something for nothing disease', passively drifting with no life purpose, accepting whatever offer is put in front of them. They continue to work in a job they do not like or have outgrown so they can continue paying to live or making repayments on materialistic things they regret buying and blame everyone and everything else for their life. The eternal worrier is inflexible, and very much aware that any change in their life requires effort.

If you are the eternal worrier, then even when you are prompted by some life-changing event, as discussed in the introduction, significant sustainable changes are short-lived because inevitably you stop listening to your innate wisdom again, and the desire or need to create and maintain change fades with the effort required, and your old patterns are reignited!

This inaction can be best described with one word, even if you don't like to be associated with that word — lazy. Let's face it, it is easier to accept things as they are (the gym buddy story from the introduction), and as ridiculous as it might sound, you will, for whatever reason, not consider yourself as special enough to warrant change in your life! Because of this, you don't have to put the effort into believing in yourself (laziness) or your fellow person for that matter (more laziness). Instead, you might get to sit there and criticise and blame everyone else who is doing better than you or does not see you as being special, as discussed in the previous chapter with the three payoffs (even more laziness).

As your coach, I understand that you may not like this self-discovery — that you are passively and inflexibly being the lazy drifter who blames everyone and everything else for your life! No one wants to be associated with this description, yet when you clear away all the smoke and mirrors, what's left is the reality that you unconsciously default to being the eternal worrier because you have not consciously made the choice to *Be* the eternal warrior. Each and every day that you fail to consciously make the choice of *Being* the eternal warrior, you are wiring your brain to your unconscious unhealthy bio-electric signals and cues.

I understand that behind the eternal worrier not making the choice to change is the emotion of fear — fear of the unknown and fear of making choices to change! Fear is usually the outcome when you are not listening to your innate wisdom, or you are unable to understand the messages relayed by your innate wisdom because you have never been taught to listen. This may create feelings of knowing that something needs to change, but you cannot quite identify exactly what it is or why it needs to change. If you can't trust in the changes needed, this creates fear. When you get stuck in both fear and laziness, you end up not changing your life (for the better) because you are immersed in being the eternal worrier, and this does not allow you to live your life optimally or purposefully!

If you feel that this assertion sounds unreasonable, then consider what's changed in your life over the past five years. Consider how you woke up this morning — did you wake up full of energy, inspired to be living because you are *Being* your optimal self and living your life's purpose? It's a simple answer of Yes or No, but I predict that you might say that you are 'trying to be ... [insert your own answer]. The 'trying' answer is inadequate! It's like using your credit card in an EFTPOS terminal, you will either have money in your account to pay for your purchase or you will not; you cannot be trying to have money in the account! Imagine for a moment what you would say to your significant other or children if they told you they did not want to go to work or school because they were fearful? Imagine yourself convincing them there is nothing to be fearful of, but they then tell you they don't wish to go to work or school because they are lazy, and they blame others for their fear of not going to work or school. What would you say? Would you encourage them to be the eternal warrior or to continue being the eternal worrier?

Imagine now a different scenario in which you have, for example, a child who tells you that they have it all worked out. They tell you that if they go to school and work hard, they will achieve good grades, and if they get good grades, they can obtain a scholarship. When they obtain their scholarship, they must achieve more, which will result in them getting even higher grades so that a company will headhunt them and they will obtain a job with a big multinational. They will then have to work harder while earning the dollars to live a comfortable life. Sounds like a reasonable career pathway, but then the child tells you that this all sounds too hard, they would rather be lazy and are fearful of failing, and it's what our society demands of us and they are not interested in conforming to society's dogma! What would you say? The chances are you would be conflicted with your answer!

Firstly, you would not allow your child to use the 'I am lazy and it all sounds too hard and fearful' reasons as a legitimate excuse for not going to school and doing their best, yet you would not want them to do something in their life only to conform to society's dogma. You know that they need to be doing something they are inspired about, because you innately know that when inspiration is the driving force to creating change in life, not only do things flow better, but you start listening and trusting in your innate wisdom.

Why then should laziness, fear, blaming others and 'it's all too hard' be acceptable for you? The answer to this is the fear of the unknown and the acceptance of the three payoff reasons discussed in the introduction, with the outcome of you getting to avoid failure. The fear of failure, however, keeps you stuck in being the eternal worrier.

This is where I need to assist you in redefining your fear of failing. The main reason you are being the worrier, using the above excuses, is because you are, by default, programmed with the software of fear. From the evolutionary point of view, our fears are built into us to assist us to stay alive. We do not acquire the complete life skills to ensure survival alone when born, unlike other mammals. You, and every other person born, is less than capable of surviving alone immediately after birth, and for at least the first ten months post birth, without the help of your mother/caregiver. However, although fear has helped to keep our ancestors alive, some of these fears are now outdated; for example, being attacked by a wild animal is highly unlikely in a metropolitan city these days. It's like your brain is using an outdated fear software. We were not born to fear everything. In fact, we are born to overcome our fears. Although fear is our primitive instinct (instinctive fear), many of the specifics of fear are learned only after birth (acquired fears), such as the fear of failing. So even if you do start listening to your innate wisdom, feeling and then thinking about doing the message that you actually hear from your innate wisdom (which inspires you), the existing default neural pathway associated with your acquired fear of failure activates. You immediately stop doing it because you have connected up in your mind that taking this inspired action will automatically lead to failure even before you try! Your overwhelming fear that you may fail, or the fear that these changes may not be understood or supported by others in your life, or the fear that these changes may appear to be uncharacteristic of you, takes over and leaves you impotent.

Essentially, you are making failing mean something (a self-imposed limiting belief system), for example, if you fail you will not be accepted by others, so the fear of failing and not being accepted is not an option! This occurs because, as previously discussed, you have been conditioned by society to fear, and you have been conditioned to believe that if you fail, something is wrong with you and you will not be accepted by others! The first step to changing this cycle is to change your self-imposed limiting belief systems about failure and acceptance. Let's use a mathematical like equation to illustrate this point:

1. You 'do' something for the first time + it didn't work = you are a failure!

2. So, by implication, the only way to achieve success is:

3. You 'do' something for the first time + it does work = you are a success!

Let's now extrapolate the logic (albeit it is faulty logic) that if you 'do' something and it doesn't work the first time, you are a failure, and therefore bad! Really? The question I ask you here is — when did you decide to personalise this? Stop for a moment and re-evaluate the equations above; wasn't it that your first attempt at doing something failed, therefore it was a bad attempt or an inadequate strategy, not *you* failing? I emphasise here that you cannot be a failure!

Although there appear to be only two outcomes from the above equations — one where you are a failure (bad), and the other where you are a success (good) — you will learn in chapter 6 that you cannot be a failure (bad) or a success (good)! This is based on faulty belief systems that you have adopted as your own (the self-imposed limiting belief systems) — you have been lied to and conned into believing this! In fact, you *do* have a choice of either 'feeling good' or 'feeling not good', irrespective of the outcome of the equations above. This will be discussed in more detail later, but what I want to present to you now is another way of looking at the above equations. There is no reason, apart from your current self-imposed limiting belief systems, why the above equations could not look more like this:

You 'do' something (for the first time) + it didn't work = lesson (the action you attempted didn't work) and you still get the choice to feel good.

You 'do' something (for the first time) + it worked = lesson (the action you attempted did work) and you still get the choice to feel good.

These equations are a more realistic interpretation of what can occur in your life. Making the choice to adopt this equation when interpreting your actions in attempting something establishes and increases the possibility of having something work — after all, how many times do you get something new right the first shot? Not many, but sometimes you do! An important equation that results from the above is:

Lesson + lesson = greater possibility of making an attempt work (and you still get to choose to feel good)

Or even better still:

Lesson = attempt works[2]

In other words, the more lessons you learn, the greater the chance of learning how to make something work, while choosing to feel good. Making the choice to feel good irrespective of the outcome is a characteristic of Being an eternal warrior!

Now that you have these new equations as a possible way of re-evaluating what you do in your life, you may be open to transforming from being the eternal worrier, who blames everyone and everything else for their life and is inflexible, to Being the eternal warrior, who is adaptable, flexible and immune to the 'something for nothing disease', and who takes responsibility for their life so that they are living an optimal life with purpose. So why, then, do you feel hesitant in embracing this new outlook on life?

Simple — as discussed above, you are fearful of failing.

This is where I want to ask you again — when was the last time you (or anyone else for that matter) attempted something and it worked flawlessly the first go? More importantly, when was the moment that you decided that by doing something and failing it meant that you had personally failed? To assist you to overcome this self-imposed limiting belief system, that only serves to breed and reinforce issues of being lazy, or fear of change or failure, I will draw your attention to some absolute masters of life who suffer none of these issues. These people are so amazing they have energy to last from dawn to dusk and are always inspired. They love new things, and rather than fear them, they embrace them and have no concerns about how they look to themselves or others. Who are these masters? Toddlers!

As previously discussed, have you ever seen a toddler think about how they look or what other people think about them? No! Have you ever observed a toddler needing motivation to get out of bed or be motivated to play? No! Toddlers are naturally curious and inquisitive, and love to explore their environment. What does this have to do with you? The answer is simple. If you want to increase your chances of making things work in your life, that is *Being* the eternal warrior so that you learn from your life's lessons, increase the childlike activity in your life. As the physicist Richard Feynman stated:

I've been caught, so to speak — like someone who was given something wonderful when he was a child, and he's always looking for it again.
I'm always looking, like a child, for the wonders I know I'm going to find — maybe not every time, but every once in a while.[2]

Similarly, the author of a number of books on human development and child development, Joseph Chilton Pearce, advocated that to play like children is to be in a mode of uninhibited growth. 'Play provides the stage for growth to happen.'

I encourage you to make playing from a childlike state, increasing the fun in your life and 'choosing to feel good' your default conscious, unconscious and subconscious setting. Allow these outcomes to interfere with your self-imposed limiting belief that failing at something means that you have failed personally by using the equations above and reactivating your inner toddler. What do I mean by being more like a toddler? Allow yourself to experience the sense of wonder at all things in the world — be the one who keeps guessing, without the negative or self-admonishing thoughts or beliefs about being wrong.

If you want to test this out, ask a toddler to pass you the 'thing' on the floor and you will observe them walking around and pointing at everything in the room and saying, 'This one?' 'No.' 'This one?' You can even give more detail like, 'To your left' or 'The white one', but they don't know left or white yet, so they will still point and ask 'This one?' They don't feel self-conscious, silly or embarrassed that their choices are incorrect. It's how they learn; it's how we all learned. At what age did you decide that you had to get it right first go every time? Holding onto this belief is crazy, and life doesn't work that way. I could go on about it, but I feel you now get the point.

Another important consideration here is to always be the first to laugh at yourself — always. Toddlers do it all the time! This is another characteristic of *Being* an eternal warrior. Warriors know that they don't have to be that serious, and *it's rarely about them*! Learn, like the warrior, to laugh at yourself, because by doing so, when someone else laughs 'at' you (not 'with' you), you will find it doesn't hurt, is not an insult, and doesn't mean you are a failure or stupid. *Being* the eternal warrior allows you to not take it personally. It rarely is. As the eternal worrier, however, you unconsciously default to make it mean something about you (your perceived expectation of reality) rather than hearing what was really said (but more on 'what is really being said' later in the book).

In the next chapter we will take a closer look as to how you got to being the eternal worrier and how you were fooled. First, let us recap with the take-home message.

The take-home message — your transformation from eternal *worrier* to eternal *warrior*

The *eternal worrier smiles* because they have been wired to avoid responsibility for changing their life. They do not try anything new, nor do they consider attempting to be like a warrior because they are unconsciously lazy (it's too much like hard work) or fearful of, for example, failing or the unknown. The eternal worrier personalises failure, so they then stop trying to make things work in their life and become stuck in being the worrier. They no longer play from a childlike place because they do not believe that this will increase their chances of making things work (succeed) in their life, so, unlike the toddler, they stop being inquisitive and continue to worry and be fearful about getting things wrong. The eternal worrier is not willing to learn from their lessons, so they continue to blame others for their actions of giving up and their reactive emotions. They give up making the choice to feel good from each of their lessons. In so doing, they reinforce their unhealthy default wiring, stop taking responsibility for their life and stop listening to their innate wisdom, feeling and thinking (as advocated by the Law of Creation). They continue to be stuck being the eternal worrier who suffers from the 'something for nothing disease', passively being the inflexible, lazy drifter, and give up their opportunity to live their life optimally and purposefully. Interestingly, the eternal worrier's poor actions of blaming, laziness and adopting payoffs for not changing result in those around them — eternal worriers and warriors alike — dreading having them around. As Ayn Rand concluded in her magnum opus *Atlas shrugged*:

> *Man cannot survive except by gaining knowledge, and reason is his only means to gain it ... Man's mind is his basic tool of survival. Life is given to him, survival is not. His body is given to him, its sustenance is not. His mind is given to him, its content is not. To remain alive, he must act, and before he can act, he must know the nature and purpose of his action. He cannot obtain his food without a knowledge of food and of the way to obtain it. He cannot dig a ditch — or build a cyclotron — without a knowledge of his aim and of the means to achieve it. To remain alive, he must think.*[4]

The *eternal warrior smiles* because they have been wired to welcome every opportunity to change and play like a toddler, welcome the opportunity to learn new lessons in life and increase their chances of making things work now and in the future, in whatever they choose to do. They know, however, that in attempting something that was unsuccessful they have learned a lesson, and that they personally did not fail — only their attempt at giving it a go did not work. They are willing to learn from their lessons, and continue until they make it work, knowing that they are responsible for what they are feeling, so they make the choice to feel good with each of their lessons. In so doing, they reinforce their healthy wiring, take responsibility for their life, and listening to their innate wisdom, feeling and thinking (based on the Law of Creation). They are *Being* the eternal warrior, who is immune to the 'something for nothing disease', actively *Being* the inspired adaptable go-getter paddler so that they are living their life optimally and purposefully.

CHAPTER 2

Needs and fear

What is it that you want?

It seems like a hard question, but that is because you, being the eternal worrier, overcomplicate things. I bring your attention to Maslow's (1908–1970) hierarchy of needs, where the basic needs (e.g. physiological and safety needs) take precedence over higher needs (for example self-transcendence needs), shown in Figure 2.1.

Figure 2.1. Maslow's hierarchy of needs.

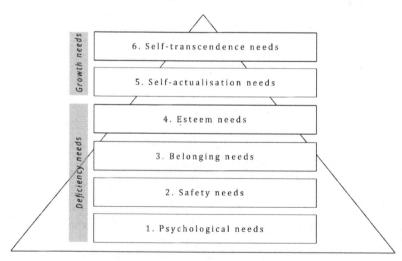

The first four levels are referred to as deficiency needs, and are associated with the feeling of discomfort when you don't have enough of something vital to your existence. Although Maslow's writings imply that we are all genetically wired this way, I want to remind you that who *you* are choosing to be (i.e. being an eternal worrier or *Being* an eternal warrior) is determined by you and not your genetics, as discussed in more detail in chapter 4. What you need to create change in your life is to first accept that you have been lied to and conned into adopting self-imposed limiting belief systems (as explained with the flea in the glass jar analogy), which keeps you stuck in being the eternal worrier and stops you from listening to your innate wisdom. If you believe that the inevitable outcome of your life is determined by your genetics, this self-imposed limiting belief system will also contribute to keeping you stuck. When you apply this to Maslow's hierarchy of needs, by being the eternal worrier, you will be forever stuck in Maslow's deficiency needs, and will be kept in Maslow's first level because you are eternally worrying about fulfilling your physiological needs!

By *Being* the eternal warrior, you are *already* actively listening to your innate wisdom, inspired and focused on fulfilling your life's purpose, while being flexible (the third and fourth elements of the awakening process respectively) in your life. When applying Maslow's hierarchy of needs to the eternal warrior, there are no deficiency needs, only needs, and as such the eternal warrior is *already* self-actualised and self-transcended!

Essentially, eternal warriors don't need to follow Maslow's hierarchy of needs because they are already adaptable and living their life optimally and purposefully. They do not think about, let alone worry about, Maslow's six levels!

You, however, have determined that you have so far been the eternal worrier in your life, and may think that you are meant to follow Maslow's hierarchy of needs in the order described above. The issue that all eternal worriers face is that the opportunity to bypass deficiency needs to self-actualisation and self-transcendence becomes almost impossible because you are worrying about meeting the first four deficiency needs!

Knowing that you find yourself living your life from one or more of Maslow's deficiency need states is not a judgement on you (or anyone else for that matter) because, like the flea in the jar, the glass lid (the self-imposed limiting belief systems) conditioned you to live your life sub-optimally. This will continue until someone else, like me, without those self-imposed limiting belief systems, shows you that it can be done, just like new fleas introduced to the glass jar. They would not have been conditioned by the glass lid, so they would jump optimally, and to the surprise of the conditioned flea, jump out of the jar! I ask you the question: Are you ready to jump out of your jar?

The purpose of this book is to not only highlight that you are living your life sub-optimally, without purpose and inflexibly, but to also demonstrate that you, like me, may learn to be flexible and live optimally with purpose, by offering you the skills and resources that will allow you to relearn, like the conditioned flea, how to jump optimally again by *Being* the eternal warrior!

As you may now realise, *Being* the warrior of your life is the only option to choose if you are to live your life of purpose optimally and flexibly, where you are no longer bound to the dogma of Maslow's hierarchy or any other rigid belief system. Although Maslow's hierarchy had its purpose, by *Being* the warrior of your life, listening to your innate wisdom, applying the Law of Creation and actioning changes as they present in life, you do not have to wait a lifetime before achieving and eternally maintaining Maslow's highest level of self-transcendence and beyond. Although there are many who support and adopt Maslow's work, there are also those who criticise him.

Irrespective of which side of the fence you sit on, by *Being* an eternal warrior, you are not limited to Maslow's hierarchy of needs, and I will show you why.

Simply put, it stands to reason that in order to survive essentially you need food, water and adequate shelter, as advocated by Maslow's physiological and safety deficiency needs, but unlike Maslow's understanding, when you are actively *Being* the eternal warrior, you are able to meet these essential needs while innately knowing your life's purpose, feeling safe, innately knowing that you belong, and having high self-esteem because you are immune to the 'something for nothing disease'. You take responsibility for your life so that you are living optimally and purposefully, progressing beyond self-actualisation and self-transcendence.

Let's now frame this to you in another way with the following scenario, where you are shipwrecked on an island with other survivors, to further explain the dynamics of *Being* an eternal warrior compared to an eternal worrier.

There can only be two outcomes if you are shipwrecked on an island — you either survive or perish. An eternal warrior would see the shipwreck in the same way as the strong current in the river in the canoe ride analogy. Shipwrecked on an island with other survivors would not stop an eternal warrior from living their life optimally, purposefully and flexibly, as they do not see Maslow's deficiency needs as a prerequisite to self-transcendence! An eternal worrier, however, being shipwrecked on an island, would be consumed in worrying about how they are going to get back home to their family, friends and work, worrying about having no food, no water, no shelter, no security, trusting the other survivors, and so on. While the eternal worrier is stuck in worry or fear, the eternal warrior has become familiar with their new surroundings, established the necessities for life based on the circumstances and resources available, and begun putting things into action, never losing sight of their life purpose.

This is where I ask you to pause for a moment to recall the river and canoe analogy, and to ask yourself the following two questions: What type of canoeist do you want to be? What type of canoeist would you want to have with you on this island? It's a no brainer! If you are to survive this shipwreck, you cannot be paralysed by your own worry or fear, let alone by someone's worry and fear — you would all perish immediately! You would need to be, along with the other survivors, making the choice of *Being* the warrior, so that, collectively, you could work together, inspired by the common goal of meeting the basic needs for human survival! Any other way would jeopardise any chances of survival and rescue!

Although you are not shipwrecked on an island, this scenario may be familiar to you. I ask you to let your imagination be free for just a moment and replace the words 'shipwrecked' with 'born', 'island' with 'planet Earth', and 'survivors' with 'people'. So instead of being shipwrecked on an island with other survivors, picture a scenario where you feel yourself being born on planet Earth with other people. This is no longer a scenario; it is your reality. You were born on planet Earth with other people! Earth, in the context of the solar system and galaxy, could be compared to an island. Your mother could be compared to the vessel (the ship) that brought you to Earth (the island) (although your mother is not really a ship, nor was she shipwrecked) — metaphorically speaking, you understand the point.

You were born on Earth with other people, and as a child, you were taught various skills to 'survive' on Earth. What did you need to do again in the 'shipwrecked on an island' scenario? That's right — as the worrier, you needed to survive, as the warrior — thrive! What then is the common theme in both the shipwreck scenario and the reality that you were born on planet Earth? Survive and then thrive! What do you need to survive and thrive? *Be* the warrior! But if you are being the worrier, having to consistently worry about working to earn an income to purchase food, to maintain your security (pay rent or a mortgage), to maintain the essential services and upkeep for your home while trying to find a work–life balance, it's as if you are waiting for someone to *rescue* you and set you free from your current situation! Rescuing you from your life and setting you free (financially) is often used as the hook by many of these self-help motivators who are relying on your reactionary insecurity, that is being the worrier, to extract money from you! However, if you (and all other people born on Earth with you) were truly *Being* the warrior in life, there would be no one for these so-called self-help motivators to market the 'I will rescue you and set you free' message too!

This is where I would like to draw your attention to an interesting aside here. Recall from the introduction the three payoff reasons? They were:

1.   being able to avoid responsibility or consequence
2.   being able to avoid success or failure
3.   being able to avoid failure but can claim success (the coat-tail rider).

These are the reason you might become lazy, blame others and not change when you are being the worrier in life, and it is fear that keeps you from interrupting and rewiring your unhealthy default neural pathway! When you are being the worrier, immersed in fear, you have a tendency to be lazy and blame others. You get to falsely believe that you can avoid consequences and responsibilities, success or failure while opportunistically looking to ride on someone else's success and claim it as your own. Furthermore, do you also recall me making the point a couple of times that you have been lied to, conned and duped? Well, I will now reveal how this keeps you being a worrier.

Look again closely at Figure 2.1. Maslow's hierarchy of needs — what is need number 2? It's the need to feel safe. Do you feel safe? If you felt safe, you wouldn't have read or paid those self-help motivators that claim to be able to rescue you from your life! If you still answered yes, then I ask you to think again! What would the consequences be if you did not have an income to pay your rent or mortgage, or everyday expenses like food, water, essential services, clothing and so on. Still feel safe? What about watching the news tonight — then re-evaluate your feeling of safety. Do you feel inspired to leave your car, home and workplace unsecured? Not if you listen to the media and news reports! The media have a habit of reporting news associated with some bird or animal flu, people being killed, car accidents, fires, the coming recession, and so on.

This does not create a feeling of safety, and this occurs every night with all sorts of media - TV, print, radio and internet! If you feel this is an unreasonable observation, I encourage you to do this experiment —deliberately do not watch the news for three weeks before tuning in again to see if it has changed. Guess what? You will find, as I did, that it hasn't. Even after three months of not watching the news on TV, it still did not change. The stories and characters may change, but the overall theme of 'doom and gloom' impacting on your perceptions of feeling unsafe does not change, so this continues to reinforce a worrier's faulty default wiring thereby ensuring that they remain stuck in fear. In this state, the worrier will not achieve Maslow's second deficiency need of safety.

This experiment is by no means telling you to put your head in the sand. That would be the behaviour of the worrier! The reality is that it pays to be informed when living in your current urbanised environment; however, looking at the news on TV and other sources of media, and being preoccupied with working to earn an income to make ends meet, means you end up living in *fear*. Based on Maslow's hierarchy, you can't meet level 3 needs if you are stuck at level 2. Fear, as reported through the media, is one of the reasons why people are not evolving. To validate to you that this media-induced fear is real, I will share with you one of the more brilliant ways that was used to establish this over-hyped fear generated by the media. Michael Moore and Barry Glassner, the author of *The culture of fear*, visited the street corner of Florence and Normandie in 2003 while filming Moore's movie *Bowling for Columbine*. The film is about guns, so Moore came to a place with a reputation for murder. Glassner dispelled this myth with a simple truth — you are more likely to die from the air quality at the intersection of Florence and Normandie than from a bullet! The point that this demonstrated was that the media had over-portrayed the risk to a person's safety by playing on fear. There is, of course, a cost to this 'living in fear', and this cost is outlined in the next section.

We are being lied to about how unsafe the world is, and what's worse, we are the ones who ask for it in our films, TV shows, newspapers and so on. When we buy the papers or magazines that sensationalise fear, we are telling the media to feed our need for fear! The media will continue to report and sensationalise fear as long as we are buying because there is money to be made.

Which brings us to a cornerstone of fear — money. Remember, *deficiency* needs must be met first. Think about it — if you are constantly worrying about money, what then are you being? A worrier! This means that you cannot be focused on living optimally and purposefully, let alone implement the Law of Creation. The chances are that, as a worrier, you are most probably looking at money through a *deficiency* mindset or 'lack of' mindset, such as how far you are in debt or how little money you have to make ends meet. All you need to do to reinforce your fear around money is to replay many of the commonly held and often heard beliefs about money:

- it doesn't grow on trees
- you have to work hard for it
- it doesn't come easy
- it can't buy happiness
- it can't buy love
- money ruins people
- you're nothing without money
- it's the root of all evil.

You can see that some of these beliefs are in conflict with each other. For example, money cannot buy happiness or love, but you are nothing without it and it's the root of all evil. Needless to say, this incongruence may cause you stress and confusion, particularly so when you are being the worrier, rigidly holding onto these conflicting money beliefs.

When it comes to money, no matter how much money you have, do you honestly believe you will ever stop wanting more? What is your cut-off point? Do you make a million dollars and say, 'That's it, I'm done with making money'? Remember, being the worrier is synonymous with having a 'lack of' mentality, which is based around the fear of not having enough (e.g. not enough money, not enough love, not enough respect).

This 'Lack of Mentality', 'worrier mentality' or 'fear-based mindset' is not only a distraction, it's a barrier to the change that can transform you from being the worrier to Being the warrior. If you are seeking self-transcendence, you need to find a way to escape from your deficiency needs, so that you can change your focus from being the worrier to Being the warrior.

The take-home message — your transformation from eternal *worrier* to eternal *warrior*

The *eternal worrier smiles* because they avoid living from a place of power. Instead, they live from a place of laziness, blame and fear, which only serves to keep them being the worrier and 'something for nothing' sufferer. This means that they are consistently in a state of poor clarity of thought because they are only surviving, and as such never get to address their deficiency needs, as they are immersed in worrying about them or being fearful of them. The worrier therefore never has to ask the questions of 'Who am I?', 'What is my optimal potential?' and 'What is my purpose?' By not asking these questions and seeking out their answers, they reinforce their unhealthy default wiring which prevents them from reaching the levels of self-actualisation and self-transcendence, but they do get to blame others for not achieving these higher-level needs.

The *eternal warrior smiles* because they realise that laziness, blame and fear are a responsibility of living and need to be dealt with. By dealing with these issues, the warrior creates an abundant mentality and can resolve their needs. In doing so, they not only can ask the questions of 'Who am I?', 'What is my optimal potential?' and 'What is my purpose?', they already know the answers by having had the confidence to seek them out. By doing so, they reinforce their healthy default wiring thereby creating the possibility of living from a place of power, and therefore are able to reach beyond the levels of self-actualisation and self-transcendence. With this mindset, warriors are immune to the 'something for nothing disease', actively Being the inspired go-getter paddler who takes responsibility and adopts flexibility in life as they live optimally and purposefully.

CHAPTER 3

The effect of living in fear-induced stress and worry

Fear-induced stress and worry are common topics of everyday conversations, particularly when you are being the eternal worrier. You may find yourself worrying about and talking about your stressors with your family, friends, or colleagues, who may also share the same stressors. For example, you may be stressed by the fear of not performing well at your work, or perhaps it's the stress of having to pass exams or doing your next presentation. It could be the fear of being rejected in relationships, feeling overwhelmed with your life's obligations, not having enough money to make ends meet or even worse, the fear of losing your independence (e.g. getting burnt out, contracting some disease such as cancer, becoming a paraplegic due to some horrific accident, or simply from getting old)! These combinations of fear-induced stressors and worry serve to reinforce your unhealthy default wiring which consume you when you are being the worrier.

You most probably are already aware of the effects of prolonged fear-induced stress and worry on your physical and mental health. Doctors of traditional Chinese medicine (TCM) certainly were, as they identified seven endogenous factors (emotions) as being one of the three key categories for causing dis-harmonies/dis-ease (syndromes in TCM terms) in your body. In terms of Rhett Ogston Applications (ROAs) these seven were condensed into a set of five emotions (anger, joy/sadness, overthinking/worry, grief/ melancholy, fear – see table 3.1). In terms of TCM the other two categories that cause dis-harmonies are external pathogenic factors and non-internal/non-external factors, which are not discussed here. If you are not aware of the effects of fear-induced stress and worry, then allowing these emotions to go unchecked will contribute to a variety of physiological changes, as listed in Table 3.1, which may lead to dis-eases such as heart disease, autoimmune diseases and obesity, and may cause or exacerbate mood disorders such as depression and anxiety, bipolar disorder, cognitive (thinking) problems, personality changes and problem behaviours, which are discussed in more detail below.

Table 3.1 The physiological changes caused by emotions according to Western physiology and TCM

Emotions	Western physiological changes changes and effects on the body	TCM physiological changes and effects on the body

Anger (frustration, brooding, irritability)	· results in higher levels of C-reactive protein levels (CRP)[6]
	· triggers the body's 'fight or flight' response which activates the adrenal glands to flood the body with stress hormones, such as adrenaline and cortisol
	· when unmanaged anger has been linked to:
	  · headache
	  · digestion problems, such as abdominal pain
	  · insomnia
	  · increased anxiety
	  · depression
	  · high blood pressure
	  · skin problems, such as eczema
	  · heart attack
	  · stroke[7]
		· makes the Qi rise, particularly the Liver Qi, which may result in headaches, tinnitus, dizziness, red face, red blotches on the front part of the neck, vomiting (sometimes with blood)[8]

Joy (over excitement)/ sadness	· changes in blood pressure and heart rate[11] · increase in heart rate and headaches[12]	· weakens the Heart Qi and then weakens the Lung Qi which may result in crying, depression, tiredness, breathlessness, Blood deficiency and loss of period in women (amenorrhea)[13] · injures the Heart Qi which may result in poor concentration, restlessness, poor sleep[14]
Worry/over-thinking	· affects the movements of the stomach and colon causing increased irritability, spasticity and may produce colitis[3] · increases the risk of coronary heart disease in older men[4]	· weakens the Spleen Qi which may result in colon issues (loose stools), loss of appetite, tiredness · weakens the Spleen's transformation and transportation function which may results in phlegm and damp production, such as mucus in the stool, post nasal drip · causes Lung Qi stagnation which may result in anxiety, breathlessness and stiffness of the neck and shoulders[5]

Emotions	Western physiological changes changes and effects on the body	TCM physiological changes and effects on the body
Grief/ melancholy	• associated with neuroendocrine activation (cortisol response) • alters sleep (electroencephalography changes), • associated with immune imbalance (reduced T-lymphocyte proliferation) • associated with inflammatory cell mobilization (neutrophils) • alters prothrombotic response (platelet activation and increased vWF-ag) • associated with hemodynamic changes (heart rate and blood pressure)[9]	• causes Qi stagnation and Lung Qi deficiency which may result in low spirits, difficulty breathing and lassitude[10]
Fear (shock, fright)	• increase in cortisol levels • weakens immune system • increases cardiovascular damage • gastrointestinal problems • decreases fertility • impairs formation of long-term memories • damages certain parts of the brain, such as the hippocampus • fatigue • increases likelihood of osteoporosis and type 2 diabetes • aggravates clinical depression • accelerates ageing • may result in premature death • increase in CRP – a substance known to promote cardiovascular disease and stroke[1]	• depletes the Kidney Jing, which may result in decreased fertility, weakened immune system, weakened bones (osteoporosis), urinary dysfunction, accelerated aging and premature death • blocks the upper Jiao (burner) and may cause night sweating, palpitations, dry mouth and throat • depletes Heart qi, which may cause insomnia, mind disturbance, breathlessness, fatigue and palpitations[2]

A vicious cycle may be created when you get stuck in your fear-induced stress and worry, which stops you from actively listening and Being the eternal warrior, living an optimal life with purpose. Instead, you may become overly consumed with fear and worry, which only serves to keep you being the eternal worrier who blames everyone and everything else for their life and is inflexible, who often rests on 'She'll be right mate' in the Australian vernacular!

When your neural pathways are wired to being a worrier, living in this fear-induced stressful state occurs by default. This means that you are usually unaware of the fact that you are living in this state! The physical symptoms (listed in the table 3.1), and in particular the emotional and reactive thoughts (self-imposed belief systems) due to fear-induced stress and worry only serve to reinforce your default unhealthy wiring. Unless this can be interrupted, then your unhealthy wiring interferes with your ability to listen to your innate wisdom, implement the Law of Creation, or create the necessary changes in your life to reconnect to Being the eternal warrior. As such, you continue being the eternal worrier, existing in a continuous fear-induced stress response state.

The scientific literature defines (fear-induced) stress as an external event or stimuli that causes tension or internal arousal. It is a subjective (internal) response or physical reaction to demanding or damaging responses. It is well accepted that the 'stress response', also referred to as the 'fight or flight' response, is a physiological response designed to prepare and activate the body for survival in a potentially dangerous or life-threatening situation. Once the event ends, the stress response ends, and your physiological response returns to normal. As an eternal worrier, however, your stress response doesn't end, even when you are *not* faced with a life or death scenario! In fact, being an eternal worrier, your stress response is rarely activated by life or death situations, but rather by non-life-threatening worry associated with fear-induced stress. For example, an eternal worrier may choose to go to work every day, but they may do so because they are fearful of not having security, being judged because they do not go to work, not having a fulfilling career, or not making enough money to live or keep up with their peers.

Another example is associated with relationships. The eternal worrier may stay in a relationship because they fear being alone, not being loved by someone else, or losing what they have already have, even though it's not what they really want. The eternal worrier does not readily make changes in their life because they are fearful of change (i.e. the fear of starting something new or the fear of the unknown). These examples are perceived as fear-induced stressors, which not only keep the eternal worrier stuck in being the eternal worrier (hence the use of the term *eternal*), but also contribute to dis- harmony and dis-ease which results in the development of stress-related disease states as mentioned above.

In addition to fear-induced stress and worry, there are other reasons that may keep an eternal worrier worrying.

They include:

- being stuck in emotions other than fear and worry (as identified in Table 3.1)
- frustration caused by the obstruction to attaining goals
- conflict (of any kind)
- changes (from normal)
- the pressure caused by unrealistic goal-setting.

In fact, anything in your environment has the potential to keep you being the eternal worrier. It could be associated with physical, social or psychological issues, including being triggered by your imagination or a stimulating factor for worry. When an eternal worrier first experiences a potential stressor (e.g. fear or worry), instead of making an appraisal of the stressor, they react! It is common for eternal worriers to have a primary and secondary reaction (not response) to their perceived fear-induced stressor. A primary reaction could be, for example, 'That person is doing a better job than me'. A secondary reaction to this example could be, 'What do I have to do to save my job?'

Once having made these associated reactions to the identified fear-induced stressor based on their perceived expectation of reality related to that person doing a better job than them, the external worrier must now find a way of coping with this situation.

The eternal worrier is usually stuck, immersed in their fear-induced stress or other factors, which are all based on their perceived expectation of reality. Living life from this space means that the eternal worrier is unable to effectively initiate the coping phase of stress, which is defined as a constructive attempt at solving the problem or adjusting to it. Your coach brings to your attention that, to be effective at coping, you need to be solution-oriented, make use of social support, be realistic (know your strengths and your weaknesses), monitor yourself (feelings and surroundings), and anticipate (learn from past experiences). These are all characteristic traits of *Being* the eternal warrior who takes responsibility for their life. By being the eternal worrier, you are not effectively initiating the coping phase of stress, that is, you are unable to be solution orientated because you are focused on worry and fear, and because of your eternal worrier payoffs, you are unable to effectively make use of your social support, as you have already burned those networks!

Eternal worriers then experience the stress response both physiologically (e.g. sympathetic nerve stimulation, increased cortisol release, increased blood pressure, increased heart rate, muscle tightness and decreased immunocompetence) and psychologically. Psychological responses might include defences such as:

- repression – blocking from consciousness
- projection – undesirable traits onto others
- displacement – resentment at boss, which may be taken out on our own children
- reaction formation – opposite behaviour, such as love and hate
- regression – back to earlier development
- inability to exercise rationalisation – unreasonable excuses
- denial – fail everything but still sit last exam
- inability to exercise sublimation – not able to take socially unacceptable behaviour and channel it into something that is acceptable.

As your coach I want to highlight that in both physical and emotional reactions to stressors, there is a release of various mediators such as cortisol, a glucocorticoid steroid hormone produced by the adrenal gland, as outlined in Table 3.1. Although the release of cortisol is a natural physiological response to stress as well as to low blood-glucose concentration, it is essential for an effective fight or flight/stress response, but it was never meant to be released constantly. It is well established that chronically elevated cortisol levels interfere with learning and memory function, lower immune system response and bone density, initiate premature ageing, increase weight gain, blood pressure, cholesterol levels and heart disease — and the list goes on and on. This is what is occurring when you are being the eternal worrier; you are literally bathing your cells in excessive cortisol, which not only interferes with normal cell growth and development, but also negatively impacts on the biofield activity of your cells and genes.

The biofield is an energy field that surrounds and moves through all cells, and is influenced by bio-electric signals and cues, which in turn influences cell and gene expression. Each of the emotional states (our examples of fear-induced stress or worry) referred to above is what I collectively refer to as unhealthy bio-electric signals and cues, which result in an unhealthy biofield.

The implications of this are explained by my 'Stem cell and biofield hypothesis', which states:

> *A healthy stem cell has a healthy biofield, and a healthy biofield will generate a healthy cell.*

What this means is that for a cell to be expressed (genes) as a healthy cell, it requires a healthy biofield and bio-electric code. This is influenced by healthy bio-electric signals and cues. I want to highlight the importance of this based on the understanding that all living cells are considered to be binary in nature. This means that any cell has one of two possible responses or outcomes for any given life situation they face — it's either a 0 or 1, or said another way, it's either on or off. To give you an example of what this means, consider a cell's movement. There can only be two main directions that a cell moves in: (0) forward (toward food, growth and development, all of which are examples of healthy bio-electric signals and cues) or (1) backward (away from a potential stressor, e.g. toxins, an unhealthy bio-electric signal and cue). Cells can alternate between the two directions (i.e. forward and backward), but they cannot travel in both directions at the same time. That would be like getting your car to drive in both reverse and drive at the same time, which is impossible!

This understanding can be applied to a cell's response to its environment — it is either in what I refer to as a 'growth/reproduce/thrive phase' or a 'static/defensive/survive phase'. Cells can alternate between these two phases (i.e. be in growth/reproduce/thrive phases when the signals and cues of their environment indicate safety, and static/defensive/survive phase when the signals and cues in their environment indicate danger), but they cannot be in both phases at the same time. It stands to reason that a cell, when continually exposed to signals and cues in its environment that initiate the static/defence/survive phase, cannot sustain this phase without causing cell damage, which can only be effectively repaired during the growth/reproduce/thrive phase.

As your coach I want to remind you that you are made up of a collection of cells! Yes, that's correct, you are a highly specialised multicellular organism. Every part of you is made of cells (there isn't a physical part of you that is not made up cells), which function in a similar way as single cells to environmental signals and cues. I took this into consideration with my 'Stem cell and biofield hypothesis', so when you upscale this hypothesis from stem cells to humans, it is possible to postulate that:

A healthy individual has a healthy biofield and a healthy biofield creates a healthy individual.

When this hypothesis is upscaled again:

Healthy individuals collectively have a healthy biofield and this collective healthy biofield creates healthy communities.

This can be upscaled further, and you can see the potential ongoing effect — healthy communities collectively have a healthy biofield, which creates healthy countries.

Healthy countries collectively have a healthy biofield, which creates a healthy world. A healthy world has a healthy biofield, which creates a healthy planet — and without a healthy planet, human life will cease to function in the way we have become accustomed to.

Although the impact of this book goes beyond you to everyone living on planet Earth, it is still necessary to start with you, as stated at the beginning of this book: 'The potential of humankind starts with you — especially you!' Knowing this truth, I remind you that for you to achieve this outcome, you need to be functioning optimally with a life purpose that includes *Being* the eternal warrior. This is, however, not possible when you are being an eternal worrier following (without listening or thought) an unhealthy lifestyle that impacts on your cells!

It is documented that cellular damage, such as changes in telomere length and telomerase activity, might occur through unhealthy diets, sedentary lifestyles, alcohol, poor sleep patterns, unhealthy fast living, pharmaceutical and other drug use, electromagnetic radiation, poor social networks and how you perceive your reality, all of which may be considered unhealthy bio-electric signals and cues. Telomeres are the protective caps found on the ends of chromosomes that affect how quickly cells age and die. The unhealthy lifestyles outlined above may cause telomeres to prematurely shorten, which reduces the lifespan of cells, while telomerase activity also reduces, impacting on cellular health and longevity (both are reduced). But healthy lifestyle behaviours may increase telomere length, as will be explained in more detail in chapter 4.

What would you say if I shared with you that you *can* master your own internal world by changing both your genetic programming and bio-electric signals and cues so that you form a healthy biofield with the healthy expression of the bio-electric code, and as a result, experience less worry and fear-induced stress, and therefore fewer fear-induced dis-ease states, while increasing your probability of transforming from the eternal worrier to *Being* the eternal warrior? We will explain this in chapter 4, after we look at the take-home message.

The take-home message — your transformation from eternal *worrier* to eternal *warrior*

The *eternal worrier smiles* because they have to cover their reactionary behaviours to fear-induced stress, cover their worry and frustrations that arise from having consistent conflict in their life, when being obstructed from attaining their goals due to the pressures of unrealistic goal-setting and not accepting change (from normal). This creates the scene for consistent fear-induced stress reactions, worry and frustrations in life, which keeps them in a fight or flight/stress response, which contributes to unhealthy bio-electric signals and cues, an unhealthy biofield and the unhealthy expression of the bio-electric code, which causes dis-harmony and dis-ease thereby acting as triggers to generating numerous disease states by initiating unhealthy changes with the worrier's cells and genes.

The *eternal warrior smiles* because they choose to be relaxed. They respond rather than react to life situations, as opposed to entering a state of fear-induced stress. They choose to take active action towards attainment of goals, and actively find solutions to obstructions to achieve their goals. This removes emotional frustrations from their life because they are actively 'doing' something to remove these obstructions. They make the choice to avoid conflict and to welcome changes (from normal), which allows for personal growth and the ability to review and set realistic goals (please refer to my book *Real health: The system that needs an overhaul* for more about realistic goal-setting), which limits any feelings of pressure around attaining goals. This choice allows their body to remain in a permanently relaxed state, and they avoid the perceptions of life stressors, which encourages healthy bio-electric signals and cues, a healthy biofield and the healthy expression of the bio-electric code, liberating them from dis-harmony, dis-ease and the development of disease states associated with stress by initiating healthy functioning of cells and genes.

CHAPTER 4

Changing your genetics

This chapter is inspired by the work of: *Bruce Lipton, the author of The biology of belief, who challenged the dogma that genes (DNA) control the cell, researchers in the area of 'regenerative and developmental biology (morphological and behavioural information processing in living systems)', such as Michael Levin from Tufts University, who have challenged the dogma that DNA is solely responsible for what is expressed bio informaticists such as Nick Goldman, a group leader at the European Bioinformatics Institute in Hinxton UK, who challenged the dogma that DNA can only store genetic information.*

The research listed above supports what I know: your genes are changeable and are influenced by environmental triggers. Lipton's work suggests that the nucleus of the cell, which contains the DNA, is not the only controller of the cell as once believed, albeit all the genetic codes (the cell's genetic blueprint) are contained within the nucleus. Lipton believes that, based on his observations of cell behaviour in relation to environmental triggers, your cells, and hence your destiny, are not totally at the mercy of what you inherited from your family (your genetics)![1]

Although it is accepted by science that proteins are made with instruction from DNA, and that specific proteins regulate the expression of certain genes, the strongly held belief that DNA (the material contained in the nucleus) is totally in control of the cell, yet is subject to random mutations, is challenged by Lipton. Despite the pseudoscience allegations made against Lipton to discredit this challenge, his work has stimulated thought that your environment has a role to play (possibly a bigger role than what the current dogma wants you to believe) in shaping you.[2] If Lipton's assertion is true, then the natural environment may also be a factor in the genetic code (genotype) expression (phenotype), and as such, random mutations may not be as random as currently believed.

Unlike what you may have been taught at school or possibly thought, Lipton suggests that, although DNA contains the blueprint codes and is therefore believed to be in total control of your cells (you), this scientific dogma cannot hold true because DNA is not the only factor for determining gene expression. Lipton stands his ground in challenging this scientific dogma, despite the critics mocking his work. Lipton firmly believes that mutations are a deliberate action undertaken by a cell to adapt to its natural environment, and the information stored within the DNA (the cell's genetic blueprint) can be accessed by the cell to allow for these changes to occur, once influenced by its natural environment.[3]

To demonstrate that the environment influences cell behaviour and gene expression, Lipton cites research from British geneticist, John Cairns, which was published in 1988 titled 'The origin of mutants'.[4] This research was on bacteria that had a defective gene for an enzyme called lactase (responsible for breaking down a sugar called lactose). Knowing that these specific bacteria had a defective lactase enzyme, the hypothesis was that, by supplying lactose as the only source of food to these bacteria, they would be unable to convert the lactose into energy for life, growth and reproduction, and as such they would die. This assumption makes perfect sense if you accept the current science that gene mutation is a random event, and that environment-directed mutation, such as that for the specific lactase gene, was not possible. What Cairns observed, however, was that, within a few days, there were bacterial colonies growing in every experiment.

How was this possible when the initial colony of bacteria was destined to die? Was it merely fate based on random mutation that they survived? To understand these outcomes, Cairns investigated the DNA of the original bacterial colony and found that there was no random change with their DNA. Instead, he observed that there were numerous specific genetic mutations for the defective lactase gene! Based on these observations, Cairns could only conclude that the bacteria had deliberately changed only the lactase gene given their lactose-rich environment, before they actually began dividing into new colonies. The bacteria needed to survive, and they found a way to do that by changing their genetic material to suit their environment.

This conclusion, however, sparked controversy within this field, and the debate was on between the teleological (Cairns' directed mutation beliefs) and non-teleological models (Darwin's random mutation beliefs), and for the next ten years, the teleological model appeared to reign with this new explanation of mutation (directed mutations) displacing the existing one (random mutations), all sparked by Cairns' 1988 study.

However, not to be outdone, the non-teleological advocates gradually accumulated evidence so that by 1998, essentially everyone in the field, including Cairns and his closest collaborators, re-evaluated Cairns' original 1988 observations, which now appeared to no longer support directed mutations, and so the non-teleological model regained its place as the accepted model of mutation.

What the advocates for the teleological model believed to be the evidence for directed mutations were now considered an inaccurate interpretation of Cairns' data. Instead, Cairns' observations fell within the accepted Darwinian (non-teleological) framework - the ten-year period where a new phenomenon appeared to dominate was seemingly disproven. In those ten years, however, two key new features of bacterial biology were discovered that served to disprove the directed mutation explanation:

- When bacteria are starved, as they were in the Cairns study, it is believed that they would have entered what is termed a 'hypermutable state'. In this state, high levels of mutations are introduced throughout the bacterial genome, but selection for specific mutants makes it appear as if the environmental conditions preferentially targeted mutations to the selected gene.
- The other feature discovered was amplification, which occurs to crippled genes, such as the defective lactase gene in Cairns' experiment, where a multiplication of the copies of the crippled gene is first favourably selected because it leads to a small but detectable increase in its product's minimal activity. Because of this massive gene amplification, it makes for better chances of mutation, and when these occur, the extra gene copies become a burden, and are eliminated by selection. The result, as advocated by the non-teleological model, is the appearance of highly targeted mutations. In other words, Cairns' lactase gene defective bacteria, when placed in a lactose rich environment, randomly selected this specific lactase defective gene to amplify so that a random mutation occurred, and these bacteria were randomly able to survive in an otherwise hostile environment, in which death was certain if the lactase defective enzyme was not randomly corrected by this random mutation process.

This all sounds very coincidental to occur randomly, but these two non-teleological explanations were sufficient to allow the random mutation selection model to regain its place as the accepted mutation explanation, although the term 'adaptive mutations' had replaced directed mutations during this process, much to the disapproval of the random mutation advocates.

As your coach, I'd ask you to put aside these two opposing views and consider the possibility suggested by researchers such as Lipton that your natural environment has the potential to influence your genetic expression. If it were not for the lactose only food supply in Cairns' experiment, would the random mutations that rectified the defective lactase gene have occurred? Said another way, would well-fed bacteria with the same defective lactase gene go into a hypermutable state, and would amplification have initiated the mutation changes so that the bacteria's defective lactase gene was randomly replaced with a functional lactase gene? Although random mutation is now credited for the changes Cairns observed, it took a hostile environment where bacteria were starving due to a specific gene defect for these random mutations to have been initiated. This does sound like it was the natural environment that initiated the trigger for this supposedly random mutation!

Despite the predominance of the random mutation model, pioneering research from the Levin Lab at Tufts University suggests otherwise. Rather than researching gene expression networks and biochemical signalling factors as other research groups are doing, this team is pursuing, at a molecular level, the roles of endogenous voltages, pH gradients and ion fluxes as epigenetic carriers of morphological information. The bio-electricity projects that the Levin Lab are currently include inducing regeneration of limbs, eyes, tails and craniofacial structures in normally non-regenerating species by providing the appropriate bio-electric signals and cues to the cells at the wound site.

While ion flows control cell-level behaviours such as migration, differentiation and proliferation, bio-electric signals also function as master regulators of large-scale shape in many contexts — a simple signal can induce complex, highly orchestrated, self-limiting downstream morphogenetic cascades. Using gain- and loss-of-function techniques to specifically modulate cells' ion flow, researchers at the Levin Lab can regulate large-scale morphogenetic events relevant to, for example, limb formation and eye induction, which will be discussed in more detail below.[5]

Although this research is limited to animal cells, the fact remains that bio-electric signals and cues have been reported to function as regulators of morphogenetic change. This implies that genes are not always the trigger for morphogenetic changes! The ideas presented by the Levin Lab inspired me to investigate this area in relation to my work, and as such, my 'Stem cell and biofield hypothesis', introduced in chapter 3, was born.

As your coach, I'd like to bring to your awareness the following possibilities based on the above information. Lipton upscales what he observed in cells to you (a human, made up of cells), and emphasises that, unlike cells, your natural environment is not only where you reside but, more importantly, how you perceive your natural environment to be. Your beliefs and perceptions about your environment may then have the potential to influence your genetic expression. Based on this emphasis, what you think, consciously or subconsciously, does matter. Lipton, however, does not discuss thinking, your perceptions, beliefs systems and emotions as examples of bio-electric signals and cues, as those in the field of optogenetics and cybernetics do (which will be discussed in more detail below).

We do know from the Levin Lab that bio-electric signals and cues are master regulators of morphogenetic change, albeit in animal models, but what if these changes also impact on your cells, and hence you as a human? This is exactly what is postulated by my 'Stem cell and biofield hypothesis', and the upscaling of this hypothesis to humans, as previously discussed. Although the 'Stem cell and biofield hypothesis' has yet to be scientifically validated, a theoretical model does exist for this based on bio-electric signals and cues produced from brainwaves and generated by your perceptions of your natural environment that may essentially 'shape' you based on the morphogenetic changes observed in animal models. Let's say, for example, you are making the choice of Being the eternal warrior as previously discussed. This would be interpreted as generating healthy bio-electric signals and cues that would then have the capacity to both shape and maintain you as Being the eternal warrior. You, however have already established that you are being the eternal worrier, and as such, this generates brainwaves that are unhealthy bio-electric signals and cues, which shape you as the worrier until the conscious choice occurs to change who you are being/Being.

This may sound a little 'out there', but so was the suggestion that DNA could store anything other than genetic material. Nick Goldman (a group leader at the European Bioinformatics Institute in Hinxton, UK) was tossing around ideas with his colleagues for a solution for storing the reams of genome sequences and other data the world was throwing at them, in a practical and affordable way given the current expense and limitations of conventional computing technology. Sci-fi alternatives were jokingly offered as a solution when the reality of what was suggested was realised. Considering that DNA stores genetic material, what about using DNA to store information![6] This insight into converting DNA's role being only storage for genetic material to being a storage for information is now a reality. This proposition was taken very seriously by Microsoft Research, which has made an early move in DNA storage, having ordered 10 million strings from Twist Bioscience, a DNA synthesis start-up company in San Francisco, California. This may then help to create the necessary demand. Not only does this reinforce that DNA is more than a storage facility for genetic data, despite random mutations, it highlights how something that was once never considered possible now is possible. This may assist in bringing down the walls of limitations in the hope of progress and understanding, and as such open the possibility for my 'Stem cell and biofield hypothesis' to be seriously considered.

This is where I would like you to understand the possibility that your cells and genes (your DNA) are strongly influenced by how you perceive your natural environment. The question that arises is — what is your natural environment? How you answer this question will be influenced by your own definition, knowledge and perceptions about your 'natural environment'. You have two general natural environments: your internal and external environments. The internal environment is inside you, and is essentially where your cells live, function, divide and keep you alive. You (your conscious mind) has very little idea, if any, about your internal environment and how it works, but it still functions irrespective of how much you know! If you really think you know how your internal environment functions, you will have no problems in monitoring your stress response state by detecting your cortisol levels without using external measuring tools such as a saliva or blood cortisol tests. You would be able to measure and regulate the absorption of every signal nutrient and manage the detoxification process for every single chemical (e.g. pesticides, herbicides, artificial colouring, flavouring and so on) that finds its way into your body from the foods you eat and liquids you drink.

I could go on, but these two examples are sufficient to demonstrate you are not consciously in control of what's occurring within your internal environment, although you can certainly influence it. Let's use cortisol (the stress response hormone we discussed in relation to fear induced stress above) to further illustrate this point. Your internal environment, such as the extra- and intra-cellular fluids, become flooded with cortisol when triggered by your stress response. This release of cortisol is out of your conscious control, and it is a natural and essential reaction to the fight or flight response to keep you alive! As previously discussed, it is well documented that when cortisol levels are maintained at high concentrations for prolonged periods of time within your internal environment, it will cause disease states. Your conscious mind, however, does not have specific control over your cortisol levels. If it did, wouldn't you ensure that your cortisol levels were cleared as soon as your fight or flight response state was over?

This is where, as your coach, I encourage you to be once again open to the possibility of changing another self-imposed limiting belief, that is, your belief that your internal environment cannot be changed by your perceptions of your external environment.

Your external environment is where you live, and it exerts a level of control over you. Why? Because no matter what signals and cues are presented to you by your external environment, *you* must adjust to them. It does not work the other way around. For example, you must get out of the rain when it's raining (an external environment signal and cue) if you don't want get wet — it doesn't stop raining because you don't want to get wet! When the weather is cold (an external environmental signal and cue), you need to adapt your behaviour to stay warm — the cold weather doesn't stop because you want to stay warm! You, like every other living species on Earth, need to adapt to the signals and cues from your external environment. Your perceptions, however, of the signals and cues from your external environment will influence whether or not you are creating unhealthy bio-electric signals and cues by being reactionary to it (such as when you are being the eternal worrier) or creating healthy bio-electric signals and cues by Being responsive to it (such as when you are Being the eternal warrior). Both of these scenarios have the capacity to influence gene expression (your genetics) in either a healthy or unhealthy way.

By adjusting how you perceive the signals and cues from your external environment, you may change your behaviour which, over time, may have the potential to act as a trigger for your genes. This may be considered similar to Cairns' lactase-deficient bacteria adjusting to their environmental signals[7], albeit it is assumed that bacteria do not perceive their environment in the same way as you do. It is therefore possible that external environmental signals and cues may elicit the necessary gene action or change in gene expression, which in humans may also be influenced by the their perceived expectations of reality of their external environment, albeit it is considered by some to be a random mutation and by others as an adaptive mutation.

An example of this is associated with sunlight exposure and melanin (the pigment that gives human skin its colour and protects against damage from the sun) secretion into the skin. Ultraviolet rays from the sun stimulate melanocytes within the skin to produce melanin. The more time spent exposed to the sun, the more melanin is released. If a person living in an area of low sunlight, such as England, moves to an area of greater sunlight, such as Australia, this environmental change (greater sunlight exposure) would begin to select genes that allow for increased melanin production, irrespective of how the person perceives their external environment. Although melanin release will naturally occur in response to the change in the person's external environment, their perception of this change may further influence their internal environment.

If the person was being an eternal worrier, then being fair-skinned from England, they may have a perception of reality that creates a fear-induced stress about getting sunburnt under the Australian sun, based on the association of fair skin, sun exposure, easily getting burnt and increased risk of death due to malignant melanoma (skin cancer). This would, as previously stated, flood their internal environment with cortisol, even though they are not facing any immediate situation requiring a fight or flight response. This would not only impact on their general health and wellbeing with sustained cortisol levels, but cortisol may sensitise the skin and trigger inflammation of the skin, which may affect the healthy natural release of melanin.

The opposite would also hold true. If the same person was making the transition from England to Australia, but were instead *Being* the eternal warrior, this would result in a healthy bio-electric signal and cue resulting in a healthy biofield and expression of the bio-electric code and genes, such as those that release melanin. Based on my 'Stem cell and biofield hypothesis', this would allow for a healthy, natural release of melanin in response to the external environment change from sun-poor England to sun-rich Australia, without the potential skin sensitivities from prematurely sustained levels of cortisol arising from the fear-induced, eternal worrier mindset, where the self-talk might be 'I will get burnt' or 'I will not get burnt'. I want to highlight here that this eternal worrier mindset of getting burnt or not getting burnt is still focused on the negative 'burnt'. *Being* the eternal warrior, with the matching mindset, means there would be no fear-induced stress about getting burnt, which means no cortisol release in relation to sunlight. They would be actively listening to their innate wisdom by *Being* (in alignment, synergy, synergism and authenticity) and by doing so naturally and effortlessly would be prepared with the appropriate precautions to respond to the Australian sun. This then allows for the healthy expression of their bio-electric code and the healthy expression of those genes that naturally increases melanin in response to sunlight.

Sunlight is an example of an environmentally generated bio-electric signal and cue. Others include things such as 'geomagnetic' fields, gravity and Schumann's resonance. Not only are bio-electric signals and cues generated externally, they are generated by all living cells, in particular human brain and heart cells. Bio-electric signals and cues are also referred to in traditional medicines, such the meridian system in TCM and chakras in Ayurveda. There are also man-made, artificially generated bio-electric signals and cues, such as power lines, computers, mobile phones, microwaves and other 'technology' devices. All bio-electric signals and cues, whether generated internally, externally or man-made, will influence you in some way. This is explained by my 'Stem cell and biofield hypothesis', which postulates that bio-electric signals and cues influence your biofield, which in turn influences your bio-electric code expression, and this may impact on your genetic expression.

As your coach, I want to introduce you to the research of Professor Irena Ćosić and her team from the School of Electrical and Computer Engineering at RMIT University. This group of researchers may validate the TCM reference of 'chi' (an energy field) and meridians, based on research where they compare the experimental findings from human electrophysiological signal responses to environmental 'geomagnetic' and artificial extremely low frequency electromagnetic fields (EMFs) in order to determine the transfer characteristic from acupuncture meridian analysis and electroencephalogram (EEG) studies. They analysed meridian and point characteristics that have been documented in TCM literature for over 5000 years, with specific computer programs, high sample rate and resolution analogue to digital converters, and the development of complex and powerful mathematical analysis algorithms. This provided a greater scientific understanding of these complex traditional medicine energy systems. These researchers propose that the meridian system allows for efficient administration of energy and 'possibly in the future for the development of diagnostic tools based on the state of the meridians and energetic balance of the overall system'.[8]

Ćosić and her team of researchers also assert that, as the frequency of the meridian system closely correlates with the nature's own resonant frequency (Schuman's resonance — another bio-electric signal and cue), this correlation:

> may indicate a relationship between one's existence and functioning as an integral part of nature and the universe. It could also help explain the sensitivity of our bodies and minds to

> *changes in the environment and even the universe, which has*
> *been used by our ancestors throughout time as a form of spiritual*
> *guidance and a form of healing.*[9]

Although this correlation does not specifically discuss genetic changes in relation to the meridian system, it does offer a lead into the possibility that the interaction between bio-electric signals and cues, that is, the meridian system, may modify the bio-electric signals and cues from the external environment, which may then influence the bio-electric signals and cues of the internal environment (your cells).

The idea that cells have their own bio-electric signals and cues is well documented. It has been observed that, when injured, cells will generate electric currents (a bio-electric signal and cue) in the vicinity of the problem areas. These have been referred to as injury currents.[10] Further, at some point in time, there is a trigger (another bio-electric signal and cue) that initiates an 'injury current polarity reversal', in which a 'healing current' (another bio-electric signal and cue) is produced. This means that the cells of the injured tissue are now actively engaged in the repair and healing process. Although genes are not specifically referred to here, one can only assume that the information for cellular healing comes from the cell's genes, stored within its nucleus, and as such, the injury current polarity reversal and subsequent healing current must access the appropriate information from its genes for the cell to know how to heal itself.

I would bring to your attention that a disturbance in the integrity of living tissue has also been observed to arise from non-physical events. The scientific literature reports that unhealthy energy fields (bio-electric signals and cues), such as an increase in EMF body exposure 'may have adverse consequences on health'.[11] It has been argued that even the EMF emitted by laptop computers (LTCs) may have the potential to be unhealthy to foetal development. It is suggested that the use of the word 'laptop' is misleading, because 'evidence shows that an incorrect use of the LTC can cause an increased EMF body exposure'.[12] These researchers are possibly alluding to, while not specifically implying, that foetal development (healthy cells and stem cells) are influenced by EMF such as those emitted by LTCs (unhealthy bio-electric signals and cues), which affects healthy gene expression.

This example of healthy foetal cells being 'injured' by a non-physical event (EMFs emitted by an LTC) may also be explained by my 'Stem cell and biofield hypothesis' that 'A healthy stem cell (bio-electric code) has a healthy biofield, and a healthy biofield will generate a healthy cell (bio-electric code). The man-made, unhealthy bio-electric signal and cue (EMF from LTC) may lead to an unhealthy foetal biofield. When this is prolonged and unchanged, this will lead to an unhealthy bio-electric code, which may then result in unhealthy gene expression, that is, unhealthy foetal cell development.

When the biofield is interfered with by unhealthy bio-electric signals and cues, this will generate an unhealthy cell (bio-electric code), which in this example is unhealthy foetal cell development. The foetal cells are unable to express their 'optimal self', and as such are unable to fulfil their life's purpose of Being, which are healthy foetal cells. The life purpose of Being optimal foetal cells is to develop into a healthy human Being with a healthy and optimal bio-electric code.

The healthy gene expression that creates life cannot occur when interfered with. This is exactly what the pioneering research of Michael Levin and his team of researchers from the Department of Biology and Tufts Center for Regenerative and Developmental Biology have demonstrated, as previously discussed. Levin and Tseng published an article titled 'Cracking the bio-electric code: Probing endogenous ionic controls of pattern formation'.[13] These authors state that 'bio-electric cues function alongside chemical gradients, transcriptional networks, and haptic/tensile cues as part of the morpho-genetic field that orchestrates individual cell behaviour into large-scale anatomical pattern formation'. Levin and Tseng suggest the presence of a bio-electric code that represents and dictates a mapping of physiological properties to anatomical outcomes. This article in particular specifically challenges existing models of eye fate restriction and tissue competence maps. Levin and Tseng demonstrate their assertion based on the observation that a specific voltage range (a specific bio-electric signal and cue) is necessary for demarcation of eye fields in frog embryos. Their experiments support their assertion stating that 'remarkably, artificially setting other somatic cells to the eye-specific voltage range resulted in formation of eyes in aberrant locations, including tissues that are not in the normal anterior ectoderm lineage: eyes could be formed in the gut, on the tail, or in the lateral plate meso-derm'.

Having eyes formed in aberrant locations (unhealthy gene expression) due to specific exposure to eye-specific voltage (an unhealthy bio-electric signal and cue when used in any other area other than the area for an eye) would not be a favourable outcome. This research, however, reinforces my 'Stem cell and biofield hypothesis', that is, an unhealthy cell occurs in response to unhealthy bio-electric signals and cues. Although Levin and Tseng do not mention the biofield, my 'Stem cell and biofield hypothesis' postulates that bio-electric signals and cues (the eye-specific voltage) must first disrupt the biofield, which then influences the bio-electric code causing the unhealthy gene expression (eyes formed in aberrant locations).

The essence of this research is to demonstrate that physical stimulation (such as direct injury to a cell) and non-physical stimulation (such as the EMF and eye-specific voltage) have been independently reported to cause cell and gene changes. These cell and gene changes may be either healthy or unhealthy, depending on the type of bio-electric signal and cue. Although each of these researchers explain what they have observed differently, all of these changes may be logically explained by my 'Stem cell and biofield hypothesis'. You are literally a bundle of highly specialised cells that originate from an ovum and sperm, which, through the process of fertilisation, became a united cell. Through the processes of foetal development, this cell transforms into human life. The anticipated outcome is the birth of a healthy human being, but it is influenced by the prevailing bio-electric signals and cues generated by internal and external environmental factors.

Once you are born (the neonate), my 'Stem cell and biofield hypothesis' continues to apply — a healthy neonate (bio-electric code) has a healthy biofield, and a healthy biofield creates a healthy neonate (bio-electric code). No one can tell a neonate how to grow — it grows and develops as it is designed to do. The life purpose of a neonate is to respond to its environment (bio-electric signals and cues) so it can optimally develop into a healthy child. It is the bio-electric signals and cues within the neonate's environment (internal and external) that shape the outcome of a healthy neonate, not merely the genes that the neonate inherited, as discussed above with Cairns, and observations from researchers like Lipton about the natural environment and gene expression. The idea that the environment (bio-electric signals and cues) influences us is reinforced by the pioneering research in the field of mammalian synthetic biology.

This offers mind-blowing possibilities about genetic changes with the invention of gene switches.[14] Scientists in this field have designed gene switches that are responsive to traceless cues such as light, gas and radio waves, complex gene circuits, including oscillators, cancer-killing gene classifiers, and programmable biocomputers, as well as prosthetic gene networks that provide treatment strategies for gouty arthritis, diabetes and obesity.

Mind-controlled transgene expression is made possible by synthetic mind-genetic interfaces which allow for mind-controlled transgene expression in a living organism.

For this to occur requires different serially linked electronic, optic and genetic components, such as the brain–computer interface (BCI) to capture brain waves, as worn by human subjects, to process these electronic signals and provides a, mental state-based electronic output that switches the field generator ON and OFF. For further detail you can review Flocker et al and in particular figure 5. The human subjects wearing the BCI headset performed three different mental states: a self-trained biofeedback mental state (maintaining the observed meditation-meter values on the 10- LED indicator within a desired range); a concentration-based mental state (computer gaming); and a meditation-based mental state (relaxation).[15]

The advances in the field of cybernetics (the design of functional man–machine interfaces in which brain–computer interfaces process brainwaves to control electromechanical prostheses, such as bionic extremities and even wheelchairs) and optogenetic devices, demonstrate that mental states can indeed change gene expression and therefore change cell health. The merging of cybernetics with optogenetics technologies has created the situation where it is possible to demonstrate that brainwaves (non-physical, internal environment bio-electric signals and cues) can remotely control transgene expression and cellular behaviour in living cells! That is, your mental states, such as biofeedback, concentration and meditation, have been captured via these cybernetic and optogenetic technologies to directly control the transgene expression in living cells and mammals, which changes DNA expression. All this is achieved wirelessly, like an LTC connecting wirelessly to a modem! How amazing is this discovery! Let me state this again for you, just in case you missed it.

These researchers have shown that it is possible to wirelessly activate synthetic mind-controlled gene switches that enable human brain activities and mental states to program transgene expression in human cells![16]

These fields of research further reinforce what my 'Stem cell and biofield hypothesis' postulates — that external, non-physical bio-electric signals and cues, such as light and radio waves can impact on genes. What my hypothesis infers is that these bio-electric signals and cues first have an impact on the biofield, which then influences the bio-electric code. Changes in the bio-electric code then have the potential to activate genes, which ultimately influences cell health. This is where I would like you to become inspired and excited by the possibility that if meditation, concentration and biofeedback where demonstrated to impact on gene expression, then other external, non-physical bio-electric signals and cues, such as mental states associated with your thoughts and emotions generated by brain activity, could also have the potential to change your genes, and therefore your cell health. Having this understanding means that, when you are making the choice of *Being* the eternal warrior (a bio-electric signal and cue), you are influencing your own biofield, bio-electric code and gene expression! If mental states can achieve genetic changes within cells, then the mental state where you are consciously making the choice of *Being* an eternal warrior (a healthy, non-physical bio-electric signal and cue) should in theory have the same effect! So, making the conscious choice of *Being* the warrior (the healthy mental state) would result in a healthy biofield, which then influences the healthy expression of the bio-electric code and then the healthy expression of the genes. The opposite would be true if you default to the unhealthy, non-physical bio-electric signals and cues of being the worrier!

This all sounds amazing, but also highly technological, and on the surface, it may appear that it requires expensive equipment and a research laboratory to achieve healthy cell gene outcomes. As your coach, however, I want to remind you that other ways are possible, particularly so when you understand how to implement the 'Stem cell and biofield hypothesis' and *Being* (alignment, synergy, authentic and synergism) the eternal warrior.

Other research scientists have demonstrated that it is possible to influence your genes without the need for high-tech gadgetry. *The Lancet Oncology* published an article titled 'Effect of comprehensive lifestyle changes on telomerase activity and telomere length in men with biopsy-proven low-risk prostate cancer: 5-year follow-up of a descriptive pilot study'.[17] This small pilot study demonstrated for the first time that changes in diet, exercise, stress management and social support (all of which are examples of bio-electric signals and cues) can influence human gene expression by influencing telomeres.

Telomeres are the protective caps on the ends of chromosomes that affect how quickly cells age and die. Picture a shoelace and the plastic tips on the end that make it easier to thread the lace. The plastic tip represents telomeres, which protect the ends of chromosomes and help them remain stable. As they become shorter, and as their structural integrity weakens, the cells age and die quicker. In recent years, shorter telomeres have become associated with a broad range of aging-related diseases, including many forms of cancer, stroke, vascular dementia, cardiovascular disease, obesity, osteoporosis and diabetes. These findings have sparked interest from other researchers to perform intervention studies that examine telomeres as well was telomerase activity (the enzyme that make telomeres longer) in healthy volunteers, carers of patients with Alzheimer's disease, individuals with obesity, and breast cancer patients.[18]

One interesting observation from each of these intervention studies — they all involve using the non-physical bio-electric signal and cue of mental state. In these cases, it was meditation as the intervention that demonstrated, to varying degrees of success, increases in telomerase activity and subtle changes in telomere length. These independent studies provide further support for my 'Stem cell and biofield hypothesis' - a healthy bio-electric signal and cue (e.g. meditation) results in a healthy biofield, which influences the healthy expression of the bio-electric code, allowing for healthy gene expression (changes in telomerase activity and telomere length), thereby improving cell function, which ultimately improves your health and wellbeing.

Although the mental state of meditation may generate a sense of calm and peace, imagine if you made the choice to implement the mental state of Being the eternal warrior — this might literally change your life. However, you established at the beginning of this book that you were, in fact, being the eternal worrier, without making the conscious choice! How much of living your life's purpose optimally have you missed out on by not making that choice?

The idea that non-physical bio-electric signals and cues can influence genetic material has also been observed by the preliminary clinical research of Scott C Kelsey, a graduate assistant at the Department of Biomedical Sciences at Missouri State University in his report titled *Qualification and quantification of telomeric elongation due to electromagnetic resonance exposure.*[19] He proposes that if telomerase can be activated via electromagnetic resonance exposure (a non-physical bio-electric signal and cue) within the cell, it could lead to an increase in cellular upkeep without the administration of pharmaceutical drugs.

The data from Kelsey's preliminary experiments appear to support that non-physical bio-electric signals and cues (electromagnetic exposure) at a certain frequency somehow influences telomeric maintenance. According to his report, telomeric lengths are maintained and, in some instances, elongated. Not only was this observed, but the cell cultures he was studying displayed prolonged life. The critical point of about twenty to thirty passages in culture telomeres where you would normally expect the triggers that signal the cells to enter senescence (the condition or process of deterioration with age, the loss of a cell's power of division and growth) did not occur. Kelsey observed the maintenance of telomere length even into the relatively old age of the cell cultures. Although larger clinical trials are required to further validate this observation, Kelsey's results appear to indicate telomere maintenance and subtle elongation can occur in response to a specific electromagnetic resonance exposure.

All this research demonstrates that your genes cannot possibly be the only factor in control of gene expression, or of being switched on or off.

Although it is believed that your genes are self-regulating, with random mutations occurring, the above collection of information inadvertently challenges this belief. As demonstrated above, there are both non-physical and physical environmental bio-electrical signals and cues that may influence cellular and gene changes. As your coach, I have been guiding you towards the understanding that there is one very influential non-physical bio-electric signal and cue that may bring about these changes within you, and it is free for you to access. It is your mental state/thoughts. As previously discussed, your perceived expectations of reality, and what you are consciously choosing to feel in your present moment, will influence whether or not you are *Being* the eternal warrior. Not enough emphasis is placed on the importance of making this conscious choice of *Being* the eternal warrior, let alone having confidence in the outcome after making this choice.

Even at a cellular level, your perceptions have an impact on gene and cell health. This observation is made contrary to what has been dubbed 'the primacy of DNA' stemming from the 1953 discovery of DNA by Watson and Crick, which later determined that DNA was necessary as the blueprint for making proteins. Along with this finding was the misperception that DNA had to be the 'brain of the cell'. According to Lipton's observations when he first began cloning stem cells in 1968, when stem cells were put in culture dishes with the conditions that support muscle growth, the muscle cells evolved, and when he put the same stem cells in an altered environment, for example, one that supports bone growth, they would evolve into bone cells. Lipton repeated these observations by being able to make the stem cells evolve into fat (adipose) cells by again changing the environment to one that supports adipose cells. Although Lipton's stem cells were genetically identical, their fate was controlled by the environment in which Lipton placed them. From these observations, Lipton came to the realisation that the stem cell's membrane was like an information-processing computer chip, and the stem cell's genes were like the hard drive with all the stem cell's potential at hand. Lipton postulated that the stem cell evolved, not because of the gene programs already contained within the nucleus, but because of the feedback of information from the environment.

How then did the environment, as demonstrated by Lipton's research, activate the cell's genes via the cell membrane? Understanding cell membrane anatomy and physiology offers the answers to that question. Although it's beyond the scope of this book to teach you cellular anatomy and physiology, as your coach, I would like you to know that the cell membrane is more than just a physical barrier that keeps the cell's internal contents in and the external environment out — it's a place of great diversity and activity! The cell membrane:

- is the site for the sodium ion pump, which maintains cell volume by pumping sodium out of the cell
- selectively allows ions to pass through it
- is the site for hormone-receptor and cell signal interactions
- is a place where many reactions take place, such as oxidative phosphorylation which occurs on the cell membrane of mitochondrial cells, and protein synthesis, which occurs on the ribosomal membranes of the rough endoplasmic reticulum.

Essentially, what Lipton's 1968 experiments demonstrated, coupled with a better understanding of the cell membrane, is that what the cell perceives through its membrane is its external environment. What it perceives will be what it responds to, which then influences changes within its internal environment (cellular and gene changes). As you are made up of at least 50 trillion living cells, this means there are 50 trillion cell membranes perceiving your environment! Lipton considered the possible implications of this, and although cell membranes are an important interface between the cell's internal and external environments, Lipton postulates that cell membranes may be what makes you different from everyone else through the presence of a set of unique identifying protein keys (also referred to as receptors) on the surface of your cells. Lipton likens these surface protein receptors to a computer keyboard, which responds to environmental information via the information-processing computer chip (the cell membrane), which in turn engages the specific computer programs (the gene/DNA program). Lipton's interpretation of his observations suggests that, although you are a complex multidimensional cellular organism, your identity is derived, not from within you (your cells), but from outside you — your environment based on what your cells are perceiving! But how can your cells perceive you?

The definition of 'perceive' is to become aware or conscious of (something) or to come to realise or understand. You might question how a cell can become conscious, let alone come to realise or understand something in the same way as you can. A cell may not be seen to be conscious or understand as you do, but a collection of cells, known as a human (you!), does. Not only do you perceive, you (50 trillion cells) also have thoughts, feelings and emotions, all of which are various types of mental states. As explained above and elaborated on by my 'Stem cell and biofield hypothesis', your mental state is an example of a non-physical bio-electric signal and cue that influences the biofield that surrounds you, your organs and your cells. Your biofield acts as both a receiver and transmitter of information that influences your bio-electric code, which may possibly be filtered by the meridian system (as discussed by Ćosić's research), and then influences your cellular and genetic changes. This possibly occurs by activating one of the many cell membrane's cells signalling processes. As your coach, I remind you that this is where making the conscious choice to be in the mental state of Being the eternal warrior may be interpreted as a healthy bio-electric signal and cue, because when you are not making this choice, you are saying yes to being the eternal worrier!

When you are being the eternal worrier, you are more reactive to your external environment, and you get 'stuck' in your emotions that manifest from your rigid belief systems and perceptions of your life.

When you are living from this mental state (being the eternal worrier), which is what you have already determined at the beginning of this book, then you are living life from a reflex reactive behavioural state. This, as previously discussed, triggers the stress response and inadvertently you are living under chronic stress. When you are under stress, you lose intelligence and although this may appear to be a negative thing, in a life-death situation, it is required. Why? Because it's not a time to be thinking; it's a time to be actively listening, feeling and responding. However, when not faced with life-threatening situations, the loss of intelligence may further compound your chronic stress (unhealthy bio-electric signal and cue). As previously stated, chronic stress also initiates the same fight or flight physiological reactions, which include:

reduced blood flow to your viscera which shuts down your growth and development, your immune system works at reduced capacity to conserve energy, and you start operating from reflex behaviour rather than responding to life, and each of these responses are now seen as unhealthy bio-electric signals and cues!

Your perceptions and beliefs are the non-physical bio-electric signals and cues that allow this mental state to continue indefinitely, or until you make the change to Being the eternal warrior in your life! The evidence, as outlined above, offers the support that your genetics are not the only factor in determining who you are or what you think you are! The other factors are your mind, your perceptions, your beliefs. I want to reinforce to you that if you allow yourself to change your thoughts, beliefs and mental state, you will change your bio-electric signals and cues, your biofield, your bio-electric code, your cell membrane, your genes, and ultimately you, all by actively listening and feeling. Consider what changes could occur for you when you are *Being* the eternal warrior. Consider the potential this has to change the world. I emphasise here that you have the power to eternally change your life by making the conscious choice to change your mental state so that you are selecting your warrior genes!

Before you bring up all the excuses as to why this may seem impossible for you, as your coach, I remind you to recall chapter 1, 'Fear and laziness'. If you cannot recall it, go back and re-read that chapter. Why? Because there are no excuses for not making your choice. You can take out the 'It's my programming' or 'My family is like this' or 'It's how I am wired' excuses from your repertoire. What society has been calling genetic determinism (the genes selected for your life are totally responsible for you and all you do) is not supported by the evidence presented above. The responsibility is with you, not your genes! Why do people not like this idea? Because they don't like responsibility, and they get to blame someone or something else, as previously discussed. I am determined to get you out of this mental state of blaming, because it is an unhealthy bio-electric signal and cue that keeps you being an eternal worrier!

Blame is a mug's game, and only creates a victim consciousness. The moment you blame someone or something for anything, you immediately place that person or thing in a position of power over you, which is yet another unhealthy bio-electric signal and cue that robs you of your ability to live optimally, live purposefully!

To further explain this concept for you, I will share with you this example. Let's say that you started a job in fashion design. The building you work at is extremely stylish, and every morning in the foyer, you see a big fountain with a metal angel on top of it. You smile when you see it, and say to yourself, 'I am so lucky, I love my job and the people I work with' and so on. These are examples of self-generated bio-electric signals and cues. These signals and cues reinforce to you that this job is your dream job; the people and your boss are great, and you love it. Then the company you work for is bought out, your old boss is transferred, and the new boss has no idea what they are doing. You begin to experience problems at work due to personality conflicts between you and the new boss. Work stops being fun, and now when you walk into that building, you see the metal angel on top of the fountain and say, 'This job is no fun anymore. I hate it, everything about it, even this stupid fountain!' These, too, are self-generated bio-electric signals and cues, but they are now self-generated *unhealthy* bio-electric signals and cues. When you have drinks with your friends later on in the week, you begin to tell them your woes, and how, as soon as you see the metal angel on top of the fountain it makes you feel sad. Right there, you have become a slave to a metal angel on top of the fountain (a piece of inert metal). This angel now has the exclusive function of making you feel sad. Of course, it never had that power — it is a piece of metal and is inert — but you have attached a meaning to it that robs you of the power to choose how to feel! Paradoxically, it also robbed you of the power to choose how to feel when you believed that the angel was associated with feeling happy and lucky with your work!

You are the only person who is able to make you feel anything. No inert object on Earth, no job, holiday, person or any other thing, has the power to make you feel anything; you give that power to it. The same applies to people when we say, for example, 'John makes me feel scared!' John, like the metal angel on top of the fountain, has no such power over you. Instead, you have chosen (consciously or not) to blame him for your inability to process fear! As we have now established, your perceived expectation of reality is that you are in a fearful environment, which inevitably influences gene expression. To further illustrate this point, when a cell (or a group of cells, e.g. you) experiences a new environment (e.g. the 'John makes me feel scared' environment), it specifically adjusts its genetic readout to accommodate any environmental needs, demands and necessities (e.g. fight or flight/protection mode) to survive. Consequently, the structural and behavioural expression of the cell (you) is a reflection of the organism's environment (e.g. your cells (you) would be in protection mode) due to a perceived stressor (John). The payoff here is that, by blaming John, you are free of any responsibility for your emotions, actions, behaviour and cellular state, but the cost is never attaining mastery of your inside world, and therefore never achieving mastery over your outside world. All you do is create unhealthy bio-electric signals and cues, an unhealthy biofield resulting in the unhealthy expression of the bio-electric code, and as stated in my 'Stem cell and biofield hypothesis', this can only lead to unhealthy cells, which means an unhealthy you!

Said another way, you are in charge of and responsible for your genes and resultant state of health. Are you *Being* the eternal warrior, associated with personal growth and development, where thriving is the focus, or being the eternal worrier, which activates the fight or flight response/protection mode, where survival is the focus? If you have not made the conscious choice to *Be* the warrior, then you have said no to this, and yes to the perceptions and interactions in your life that keep you being the eternal worrier.

This is important for you to understand, because your genes adapt to your perceptions and beliefs about your environment. The flow of information from you to the environment is a two-way process — the external environment influences the internal environment and vice versa.

The information presented and examples used above serve to illustrate that you have the power to not only change your perceptions which changes your bio-electric signals and cues, your biofield and the expression of your bio-electric code but the end result of all this are changes in your genetics (the physical changes). Changing your perception and your genetics allow you to stop living from a place of fear-induced stress (being the eternal worrier) and to revive growth mode (*Being* the eternal warrior). We will explore how fear is the hurdle you need to get over in order to be open to making this change in the next chapter, after we look at the take-home message.

The take-home message — your transformation from eternal *worrier* to eternal *warrior*

The *eternal worrier smiles* because they are able to escape responsibility of their perceptions and beliefs by having the understanding that genetic mutation is random and unspecific, making them victims to their genes. They believe that DNA is the brain of the cell, is in charge, self-regulates, and can switch itself on or off independent of them. They therefore blame others (e.g. their parents or other people) or other factors (e.g. their genes) for where they are at in their life. This creates unhealthy bio-electric signals and cues, an unhealthy biofield and an unhealthy expression of their bio-electric code, which the worrier believes they are powerless to change. They are unable to change their DNA and their predetermined genetic outcome and use this as an excuse to live an unhealthy lifestyle, blaming others for their perceived lack of control or their choices in their life. They experience life as a victim and justify their reasons for living in a fear-induced state, avoiding taking any responsibility for the actions and outcomes of their life.

The *eternal warrior smiles* because they know genes may mutate specifically and deliberately to adapt to their perceptions of their environment. They understand that DNA is not the brain of the cell, and cannot be in charge, self-regulate, or switch itself on or off! Instead, the warrior knows that they can control their internal environment (including their DNA and genes) because they have the choice and responsibility for how they perceive their external environment. They know they can generate their own healthy bio-electric signals and cues, a healthy biofield and the healthy expression of their bio-electric code by knowing how to avoid ongoing fear-induced stress states by adjusting their perceptions and beliefs of their external environment, thereby mastering their internal environment. The warrior therefore chooses not to become a victim who blames others or things, like their genes, parents, any other person or inert object, for where they are at in their life. They realise and relish that they can be, and are, responsible for the direction of their life and health, because they choose to hold healthy perceptions and beliefs, which create healthy bio-electric signals and cues and a healthy biofield and bio-electric code expression, which results in a healthy environment for them to live in where they can live optimally and purposefully.

CHAPTER 5

Eliminating fear

The thought of eliminating fear may seem impossible for you to do in today's society, where you are continually bombarded with images and reports of violence, terrorist attacks, suicide bombers, pollutants, environmental disasters, financial debt, uncertainty about achieving global peace, and so on. Whether it's seeing these issues on the news (local or international), reading a newspaper, listening to the radio, watching YouTube or looking at Instagram, Facebook or twitter posts, almost everything you see and hear makes you feel the need to protect yourself. Fear-inducing images and reports are very different to the fear when you are faced with a life or death situation, yet your body will respond in the same way to both, by engaging your 'fight, flight' response so that you are ready to protect yourself. The same emotional response, however, can also make you freeze-up, becoming helpless to protect yourself!

Although most people associate the effects of fear with fight or flight, the freeze reaction is just as important to interrupt. Freezing is essentially an inability to process a sudden unexpected number of stimuli. You may not be aware that people freeze in the face of danger, but it is common. Freezing happens! Most people freeze-up when faced with the fear they feel most often. From my experience, the most common fear is based on ego and the potential harm to self-esteem. How do you know if you freeze up? Do this simple self-check — any time you find yourself in a situation where you are feeling unhappy, but still do nothing to change that feeling, confirms to you that you are frozen! The act of freezing becomes easier over time, too. I say this because the more we let our fears freeze us into inaction, the more likely we are to repeat that behaviour in the future. This is commonly known as a 'conditioned response'. You are conditioning yourself to respond to challenging or uncomfortable situations by freezing, or said another way, unhealthy fear empowers you to do nothing!

Either way, the fight, flight or freeze response is activated in the absence of life and death situations where no end is in sight, which as previously discussed is not beneficial to your health and wellbeing. The never-ending, fear-inducing images and reports occur simultaneously with the fear of failing (as discussed in chapter 1) and the fear of not meeting Maslow's hierarchy of needs (as discussed in chapter 2).

Any non-life threatening but fear-inducing event serves, not only to condition you to live your life in fear (consciously or not), but to keep you being the eternal worrier! As you may have already discovered at the beginning of this book, you are being the eternal worrier, albeit you were not making this your conscious choice. Instead, you have been automatically defaulting to being the eternal worrier based on how you were conditioned by your environment, which is reinforced and maintained by these fear-induced images and reports, fear of failing, and the fear of not meeting the basic needs of living in today's society and so on. Let's say, for example, you were not aware of the images and reports that the news, various media outlets, Instagram, twitter, Facebook, YouTube and so on publish. Apart from possibly worrying about being judged and accused of 'living under a rock', or the worry about missing out on the gossip, would you be less fearful? The saying 'out of sight, out of mind' could be applied here — being exposed less to fear-inducing images and reports may eliminate some fear, but as your coach, I would like you to recall here the earlier discussions about your perceived expectation of reality.

Although it is possible that you may eliminate some feeling of fear by not seeing these fear-inducing images and reports, it is more likely, as previously discussed, that your perceived expectation of reality predicts your actual reality — the degree of fear you experience in your present moment, irrespective of the images and reports. The probability that you will feel more fear is increased when you are being the eternal worrier, something for nothing sufferer, passively being the lazy drifter who blames everyone and everything else for their life and is inflexible, as discussed in chapter 1.

I would again highlight to you the importance of how you perceive or view yourself in your present moment. How you perceive your environment and its relationship to what you fear is not a new idea. The Roman philosopher Epictetus said two millennia ago: 'Men are disturbed not by things, but by the view which they take of them.'[1]

More recently, these words have been echoed by David Robeike, a former Director of Risk Communication at the Harvard Center for Risk Analysis, Boston. Robeike stated that: 'We must acknowledge that a significant component of risk is not the physical hazard itself, or how much of it we are exposed to, but how we perceive that hazard and exposure.'² The question I ask you to consider now is — what perceived expectation of reality are you presently making about yourself? Are you viewing yourself as *Being* the eternal warrior, who is immune to the something for nothing disease, actively *Being* the inspired and adaptable go-getter paddler, who takes responsibility for their life so that they are living their life optimally and purposefully?

It would not come as any surprise to me if you cannot currently see the choice of *Being* an eternal warrior as available to you, and instead are trapped in fear, worry or any other emotion, as discussed in chapter 4. Why am I unsurprised? When reading over the works of past great minds such as philosophers, theorists or poets, you will find a common theme — they refer to fear as being an inbuilt emotion that paralyses you, and robs you of your heart and soul, and it's something you must battle. In other words, it is believed by some that you are programmed this way! For example, the philosopher Jean Gebser theorises that fear is the natural mutational outcome from the evolution of consciousness.³ Gebser asserts that when you look back in history to a time when humans sought independence from the primordial forces of nature, at that time they observed these forces as pressing in on their awareness, and perceived them as a threat that could dissolve them if they could not gain control over them. Imagine for a moment if humans did not view nature's forces as a threat! However, as it is asserted that humans saw this as a threat, Gebser suggests that, in order for them to deal with this perceived threat from nature's forces, they needed to turn to something - sorceresses, witchcraft and wizards — in order to free themselves from the grip and spell of nature.⁴

Gebser points out that, in the beginning, when humans were still in unity with nature, there was no perceived struggle, but as human consciousness developed, the perceived struggle started, and this was where the magic man began the struggle for power that has not ceased since. This struggle was for humans, not nature, to become the maker.

Gebser believed that this ancient terror of the magic consciousness is still present in all of us, and is still readily observable in modern technology and contemporary power politics. He stated that:

> *Nature, the surrounding world, other human beings must be ruled so that man is not ruled by them. This fear that man is compelled to rule the outside world — so as not to be ruled by it — is symptomatic of our times. Every individual who fails to realize that he must rule himself falls victim to that drive.*⁵

I would state that this view of human consciousness — where you must fear being ruled and as such must strive to rule nature and others — is a big waste of time, energy and life! I ask you to be open to the possibility that to create change within yourself, you need to make a choice of how you perceive yourself and your environment. As previously discussed with my 'Stem cell and biofield hypothesis', your perceived expectation of reality is a bio-electric signal and cue that influences your biofield, your bio-electric code and your gene expression. When it is reinforcing you being the eternal worrier, every cell in your body will literally be reacting to this unhealthy bio-electric signal and cue, until you change your perceived expectation of reality to something different, that is, *Being* the eternal warrior, where the unhealthy expression of fear, worry or other emotions cannot exist.

The concept that you create your reality based on your perceived expectation of reality is not a new idea. The Irish philosopher George Berkeley is known for his theory called 'immaterialism', later referred to as 'subjective idealism'. This theory states that familiar objects like tables and chairs are only ideas in the minds of perceivers and, as a result, cannot exist without being perceived. Accordingly, Berkeley advocates that: 'The only things we perceive are our perceptions.'[6] The view that the animal observer, such as you, creates reality and not the other way around is one of the central themes of what is referred to as 'biocentrism' as advocated by Robert Lanza. This view of the world in which life and consciousness are the bottom line in understanding the larger universe—biocentrism—revolves around the way a subjective experience, which you call consciousness, relates to a physical process.[7]

What I would like you to understand is that behind every eternal worrier is an individual who has not made the choice to change their perceived expectation of reality, most probably due to their inability to process the emotion of fear (fear of the unknown and fear of making choices to change and so on)! Fear is usually the outcome when you are not listening to your innate wisdom, or are unable to understand the messages relayed by your innate wisdom because you have never been taught to listen. This may create feelings of knowing that something needs to change, but you cannot quite identify exactly what needs to change, why it needs to change, or whether you can trust in the changes needed. This then compounds your fear. When you get stuck in both fear and laziness (as discussed in chapter 1), you end up not changing your life (for the better) because you are immersed in being the eternal worrier, and this does not get you anywhere! From the previous chapter, you know that what you perceive in your environment creates your bio-electric signals and cues (either healthy or unhealthy), which influences your biofield and the expression of your bio-electric code, and consequently which genes you are expressing. It is a natural biological mechanism, so if you are surrounding yourself with fear, you are selecting genes for protection, which are the exact opposite of the genes associated with growth and thriving.

Growth is associated with your viscera (internal organs: heart, lungs, digestive system, liver, pancreas and so on). Protection is associated with your muscles and bones, and adrenal system (fight or flight response). Your adrenal system is the master switch that allows you to switch between the two modes — growth or protection. Biologically and physiologically, you cannot be in growth and protection mode at the same time. For example, if you were being chased by a lion (a bio-electric signal and cue), your adrenal system would switch from growth mode into protection mode, and you would use the fight or flight response, which would be secreting cortisol and adrenalin (stress hormones) and immediately activate your muscles and bones (protection) in order to fly or fight the lion to avoid being its lunch. It would be very unlikely that you would just sit still and digest your own lunch (growth mode using your viscera) in that situation! Ideally, you want to be out of harm's way so that you can use your own viscera in a growth state to digest your lunch!

Although you are most likely not faced with the life or death prospects of confronting a wild lion roaming around your urban environment (unless you live in the jungles of Africa), it is interesting to note that people traditionally fear public speaking more than death itself. There is no actual life or death confrontation with public speaking, but lion or not, this fear still initiates the exact same physiological response (protection mode) as if you were being chased by a lion. Recall here that fear equals protection. Your nervous/endocrine systems will switch from growth mode to protection mode, where the selection of protection genes, muscle and bone are activated, even though there is no immediate threat to life. Public speaking is not the only thing that does this. As previously stated, any fear will initiate the fight or flight response, so it may be a great time now to face both the fear of public speaking and death (or any other fears that you have, for that matter). Why? Because both, when perceived as unhealthy bio-electric signals and cues in your environment, result in an unhealthy biofield and unhealthy expression of the bio-electric code, which leads to the unhealthy expression of protection genes (not growth genes), increasing the likelihood of succumbing to stress-induced disease states. Remember that it is your perception of 'something' and the fear of that perception that is an unhealthy bio-electric signal and cue, and not the 'something' itself as discussed above.

There is another place that fear shows up constantly and seems to be counterproductive to the goal, that is, in allopathic (Western) medicine. If you consult an allopathic medical practitioner (your GP), and if you were diagnosed with cancer, you would be strongly recommended to partake in chemotherapy or radiotherapy. If you choose for yourself that there may be other alternatives, you may be met with the argument that if you don't get the treatment that is being recommended to you, you could die. And just like that, there is that number two fear — fear of death — at the precise moment when you least need it. This further activates your fight or flight response, and enhances being the eternal worrier. How can you possibly begin to select the genes that would kickstart you into growth and healing when you are fearful and worrying about dying, uncertain of life itself, and possibly fearful of everyone around you (your environment), when fear is promoted right in front of you? You cannot, unless that is, you make the conscious choice to *Be* the eternal warrior.

As your coach, I ask you this question: Why would anyone want you in a fear-based state? Simple. When you are fearful, you are easier to control. If you are living in fear, you will rarely ask why. You just accept what is put in front of you and do as you are told, after all, you do not know any better, nor do you have the time to find out for yourself. This may be evident in the USA, where they have achieved a whole new level of fear with their proclaimed war on terror. The US government (well, at first anyway) gave reasons for issuing its terror warnings, however superficial they were! Nowadays, though, they don't even bother with a reason! It is almost as if the moment someone suspects the populace is beginning to ask questions, they issue a heightened security threat, ensuring that there should now be less focus on how the country is being governed.

Another perceived expectation of reality that needs to shift, with some assistance from me as your coach, is one that many of us have, and may be one of the largest perceptions of reality — your perceptions around money. I want to shift this perception for as many people as possible because the fear of scarcity limits people and keeps them living from pay cheque to pay cheque because they have to focus on surviving!

When you are in this state, you are so much easier to manipulate and control. Setting you free of this perception makes you more independent and truly starts to shift you from worrier to warrior. Regardless of what your perception of money is, let's try a new perception (it is just a perception, not fact, so you really you have nothing to lose if you choose to play along). Your new perceived expectation of reality is that 'money comes easily to me'. See how this works for you — try it out. Say this phrase to yourself five to ten times. After having focused on saying this phrase, stop and see what it feels like to you knowing that money comes easily to you. If you are not feeling good or excited about your new perceived expectation of reality regarding money, I encourage you to try again, and stop thinking that this will never happen to you! Again, you have nothing to lose here. Be open to the possibility that you can allow yourself to create a new perception around money, that is, 'money comes easily to me'. I encourage you to keep repeating this statement until you feel good or feel a sense of lightness in yourself.

I would like you to expand on your perceived expectation of reality about money by incorporating another new understanding: 'Money is a storehouse of energy that you exchange for stuff you need or experiences that you want.' I encourage you to repeat this phrase to yourself, as you did above, five to ten times, or until you start feeling that sense of lightness and feeling good and better about yourself and your place in life. You can repeat both phrases together if you like. Give it a try and see how you are feeling about money now. You should be feeling a sense of change. How, then, can you explain this change in yourself now? You didn't change your place or position in life.

You didn't change the amount of money you currently have in your bank account. All you did was adopt two phrases that created a change in your perceived expectation of reality around money, and when it feels good, as it does, it's usually right, right? When it comes to money, take the emotional pressure off yourself by making the choice to maintain this new perception. Making this choice is easier when you are *Being* the eternal warrior! If you didn't feel a change, read on, as I will introduce you to a technique that may assist you in processing your fear (or any other emotional block) about money. If, however, you did experience a change and feel that you are starting to get the hang of changing your perceived expectation of reality, I encourage you to add another phrase to your new money perception: 'Money is power to do what I would like to do and represents freedom to pursue my dreams.'

Again, repeat this phrase to yourself five to ten times and as you did before. You should now be feeling jazzed up, excited and pumped. Why? Because your new perceived expectation of reality of money is now: 'Money comes easily to me, money is a storehouse of energy that I exchange for things or experiences that I want, which offers me the power to do what I would like to do and gives me the freedom to pursue my dreams.' If this is what money represents to you, then this will naturally increase your desire to acquire money, allowing you to focus on having money, so once you obtain it, you can then use it however you see fit for yourself. This may include using money charitably, such as supporting homeless children and so on. It's up to you how you use it, because it is your perceived expectation of reality, but if you don't have money, how can you use it?

The key point here is that, in order for you to acquire money, you must first remove yourself from the 'fear treadmill'. That is, you need to clear your negative perceptions around money and the negative perception portrayed about money from your environment. For example, you have the option to listen to the 'news' and grow more afraid every day and continue to perceive that the invisible threat is real, or you can do something different. If you continue down the invisible fear pathway, your health and your life automatically are in second place — you will continue be the eternal worrier. The irony here is that how you live, whether that is in peace and growth (*Being the eternal warrior*) or in fear and protection (being the eternal worrier), is completely up to you! Your perceived expectation of reality will change as soon as you make the choice to change it, as I demonstrated with you about money.

Now that you understand a little about fear (and emotions), and even if you did not feel any change with the money exercise above, I will now introduce you to two Rhett Ogston Applications (ROAs) in the form of two techniques that may assist you to eliminate fear and achieve emotional harmony. One is called the emotionally charged memory (ECM) technique, and it is based on neuroscience, neuro-linguistic programming (NLP) and Ned Herrmanns' dominant whole brain theory. The other is called universal emotional freedom technique (UEFT), and it has evolved from thought field therapy (TFT) and emotional freedom technique (EFT).

ECM technique from FlameTree: *the personal development & healing system*

Although this method will work well with very intense fears or phobias, I highly recommend that you learn the process thoroughly, using a moderately fearful situation and following the steps below. This technique may also be used for any emotion, but fear is used here as an example.

While doing the following 'thought exercise', once you are feeling the fear, you are required to roll your eyes four times clockwise, and then four times anticlockwise to ensure all memories, regardless of where they are located in the brain (e.g. visual lobe, auditory lobe), are available to be expunged, based on Ned Hermann's dominant-whole-brain theory.

ECM procedure

1. **Fearful situation (an unhealthy bio-electric signal and cue).** Take a minute and think of the situation that makes you moderately fearful. This could be public speaking, making a cold call, making a presentation, or any other situation that makes you afraid. Think about the situation just long enough to get a little bit of the feeling of fear. You want to be sure that you get access to the part of you that creates the fear. Roll your eyes as instructed above.

2. **Movie theatre.** Now, in your mind's eye, imagine you are sitting in a large movie theatre. See yourself up on the screen in a still picture just before you had the fearful response for the first time. (If you can't think of the first time you experienced this fear, think of a time that you have intensely had this kind of fear response).

3. **Leave your body.** Now imagine floating out of your body. Go up into the projection booth so that now you can look out and see yourself watching yourself on the screen. (If you have a height phobia, instead of going up into a projection booth, imagine yourself moving back ten rows in the theatre.) You need to remain in the projection booth until instructed to leave it.

4. **Watch a movie.** You now need to watch yourself watching yourself, and then begin to run a black and white movie of what actually occurred in the fearful situation. You need to see yourself going through the experience, and continue watching your movie from the projection booth, until you have reached the end of this situation, when the trauma was over, and you can tell from the movie that you are safe again. At this point you stop the movie and make it into a still picture of yourself after the trauma was over.

5. **Run the movie backward.** You now need to leave the projection booth and step into the picture on the screen. Go through the experience backward, in colour, just as if time was reversed and you were being sucked back through it by a giant vacuum cleaner. Do this very quickly, in about one and a half seconds or less. Do this several more times if you believe it would be helpful.

6. **Get up and move.** When you are finished, physically get up and move your body around. Shake your arms and take a deep breath. Place one hand over the mid line of the vertex of your head and simultaneously place the other hand over your sternum. While maintaining the hand positions, observe the emotion

being disassociated from the memory, thereby making the memory of being fearful passive (a healthy bio-electric signal and cue), which allows you to be able to recall the memory later without the emotional charge.

7. **Checking.** Now think of the experience again and notice your response in your mind. Rate the fear on a scale of one to ten, with ten being the worst. If it's more than a two, repeat the entire process, being careful to do each step thoroughly.

It is important to be cautious when you test the change you've just created in the real world. For example, if your fear was of heights, you might go to a fairly high place, look out the window and notice how your fear has changed. Test yourself gently and carefully, with respect for your own personal safety. Use appropriate caution in dangerous situations. In the above example of fear, the fear of heights has probably kept you out situations of being high up, so you don't have much experience in how to cope with being high up. Some situations do have inherent danger, so it is important to respect this and learn how to deal with them cautiously and resourcefully.

Possible positive changes from using the ECM technique

The most common observation is changes to bowel movements, in addition to clarity of mind, and seeing other sides to a story or opportunities that could not be seen before. Elimination of emotions provides emotional freedom from the story, so that a story can just be told for the sake of sharing information, and not stirring up old demons or opening old wounds. A life of emotional freedom is amazingly liberating. Be prepared to be more at peace with yourself and life in general.

UEFT technique from Advanced FlameTree: *the personal development & healing system*

The UEFT course is taught by Qi Health Clinic Pty Ltd certified instructors, and is also available as a self-directed course through www.rhettogston.com. The benefits of this course are freedom from any and all emotions by performing a simple twelve-step procedure. Once you have learned the procedure, you can perform UEFT in seconds. As it only takes two hours to learn the UEFT course (self-directed or live), it will not do it justice by presenting it here. If you would like more information about UEFT, or are interested in purchasing the online course for your personal reference or joining a live event, please visit www.rhettogston.com.

I realise that you may not always have 60–90 seconds to perform UEFT to eliminate fear, seven minutes to perform the 409 Degrees – *Just hold it* moves to energise you to assist in eliminating fear, or time to visit your certified FlameTree healer, so ROAs also offer you a no fuss, quick and easy way to stabilise emotions and spirit. pro·m·emo essences are a synergistic and interactive blend of traditional Chinese medicine, naturopathy (Western herbal medicine), flower essences, bio-energetic medicine and homeopathy, combined into six essences to again further empower you to process your emotions and lead a life free from fear, worry, moodiness, nervousness, sadness, restlessness, fatigue, and bitterness and so on. You can find this product at www.rhettogston.com and www.promemo.com.au.

The take-home message — your transformation from eternal *worrier* to eternal *warrior*

The *eternal worrier smiles* because their perceived expectation of reality induces fear (unhealthy bio-electric signals and cues), which allows them to maintain the perceived safety of their victim-state mentality so they can avoid being responsible for creating a better life. Living with this consistent fear, however, induces the physiological protection mode, an unhealthy biofield and the unhealthy expression of the bio-electric code, which activates their protection genes. The consequence of activating these genes leads to sub-optimal health because the growth-mode genes cannot operate simultaneously with the protection mode genes. They do not make the choice to actively use ROAs such as the ECM technique, pro·m·emo, UEFT, or any other method to harmonise their emotional states, so their protection genes remain active, increasing their exposure to the deleterious effects of unhealthy bio-electric signals and cues, which inevitably leads to stress-induced disease states, which then becomes a continual cycle.

The *eternal warrior smiles* because they take responsibility for their perceived expectation of reality, and choose to live from a place of peace, love and harmony (healthy bio-electric signals and cues), which creates a healthy biofield and expression of the bio-electric code. Choosing to live from this state physiologically activates their growth genes. The expression of these growth genes allows their body to actively repair itself and express optimal health. The eternal warrior chooses to live in control of their perceptions and eliminate faulty perceptions that induce fear. They are in control of their internal environment by monitoring and regulating their external environment.

Their perceptions induce love and growth. They make the choice to actively use ROAs such as the ECM technique, UEFT, pro·m·emo or any other method to harmonise their emotional states so that their growth genes remain in their active state, thereby saving them from the deleterious effects of unnecessarily activating unhealthy bio–electric signals and cues and protection genes.

CHAPTER 6

Are we all a bunch of energy?

As science and technology progress, so too does our understanding of the world around us. Gone are the days when you would look at the periodic table (chemistry) for atomic mass and structure; here are the days when you read about electrical charges and volts. It is now understood that every atom and molecule emit and absorbs light of characteristic wavelengths. Every atom is vibrating, giving off and receiving energy from the environment. When I was first studying chemistry, I was taught that electrons stayed in a shell configuration, then later I was taught about cloud configurations, and the current understanding is that it's more of a probability where the electron will be. This clearly demonstrates that things change in the field of science. It is now well accepted by science that each atom has a unique frequency or vibration signature that separates it from other atoms. It's like a fingerprint — just as everyone has a unique fingerprint and can be identified from it, it is now possible to identify all matter via its unique 'frequency fingerprint'. Modern Western medicine is already using this technology to identify different tissues of the body, through CAT scans (an X-ray image made using computerised axial tomography) and MRIs (magnetic resonance imaging). For example, this technology can distinguish bone tissue from organ tissue (e.g. a heart or kidney) based on each tissue type's unique frequency, so that a liver appears different to bone in an MRI.

Knowing that matter can be identified by its unique frequency fingerprint, can this principle be applied to non-matter things, such as emotions, beliefs and perceptions? It makes sense that emotions, beliefs and perceptions would also have their unique 'frequency fingerprint', which I refer to as bio-electric signals and cues. Emotions such as fear, worry, joy and so on are all different bio-electric signals and cues (unique frequency fingerprints) that influence your biofield, as discussed in Chapter 4. In other words, you are continually emitting your own unique 'frequency fingerprint' based on your current perceived expectation of reality, which is influenced by your beliefs, perceptions, emotions and so on.

Let's say, for example, that you are emitting the unique bio-electric signal and cue for anger — based on the theory of resonance (a quality of evoking a response), you will inadvertently be stimulating anything else in your environment that has anger qualities. This means that you would be more likely to encounter the bio-electric signals and cues specific for anger in your environment than the bio-electric signals and cues associated with other emotions, and attract something or someone else that is emitting the same unique bio-electric signal and cue relating to anger. Said simply, you get back what you put out (consciously or not)! You end up attracting the frequency (bio-electric signal and cue) you put out, which can either have a healthy or unhealthy impact on your life. This makes sense because biology works in the same way.

Firstly, you need to be aware that you, your cells and your receptors are exactly like tuning forks. If you have two tuning forks that resonate at the same frequency and you activate one of those forks, the other will automatically be activated without you having to touch it. Why? Because they resonate at the same frequency! This is what professor Ćosić refers to as cell membrane resonance, which includes many types of molecular processes, such as electronic excitation, polarisation, field-generated force effects, heat, and resonant processes such as dipoles vibration, as explained by Froehlich theory. Froehlich first proposed his theory explaining resonant processes in 1968. He stated that biological systems are expected to have a branch of longitudinal electric modes in a frequency region between 10^{11} and 10^{12} sec^{-1}.[1] They are based on the dipolar properties of cell membranes, which, if energy is supplied above a certain mean rate, are very strongly excited.

Froehlich's concept has been the basis for explaining the extraordinarily high sensitivity of certain biological systems to extremely weak electromagnetic signals. In Froehlich's model, long-range collective interactions within the membranes may lead to oscillatory biochemical reactions, for example, enzyme-substrate interactions in the greater membrane of the brain. The resulting slow chemical oscillation is connected to a corresponding electric vibration by means of the large dipole moments of reaction-activated enzymes. Thus, a macroscopic oscillating polarisation is built up, causing large regions to oscillate coherently in the 10 to 100 Hz region (e.g. EEG activity). It is suggested that the Froehlich theory is applied to explain resonance processes associated with cell–cell signalling, brainwaves and enzymatic chemical reactions, particularly with cancer proliferation.[2]

This means that anything else in the immediate environment that has the same frequency could also be activated.

Now that you have a greater understanding of resonance, do you honestly believe that it is a coincidence that you meet people all the time who have the same interests as you? Why do you instantly 'click' with someone that you have only just met? As previously stated, it is because you are attracting what you resonate. Why is this understanding essential for you to take on board and immediately implement in your life? I offer you three reasons to consider.

Reason 1. If you are, for example, consistently in fear-induced stress, or any other emotionally-induced stress, you will be resonating the unique frequency fingerprint, or what I call the unique bio-electric signals and cues for fear. When you are being the eternal worrier, you are more susceptible to getting stuck in your emotions, such as fear, and this is what I refer to as unhealthy bio-electric signals and cues. Applying the law of resonance, you will also be attracting more fear-inducing stress into your life. I am sure that you can relate to this and can recall a time when you 'just knew' or 'felt it in your gut' that something wrong or bad would occur and it did! For example, if you felt your car would get stolen, what do you believe will happen? The interesting aspect here is that the stronger the fear, the stronger the bio-electric signal and cue, the stronger the resonance and hence attraction.

Reason 2. This works on the physiological principle of tachyphalatic tolerance. Tachyphylaxis (also known as tolerance) is a falling off in the effects produced by a drug during continuous use or constantly repeated administration. For example, where continuous administration of a drug is taking place, it has been observed both in vivo and in vitro that the patient develops tachyphylaxis to the drug. Tachyphylaxis is thought to arise from desensitisation associated with conformational changes or modifications (such as phosphorylation) in the receptor.[3] A second cause of tachyphylaxis is thought to be associated with the down regulation of the receptor (or other components in the targeted signalling pathway) for the drug in question.[4]

Down regulation of the receptor decreases the number of receptor system molecules on a cell, decreasing the response to continued administration of the therapeutic agent. What is the significance of knowing this? I propose that your perceptions of fear-induced stress (or other emotions that you get stuck in) in life act in the same way as the continued administration of a therapeutic agent. I stress the term 'continued' because, as previously described, the non-life threatening, fear-induced stress response never disappears from your life. I want to reinforce here that I am not referring to your perception of fear-induced stress associated with an immediate life-or-death situation. If a person is standing with a gun pointed at your head, your perception matches your reality — there is a person standing with a gun at your head! This is a life-or-death situation and will induce the natural fight-or-flight response. Based on this example, there are some possible outcomes:

(1) You fight, the offending person is disarmed and then taken away by the authorities. This means that your immediate fear is no longer in your life, so you can return to your state before this event!

(2) You fight and are shot and your life ceases, along with your perceptions and your real-life stressors.

(3) You fly (flight), that is, you somehow manage to get away. The stress of this situation is gone once you perceive you are safe.

(4) You fly (flight), but you do not manage to get away and are shot and your life ceases, along with your perceptions and your real-life stressors.

(5) You freeze and but the person leaves and you are safe. The stress of this situation is gone once you perceive you are safe.

(6) You freeze and are shot and your life ceases, along with your perceptions and your real-life stressors.

Conversely, what I am referring to here is living in a continual perceived state of fear-induced stress that is not an immediate life-or-death situation, but instead is based on your perceived expectation of reality and is creating unhealthy bio-electric signals and cues. This occurs as a result of your own faulty perceptions about your life and what you perceive as stressors in your life. This allows for the unique fear-induced stress frequency fingerprint to continue to be transmitted from you as an unhealthy bio-electric signal and cue, which, through resonance, attracts similar unhealthy bio-electric signals and cues. For example, being an eternal worrier paying your gas bill could be seen as a fear-inducing, stressful event if your bank balance is very low, and through resonance, this unhealthy bio-electric signal and cue attracts to you more expenses that need to be paid when you do not have money! Being the eternal warrior, you could have seen how great it is that you have the opportunity to live with the benefits of gas, such as heating or cooking, and to have the means to pay for the gas bill.

The gas bill, however, is not the issue, nor is it the stressor; it is how you perceive the gas bill that counts — your perceived expectation of reality. I propose that being the eternal worrier, with ongoing faulty perceptions of these stressors in your life, may indeed induce an emotional tachyphalatic tolerance. Although tachyphalatic tolerance is one of the body's many natural protective mechanisms, designed to allow you to cope with ongoing stressors in your life, perceived or real, the effectiveness of this response is limited because:

1. you cannot eliminate all receptors to fear-induced stress or other emotions (you still need the fight-or-flight response to be functional for those true life or death situations)

2. all the by-products of cellular reactions that are generated in response to your perceived stressors are still present within your body, irrespective of how many receptors you have present. Inevitably your body will have to process these stress-induced by-products even though, through tachyphalatic tolerance, there are fewer stress receptors

3. the remaining receptors never get a chance to rest as they will continually be stimulated by the perceived stressor(s). The end result of this continual stress (if left unresolved) will be that your 'stress response system' eventually becomes maxed out, which further contributes to unhealthy bio-electric signals and cues.

I will use an example here to further explain what this means. Let's say repeated administration of a drug such as morphine results in tachyphylaxis. This is a well-known concept in the development of tolerance to any substance. This results in more morphine being required to create the same effect as the first experience of using it.

However, with the higher doses of morphine going into the body, irrespective of how many down regulated receptors have resulted through tachyphalatic tolerance, the end result is an overdose. This is where a parallel can be made — your repeated ongoing negative perceptions of your life stressors may be acting in a similar way to the repeated administration of a drug such as morphine, and may therefore lead to a stress 'overdose'.

What do I mean by this and how does it apply to you? Let me further explain a drug overdose. When your body is repeatedly exposed to something that is not meant to be there — like morphine or even caffeine — your body will immediately communicate this to your conscious mind. Although morphine is a useful drug for managing pain, when repeated doses are used over a period of time, your body will let you know that you need to stop taking this substance. How does your innate wisdom inform you?

With morphine, you could experience symptoms such as changes in breathing (slowed), speech (slurred and slow), coordination (reduced), heart rate and blood pressure (decreased), alertness (confusion) and bowel function (constipation). If these symptoms are ignored and you continue to take morphine, your body will intensify these symptoms to force you to pay attention and take action. Tachyphalatic tolerance is also occurring in response to this morphine exposure so that the deleterious effects of morphine can be slowed, but this leads to tolerance and addiction to morphine, which creates the new issue of drug withdrawal.

Similarly, if your perceived expectation of reality is that of being an eternal worrier, which allows for non-life-threatening issues to continue on with no end in sight, your body will immediately communicate this to your conscious mind. Your innate wisdom is letting you know that these perceived stressors should not be there and action is required to change your current faulty perceived expectation of reality. For example, you could experience symptoms such as changes in breathing (increased), heart rate and blood pressure (increased), sleep (disturbed), emotions (anxious, angry, mood swings), and destructive behaviours (this may increase alcohol consumption, smoking or compulsive eating, or result in stopping eating). If these symptoms are ignored and the perceived stressors continue to be perceived as such, then your body will intensify these symptoms until you start to pay attention to them. As well as this, tachyphalatic tolerance occurs in response to these perceived stressors in order to diminish their impact on the body.

Although the body decreases the number of stress receptors on your cells, this is only a temporary reprieve from the effects of fear-induced and other emotional stressors. Why? Because your body and mind are still being subjected to the perceived fear-inducing or emotional stressors, which have yet to be addressed. These stressors continue to be perceived and the effects bank up! In addition to this, as discussed above, the perception that you hold is the frequency at which those perceptions will vibrate (their unique fingerprint). It is also the same frequency that is transmitted to the environment and is responsible for stimulating the same perception, via resonance, which is received back by you from your environment, which is creating and contributing to that unhealthy bio-electric signal and cue. This immediately influences your biofield and the expression of your bio-electric code. This scenario paints a picture of attracting more fear-induced or emotional stress (all of which are unhealthy bio-electric signals and cues) into your life, so that your cells see no end in sight to this stimulation bombardment!

This situation, if left unchanged, increases the risk of a stress 'overdose'. Said another way, if you do nothing to change your perceived stressors (being the eternal worrier and your perceived expectation of reality), the stress in your world will continue to grow and you will eternally be in overload from that point on. The same stressors — for example, family, job, bills, relationships, children, ageing parents, microwaves and so on — will always be present in your life, and you end up with stress 'overdose', which may progress to what is known as a nervous breakdown, self-destructive behaviours or, worse still, harming others.

Throughout this book, I will continue to direct you to ways that might assist you to free yourself from all of this, to live optimally and purposefully. I again suggest, as supported by the science discussed in chapter 4, that you are able to make the choice to change the way you perceive the stressors in your life that are currently creating, transmitting and resonating unhealthy bio-electric signals and cues. When your bio-electric signals and cues are associated with, for example, non-life threatening fear-induced stress and other emotions, then this will be your lot – unhealthy bio-electric signals and cues, unhealthy biofield, unhealthy bio-electric code and gene expression, unhealthy resonance, unhealthy creations because you are not listening to your innate wisdom or following the Law of Creation.

I am mindful here not to blame you for your perceived expectation of reality or for defaulting to being the eternal worrier. It's your conditioning that has paved the pathway for your current situation, yet this conditioning process is essential to teaching you the basic skills for surviving within your environment. This is where the real problem lies — you were taught how to survive by others who were also taught how to *survive*, rather than *Being* taught how to *thrive* in your environment. Although you were not taught how to thrive and you may feel you have no experience or guidance for thriving, you can still create changes in your life from surviving to thriving. As stated at the beginning of this book, provided you are coachable and open to the possibility of change, then this is possible, and it begins with you making the choice to create healthy bio-electric signals and cues rather than defaulting to your current unhealthy ones.

I predict that you might ask, 'But how can I do this?' Well, in chapter 5, you were introduced to various ROAs that have been specifically designed for this very purpose. You were provided with the full details of the ECM technique from FlameTree. You have also been introduced and recommended to UEFT, pro·m·emo, and to gain assistance from a certified FlameTree healer. All ROAs have been created so that they may assist you on clearing whatever resistance you have to making the choice of *Being* the eternal warrior who is thriving in your environment. I remind you that making the choice of *Being* the eternal warrior in your life will create eternal healthy bio-electric signals and cues. In so doing, you can better consciously seek and find ways to be accountable in your life, for example, by changing the meaning of 'stressors' to responsibilities, eliminating excuses, and allowing yourself to get on with the job at hand so that you are living your life optimally and purposefully. I remind you that this is attainable and realistic, even though you may never have been taught the skills for thriving.

In animal studies, it has been demonstrated that rats with a morphine 'addiction' overcame their addiction themselves, without prior experience, merely by being placed in an enriching living environment comprising enough space, good food, companionship, mating, areas for exercise and areas for privacy.[5] The rats' decent living environment is an example of healthy bio-electric signals and cues! Immerse yourself in healthy bio-electric signals and cues and changes will occur. In the case of humans, though, it's not only your external environment that needs to change, but your internal environment — your perceptions will define what an enriching environment is for you.

For example, a successful businessperson who is accustomed to staying in five-star luxury accommodation will feel that their environment is unenriched (poor) if they were to stay in a two-star hotel. However, someone who has never stayed in a hotel would believe that two-star accommodation would be luxury and would define that environment as being enriched. In both examples, nothing changed with the environments of the two-or five-star hotels, they remained the same. It was the observations and perceptions of the individuals that determined whether these hotels were perceived as enriching or not.

Reason 3. This relates to the principle of what you don't use, you lose! All cells in your body, just like muscles, will atrophy (decrease in size) if not used. Cells will also remove receptors if not used because the intelligence of the system (your body) is so superb, it works on the principle of efficiency being the basis of life. We don't, as humans, consciously know much about operating our own bodies efficiently, but your cells do! Your cells know that if a structure is not being used, they won't support it, whether that be your arm muscles, receptors in the brain, or receptors for an emotion and so on. This also explains why most of us prefer to be around 'happy' people. By being around people who emit happiness as a frequency (a bio-electric signal and cue), we allow ourselves to resonate with happiness, provided we have the belief (another bio-electric signal and cue) that we can be happy (the same frequency, like the tuning fork example — the same membrane resonance, will attract the same frequency).

Continual exposure to this frequency (the unique bio-electric signal and cue of happiness) activates your receptors so that your cells will continue to express them, so you will not lose them due to not being used. The end result is that we absorb some of the happy person's 'vibe' through resonance and feel better for it. You would be correct to question here whether we have tachyphalactic tolerance for the emotion of 'happiness', as we did for 'fear'? We do, and that is when happiness becomes an unhealthy bio-electric signal and cue. Although you may consider happiness as only a healthy bio-electric signal and cue, in TCM, 'over joy' (being overly happy) or 'over excitement' may cause dis-harmony, as explained in chapter 3. There are numerous examples of over excitement causing dis-harmony. For example, 'Beatlemania' was coined when fans became over excited about seeing the rock and roll band The Beatles! Over excited fans passed out and experienced hysteria! Another example would be the over excited child who is expecting Santa Clause to come with a big present. The child may feel restless until Christmas morning comes, and their sleep may become disturbed. These are examples of happiness being perceived as an unhealthy signal and cue. In this scenario, your body will probably down regulate the happy receptors, as it does to anything that your body deems as an unhealthy bio-electric signal and cue (or in TCM terminology, 'excessive'), whether it is fear, drugs or happiness.

By understanding the principles that I have introduced to you, and knowing that your biology has not changed (i.e. a physical molecule/substrate binds to and stimulates a physical receptor to produce a cellular change), it should now make sense to you that the physical receptor can also be stimulated to produce a cellular change by bio-electric signals and cues, whether healthy or unhealthy, such as those of emotions, intention and healing hands (which have been measured in millivolts). Said another way, just the bio-electric signals and cues (e.g. millivolts, frequency, healing intention) alone may cause the conformational change required to change the internal environment of the cell (e.g. gene transcription, elimination of waste, movement). Your cell's receptors respond not only to physical molecules but, as stated above, to energy (bio-electric signals and cues) as well. There are certain bio-electric signals and cues, such as electro-magnetic fields (EMFs) that turn on DNA synthesis and there are other bio-electric signals and cues that shut it off; other EMFs turn on cellular transcription (RNA synthesis), and there are bio-electric signals and cues that turn off RNA synthesis.

It is now well accepted by science that bio-electric signals and cues in the environment can activate cell functions. I have brought to your consciousness the evidence that bio-electric signals and cues will influence your biology, creating changes within your body in the same way that molecules do, so this may remove thoughts of quackery and doubts about the changes that can occur through changing your bio-electric signals and cues by changing your perceived expectation of reality (your perceptions) of yourself and of your environment. In essence, you are healing yourself with your own energy (bio-electric signals and cues) — energy healing. The effects of energy healing are real and measurable, and I suggest that the healthy bio-electric signals and cues generated by energy healing may influence, and are potentially more effective in controlling, biology (cells and cellular interactions) than molecules themselves, particularly when you are consciously focused on creating healthy bio-electric signals and cues, that is, *Being* the eternal warrior. The inverse to this is also true!

I would like to bring to your consciousness an article written by David Feinstein and Donna Eden titled the 'Six pillars of energy medicine: clinical strengths of a complementary paradigm'.[6] Feinstein and Eden provide evidence that the energies of a healer's hands, which are an example of a bio-electric signal and cue, are measurable in millivolts. These energies have been observed to assist in the healing of injured or diseased tissues. The part that I want to bring to your attention is that the healing effect of the energy healer is significantly increased when the healer is focused or places their intention (another example of a bio-electric signal and cue) on the healing process.

Knowing that this information and the information presented in chapter 4 all co-exist could possibly explain, not only how your energy (the healthy bio-electric signals and cues generated by your perceived expectation of reality AND *Being* the eternal warrior) can be self-healing, but how energy healings, such as FlameTree: *the personal development & healing system*, Reiki and other modalities might work.

Science has demonstrated that all cell behaviour is elicited by the receptors on the cell membrane that read environmental signals. I remind you here about what was previously discussed — if you don't use it, you lose it. Well, the cells of your body and your brain (the brain is made up of many cells) work in the exactly same way. The brain is a large processing unit comprising many different connections of neural tissue. Every time you experience something, a pathway is laid down for the specific actions that need to occur for you to 'learn' the experience. You have already experienced this but have probably called it something like 'practice makes perfect'! This is also true of your emotions — if you regularly 'feel not good', then you reinforce the 'feel-not-good pathway'. You then emit this 'feel-not-good' frequency (unhealthy bio-electric signal and cue), which results in an unhealthy biofield and the unhealthy expression of the bio-electric code for this specific 'feel-not-good' frequency. This not only begins to change your neurology by laying down and strengthening neural pathways that enable you to 'feel not good' faster and more consistently, but you also manifest, through resonance, life events and situations where you are able to 'feel not good'. In some cases, even if the situation or event is not inherently bad (not good), you perceive it to be bad because you have conditioned your neurology to perceive and taint the input in a 'feel-not-good' manner. The inverse of this is also true, where you can emit the 'feel- good' frequency. When you make the choice to 'feel good', you begin to change your neurology by laying down and strengthening neural pathways that enable you to 'feel good' faster and more consistently, but you also manifest, through resonance, life events and situations where you are able to 'feel good'.

Now that you are aware of the above information — that it's your perceptions and not your genes that control you — you can start to consciously begin framing how you feel about yourself now (if you have not already started to do so) in a healthy way to initiate your process of changing your life. I encourage you to take action now, as all you have is the present moment! But I understand that you need to be authentic when doing this, and authenticity is a non-negotiable component of Being and the Law of Creation. For example, when someone asks you how you are, and you are not feeling fantastic, you need to be authentic and acknowledge this feeling to yourself. You need to recognise that you have stopped making the choice to 'feel good' and have defaulted to past conditioned unhealthy bio-electric signals and cues. In this state — when you are being the eternal worrier — saying 'I feel fantastic' without feeling it is inauthentic and will not yield results, so the old 'fake it until you make it' usually does not work here or anywhere.

To create change, you need to make a choice — choose to 'feel good' or choose to 'feel not good', irrespective of what is occurring in your environment. I encourage you to try this experiment right now. Say out loud 'I choose to feel not good' five times and see how that feels for you. Then say out loud 'I choose to feel good' five times and see how that feels for you in comparison with the first phrase. Choosing to feel good actually feels easier to say and creates a sense of lightness in your body compared to the other phrase, but you still have the choice to feel good or not good! Once you make the choice, you have empowered yourself and taken responsibility for how you choose to feel! You cannot blame anyone else for your choice!

Although this does not change your physical environment, it does create a change in you so that, when choosing to feel good, you are better able to find solutions to whatever issue you perceived that made you not feel fantastic. The solution here is to change your perceived expectation of reality so that you are *Being* the eternal warrior who is immune to the 'something for nothing' disease, actively *Being* the inspired, flexible go-getter paddler who takes responsibility for their life so that they are living optimally and purposefully. When you are struggling to implement this healthy bio-electric signal or cue, I encourage you to ask for help. You can go back to chapter 5 and perform the ECM technique, use UEFT and pro·m·emo, or see a certified FlameTree healer to assist you to clear the space so you can process your emotions and free yourself to make that choice of feeling good. Then you can get to feeling fantastic and authentically reply, 'I am feeling fantastic!' To reach this state, you need to make the conscious decision to practise choosing to feel good so that feeling good and *Being* the eternal warrior become your perceived expectation of reality in everything you do.

Choosing to do this begins the process of changing your biofield and bio-electric code expression, so that your brain may start activating your nervous and endocrine systems to begin communicating this message to your cells, and your 'feel good' gene expression is selected so you can authentically feel good! I understand that sometimes you might need assistance beyond just consciously making the choice to change your perceived expectation of reality and *Be* the eternal warrior so that you create your own healthy bio-electric signals and cues, which is why I created ROAs such as UEFT, pro·m·emo and FlameTree to authentically assist you to fast-track this process.

Although it is possible to achieve just by making the choice, I know that when you get stuck in your emotion or overwhelmed by your situation, being supported by ROAs will assist you in getting unstuck and fast-tracking your ability to create healthy bio-electric signals and cues so that you may reach your optimal potential and live your life of purpose.

I want to reiterate here that whatever thoughts, emotions, intentions or feelings you have, whether consciously or not, your cell receptors and neural connections within your brain are responding to your perceptions (either 'feeling not good' or 'feeling good'), and your brain is acting as the translator for your prevailing perceptions — it translates your perceptions (bio-electric signals and cues) into something your body can use for information. For example, light is light; it doesn't mean much to your body until your brain converts light, via the cells of your eyes, into electromagnetic vibrations that are transmitted to nerves. Similarly, with sound. Have you ever heard the old question, 'If a tree falls in the forest, and nobody is there, does it make a sound?' The reality is that a falling tree does not make a sound, irrespective of whether you are there to observe it fall or not! If you took the stance that trees make a sound when they fall even when you are not there to observe it, you are disclosing your conditioned belief of an objective, independent reality that seems to be the prevailing mindset of a universe that it exists just as well without us as with us. 'You' are of small consequence in the cosmos, as advocated by some Western views that have roots that go back at least to Biblical times, but I consider this viewpoint an unhealthy bio-electric signal and cue.

Getting back to sound and the reality of what occurs when that tree falls in the woods without your ears, sound does not exist! When a tree falls, there is disturbance in the medium it finds itself in, in this case, the air. A falling tree creates rapid air-pressure variations, which spread out by travelling through its surrounding medium (air) and may reach up to 1207 km per hour (750 mph), until, that is, they lose their coherency, and once again the air pressure re-establishes the background evenness of air prior to the tree falling. No sound is created, only movement of air, until your ear comes to the scene, which means you need to be present when that tree is falling to hear it! The change in air pressure created by the falling tree physically causes your ear's tympanic membrane (eardrum) to vibrate. This vibration stimulates your nerves only if the air is pulsing in a range of 20 to 20,000 times a second. When this occurs, your nerves will be stimulated by the moving eardrum and will send electrical signals to a section of your brain, resulting in your cognition of a noise. Without your ear, a functioning nervous system and the changes in air pressure due to a falling tree, the pulsing of air by itself does not constitute any sort of sound.

Again, we see this with touch. Although touch is perceived as a physical pressure, it is, like vision and sound, a result of electromagnetic vibrations transmitted through your nervous system. It is your brain that converts your entire environment, including your perceived emotions, into electromagnetic vibrations, which then become your awareness. Your brain is not only creating the outcome for you to cognitively experience sight, sound, touch and so on, it is also recording the ability for you to remember that experience. Why? The answer to this question is important because, if you take your awareness and play it back through your brain, you repeat the experience again. This means that your brain is not only processing incoming bio-electric signals and cues, it is also acting as a recorder of them. Your brain is like a camera — it takes a photograph and converts that photograph into a slide. Essentially, you get a picture of what you just learned, and your awareness is the light bulb that illuminates the slide. But when you take your awareness and play it back through the slide, you recreate the behaviour and event.

It is estimated that forty million bits of information are being processed in your brain right now, at every second. Your brain can do this, but your conscious mind cannot. As you are reading this right now, tell me, how does your shirt feel on your back? What about how many beats per minute you need your heart to beat? What about the energy required to maintain your gaze so that you can read this page? Your conscious mind can only hold a fraction of what you are processing right now; the rest of the information gets filtered out if it is not necessary in your present moment. If something isn't changing or isn't perceived to be important in your present moment, your conscious mind will ignore it or forget about it. This makes sense! There is no point you thinking about how your shirt feels on your back while you are trying to process new information. This new information is important, and your brain wants to learn this or at least understand it, so it makes learning the new information the priority. You were and are, however, still feeling your shirt on your back the entire time because your nerves don't stop streaming in information, because they are always on.

Most of your behaviour is determined by your perceived expectation of reality, which is influenced by your past experiences and memories. Your behaviour is something that you seldom focus on consciously. It's like walking; you, as an adult who already knows how to walk, will not be focused on thinking about all of the different movements and coordination that goes in to each step to initiate walking, you just do it. Your behaviour basically functions in the same way — you are a 'push-button-get-response machine'. It's the difference between walking your talk and not walking your talk. Why? Your mind is like an iceberg; it has the tip poking out of the water and the other 80–90 per cent beneath the surface. This is why positive thinking and affirmations are flawed and will not work for most people.

My favourite analogy to demonstrate this is the 'streak of yellow paint on the black ball' analogy. If you have a black ball (this represents all of the pre-programmed behaviours, thoughts, ideas, concepts and so on in your head) and you decide that today you are going to lose some weight (because you are very overweight), you then start to think positively about yourself losing weight (this represents your paint brush with yellow paint on it). So, you start stroking the brush against the ball and leaving yellow streaks on it. The question that needs to be asked here: is the black ball now transforming into a yellow one? The answer is a big no! Just as the yellow paint does not make the black ball a yellow ball, that small positive thought in your head will not make you lose weight! It is a massively unfair fight! Why? Because 80–90 per cent of already pre- programmed thoughts, ideas, belief systems and so on are there from your learned experiences. You will not successfully lose weight because that little conscious streak of yellow paint (the positive thinking) says so; instead, you need to recognise that you have a weight issue because whatever learning experiences you had about your life are already programmed in there. To achieve transformation, you need to first undo the programming!

Remember that your mind and the cell only perceive the environment — the cell sends the signals from the perceived environment to the nucleus. The nucleus then adjusts the genes to complement whatever is present in your environment. The structure of the cell reflects the perception of the environment, and I again stress here that it is not the actual environment but your perception of it. Everything is present in the world — it contains all experiences and all things — all of it. Everything is available to you. The important thing here is that you will only see what you have been trained (pre-programmed by others when you were young) to see!

Stop for a moment and consider how police are trained to recall the experience of a robbery versus how a lay person, would experience the same event. A police officer would notice specific details about the perpetrator, despite the fact that they are working in a stressful environment. For example, a police officer is trained to notice that the features of certain perpetrator might be Caucasian male, 190 cm, around 45 to 50 years of age, short black hair, two ear piercings and a single tattoo of a cross on their right upper forearm. You may only notice that the perpetrator was a male about the same height as you (or shorter) with dark hair, because you have not been trained to collect information as police officers have been. Once you are trained to see things a certain way, you continue to see them that way. For example, a retired police officer will still observe a perpetrator in the same way ten years after retirement. You will only ever be able to see what you are trained to see. I'd ask you now to focus on where it was that you were first 'trained' to see/perceive your experiences? The most likely answer will be that your training started with your family, and that training is done and completed even before you can challenge the belief systems you adopt or mimic.

The next most common place you are 'taught' is from your experiences. Your experiences act as the teacher for learning about and applying 'filters'. You have already learned what filters to use to perceive your immediate environment — metaphorically, they sit on your eyes and you look through them at all you see (the same is true for your other senses). Filters will be discussed in greater detail in chapter 9 '18 common filters we use to navigate our world'. What you do not currently realise is that you go through your life with these filters tainting your perceived expectation of reality. You then perceive your environment through these filters, and that perception validates your belief system in how you view the world. You then select your reality based on the experiences through which you view the world. This changes the 'namaste' or 'as is' reality into something that you selected to perceive. The end result of what you perceive will either be healthy or unhealthy bio-electric signals and cues, which become self-sustaining.

The take-home message — your transformation from eternal *worrier* to eternal *warrior*

The *eternal worrier smiles* because they choose to live in a material world that does not include bio-electric signals and cues (energies). They see the world as static, fixed and independent of themselves, which limits possibilities, flow and change (including matter, belief systems, perceptions, and even who they are). They do not believe that they are consistently emitting their frequency fingerprint to the universe, but they believe that the universe causes things to happen to them, embracing their victim mentality. They blame the external environment for what occurs in their lives and what they attract to themselves. They are unconsciously choosing fear and stress (instead of love and peace), and as such continue being the eternal worrier. They choose to associate with whoever comes into their world, even if that person exhibits negative beliefs or energies, something that a warrior would never accept. They accept being a victim. They choose to not believe in non-invasive healing energies and to blame their emotions and how they feel on what is happening to them at that time. They believe their perception is actually their reality and are therefore doomed to suffer what the universe delivers to them (as opposed to what they want to create). They get to avoid responsibility for what they think, feel, do, emit, create and attract into their life. The eternal worrier believes that yellow paint does make the black ball a yellow ball! They are unaware that their training — the belief systems they have adopted or mimicked from their family and experiences — are changeable, and therefore blindly go through life acting out their behaviours. Should anyone ever 'call them out' on this behaviour, the eternal worrier becomes reactive and uses the fallback position of blaming their family and experiences for who they are being, rather than experience something new, all of which contributes to the manifestation of unhealthy bio-electric signals and cues, an unhealthy biofield and the unhealthy expression of the bio-electric code, which influences what genes become expressed.

The *eternal warrior smiles* because they choose to live in an energetic world of possibilities, where matter, belief systems, perceptions, who they are and so on are made up of energy. The eternal warrior knows that, because they are energy, they are consistently emitting their frequency fingerprint to the universe. They know that they are in control of what they emit and they are conscious of this fact. They carefully choose what they emit because they understand that whatever is emitted will resonate with the external environment, and they will create and attract to them those things, people or experiences that resonate with the same frequency.

The eternal warrior chooses love and peace (instead of fear and stress). They choose who they associate with, people who have positive energies (healthy bio-electric signals and cues), and do not accept being a victim, something that the eternal worrier does without consciousness. The eternal warrior chooses to believe in non-invasive healing energies and makes the choice to feel good. They understand that their brain controls their perceptions and that they are in control of their brain, therefore they are responsible for what they think, feel, do, emit, create and attract. The eternal warrior welcomes and relishes that responsibility. They know that all experiences are valid and present in the world, and that they are the only ones who can choose and create what they experience. Again, they relish this responsibility because they know they are warriors!

The eternal warrior knows that yellow paint does *not* make the black ball a yellow ball! They are aware that their training from their family and experiences is changeable, and they can go through life choosing actions and behaviours that are appropriate to their situation. Should anyone ever 'call them out' on their behaviour, the eternal warrior can, on reflection and if necessary, instantaneously change their response to experience something new, all of which contributes to the creation and maintenance of healthy bio-electric signals and cues, a healthy biofield and a healthy expression of the bio-electric code, thereby influencing the healthy expression of their genes.

CHAPTER 7

You, your identity and how you were formed

Who are you, what is your identity and how were you formed? These may be challenging questions to answer. Based on the previous chapters, who you are choosing to be in your present moment is a key component to answering these questions. Recall that your perceptions of your environment determine what genes are selected. The way in which your cells obtain signals and cues from the environment is through your cell's receptors. As it turns out, there are also receptors for your identity. This has been demonstrated by heart transplant recipients. For example, a heart transplant recipient, Claire Sylvia, states in her book, *A change of heart: A memoir*: 'I was given a young man's heart — and started craving beer and Kentucky Fried Chicken. My daughter said I even walked like a man.'[1] Claire Sylvia's case and other cases have been discussed in a post in the *Mail Online*.[2] This post tells the extraordinary story of another heart transplant recipient in America who had committed suicide, just like the man whose heart he had received twelve years previously. In another extraordinary twist, it emerged that the recipient had also married the donor's former wife.

There are many more stories like these, which then raise the question: 'Can elements of a person's character — or even their soul — be transplanted along with a heart?' To offer a possible answer to this question, I will continue with Claire Sylvia's story from above. She was a divorced mother of one. She was forty-seven and dying from a disease called primary pulmonary hypertension when, in 1988, she had a pioneering heart–lung transplant in America. She was given the organs of an eighteen-year-old boy who had been killed in a motorcycle accident near his home in Maine. Claire, a former professional dancer, then made an astonishing discovery: she seemed to be acquiring the characteristics — and cravings — of the donor. In her book, Claire explains how she became aware of the links between her life and the life of her organ donor (Tim). She reports that she noticed new behaviours, characteristics and cravings, and began to wonder if it was possible that her new heart came with its own established collection of tastes and preferences. For example, Claire reports that she 'developed a sudden fondness for certain foods I hadn't liked before: Snickers bars, green peppers, Kentucky Fried Chicken takeaway'. Claire also reports other changes associated with her feelings and personality:

> I didn't feel that same need to have a boyfriend. I was freer and more independent than before — as if I had taken on a more masculine outlook. My personality was changing too and I was becoming more masculine. I was more aggressive and assertive than I used to be, and more confident as well. I felt tougher, fitter and I stopped getting colds. Even my walk became more manly.

These changes in her behaviour and personality were validated by Claire's daughter, who would ask her: 'Why are you walking like that? You're lumbering ... like a muscle-bound football player.' Claire realised that this masculine energy was not limited to her walk — it was also impacting on her feminine energy. Claire reports that 'a certain feminine tentativeness had fallen away'. Her status as a heterosexual did not change 'in any overt way'; however, she was attracting the sexual attention of other females without realising that she was broadcasting manly sexual 'signals'. Claire also reported an interesting dream where she encountered a sandy-haired young man in a grassy outdoor setting, who went by the name of Tim. Claire reported that his name could have been Tim Leighton. In this dream, Claire recalled having a feeling of unfinished business between herself and Tim. In her dream, Tim:

> ... returned to say goodbye and we kissed. I seemed to inhale him into me in the deepest breath I had ever taken. I felt like Tim and I would be together forever. When the dream was over, something had changed. I woke up knowing that Tim L was my donor and that some parts of his spirit and personality were now within me.

Claire recalled in her book that, around the same time of having this dream, she met a gentleman called Fred, and Fred had seen the obituary of the donor. Together, Fred and Claire located the obituary and discovered that the Tim L that she had dreamt about was actually a real person, and his full name was actually Timothy Lamirande. Claire investigated the possibility that she could have heard the donor's name in surgery by asking the transplant coordinator, Gail Eddy. Gail confirmed for Claire that doctors were unaware of the donor's name. Further to this, Gail also confirmed that the surgeon, Dr Baldwin, works in silence, with nothing being spoken during the procedure. Despite the anonymity of donors, once Claire had found the donor's obituary, her desire to explain the changes she was experiencing led her to the decision to contact Tim's family. When she did, they asked her how she had found out about them. Once Claire finished the story that led her to them, the family informed her that no other organ recipient who had received Tim's other organs (which included his corneas, kidneys and liver) had been in contact with them.

Claire reported feeling a deep connection to Tim's mother and learned that Tim was described by his family as 'restless'. Tim's family also validated other behaviours that Claire had been experiencing post-operatively, such as having so much energy, drinking beer, her newfound resilience (Tim rarely suffered from colds and flus, and when he did, he recovered quickly), enjoying eating green peppers (a food that Claire had never liked, but post-operation had begun to include them in nearly every meal), and enjoying satisfying her craving for chicken nuggets (Tim loved nuggets!). The changes Claire experienced post-transplant are testament to the strong possibility that elements of a person's character, and possibly their spirit or soul, can be transplanted along with a heart and possibly a lung. The question that remains unanswered is — how was Claire connecting to Tim's life experiences?

We know that cells don't have 'memories' as such, and hence the cells of the heart and lung could not carry the actual memory of the donor as we consciously know it (mind you, in twenty years this statement may be laughed at because scientists are discovering new things about cells all the time, and one of those new discoveries could be that cells *have* memories). Another possibility that exists is that the identity of the person (in Claire's story, her donor Tim and possibly other heart donors) must be coming through the receptors on the cells, in particular the receptors on the lung and heart cells. Interestingly, unbeknown to Claire or Tim, and possibly other lung and heart donors and recipients for that matter, according to TCM, the lung has the role of storing our corporeal soul experiences (described as the somatic expression of the soul), and the heart's role is not only related to emotional and mental activity, consciousness and spiritual experiences, but it encompasses the emotional, mental and spiritual phenomena of all other organs.

In addition to this, although foreign to Western thinking, another traditional healing system from India makes reference to the chakras, which are associated with a distinct developmental theme. There are seven main chakras, and each chakra represents a specific theme; for example, survival, expressing, creativity, love and harmony, self-expression and communication, intuition, and transcendence of ego. It is suggested that it is the chakra system that offers an explanation as to why some organ transplant recipients start to exhibit the psychological characteristics of their donors. Knowing that Western biology and physiology have identified and described the possible functions of cell receptors, and that TCM has described in its medical texts the TCM concept of the lung's storage of corporeal experiences and the heart's association with all emotional, mental, and spiritual phenomena (and the memory system of the chakras and that traditional Indian medicine have referred to a memory-like storage system that they attribute to as the chakras), it is therefore logically possible that my theory can offer an answer to how recipients such as Claire are connecting to their donor's organs by uniting these ancient understandings from TCM and Indian medicine with a modern understanding from Western biology and physiology.

Based on the above organ transplant recipient experiences, in addition to the bio-electric signals and cues, biofield and bio-electric code discussed in chapter 4, I suggest that 'you' and 'your identity' are not '*really*' in your body. This proposition aligns with my 'Stem cell and biofield hypothesis', where your biofield, which is not in your body, influences your cells, biology and physiology. What does this all mean to you? Currently, you most probably believe that you reside inside your body, after all, where else could you be if you were not inside your body? This is what most people believe to be true, but the evidence is such that I suggest that what makes you 'you' is associated with your receptors, which hold the answer to your perception of being in your body. Your receptors are energetically intertwined and interconnected with the TCM organs (e.g. the energetics of heart and lung), the chakra systems, as well as bio-electric signals and cues (which you create from your feelings, emotions, thoughts and thinking, and those from your environment), your biofield and bio-electric code.

This multiple receptor stimulation from bio-electric signals and cues, your biofield, meridians and chakras that you are continually immersed in may explain how you are formed! The possibility of you forming from your environment is not so sci-fi as you may believe. Chapter 4 offered you the possible science explaining my 'Stem cell and biofield hypothesis'. Further clues are provided in the discussion of the experiences of organ transplant recipients and the explanation of cell membrane resonance and receptors. Then there is the suggestion that it's very possible that the meridian system acts as a filtering process between your cells and environment. When you combine all this information together, it is possible to assert that, when the meridian and chakra systems are in flow and you are being immersed in healthy bio-electric signals and cues with a healthy biofield and healthy expression of your bio-electric code, this may signal your receptors to receive the healthy transmission of 'you'. This transmission then becomes your perception of who you are (which is another signal and cue to be received by your receptors), and provided that this all occurs in alignment, authentically, synergy and synergism (*Being*), it will energetically and synergistically communicate with other bio-electric signals and cues (e.g. the chakras, TCM meridians, organ systems), your biofield and bio-electric code, which thereby allows you to create and maintain what you perceive to be the healthy version of yourself and all that is associated with that. This then influences and reinforces who you are *Being* (more about *Being* in chapter 8). The reverse is also true in that unhealthy bio-electrical signals and cues will signal your receptors and result in an unhealthy biofield and bio-electric code.

Whether or not this explanation resonates with you, the transmission of you and your biofield is reflected in who you are right now, and both are influencing and reinforcing who you are *Being*, whether that manifests as you living your life's purpose or not. The emergence of experimental results suggests that internal restructuring (moving from a place of unhealthy bio-electric signals and cues, or cognitive dissonance, to healthy signals and cues, or cognitive resonance and coherence) produces a healthy biofield and an external resonance, as if a pulse of 'mental energy' is emitted and propagated outward into and onto the world. This may then create the possibility of receiving the healthier transmission of you (which is already occurring from the Uni-code!). This external resonance occurs irrespective of whether we are conscious or not of what we are resonating (healthy or unhealthy bio-electric signals and cues). What this means is that we had best be careful what meaning we attach to things, and the type of bio-electric signals and cues we choose to have, because what we are feeling, thinking, believing and doing on the inside (consciously or unconsciously) will not only influence our bio-electric code and our biofield, but what version of the transmission of you your receptors receive through the process of resonance.

Let us use, for example, our immune system to demonstrate this point. Our immune system uses our receptors to distinguish between our self, that is each and every one of our cells as 'self', from foreign invaders (microbes) that are 'non-self'. Our conscious mind is not involved in this distinction between self and non-self. Western science has clearly demonstrated this in regard to organ transplants and the immune system with the discovery and identification of the major histocompatibility complex (MHC), which is a set of cell surface molecules that mediate interactions with your immune system cells, such as white blood cells (e.g. leukocytes). The interesting observation is that the MHC not only determines the compatibility of donors for organ transplant, but also distinguishes 'self' from 'non-self' in relation to autoimmune diseases (your immune system attacking your healthy cells instead of foreign cells that should not be there!).

This is one of the hurdles that Western medicine needed to overcome with organ transplants, where organ transplant recipients are usually prescribed drugs that suppress the immune system (known as immunosuppression). The reason that transplant recipients must be immunosuppressed (having their immune system chemically 'toned down') is so that the recipient's immune system does not reject the donated organ(s), which the recipient's immune system would classify as 'non-self' and hence would start attacking, leading to the donated organ being destroyed. Said another way, the host body's immune system is naturally designed to destroy anything that is 'unnatural' to the host body; this includes tissue from other people, such as donated organs.

Knowing that this differentiation of 'self' and 'non-self' occurs at the cellular level, it is therefore highly possible that your surface cell molecules (cell receptors), whose function is to recognise 'self' from 'non-self', just like the MHC, may just recognise you as you! This would be a plausible explanation as to why transplanted organs may carry 'characteristics' that we become aware of consciously, such as when an organ donor like Tim's characteristics became known to the organ recipient, Claire, after receiving her heart–lung transplant. This concept is further strengthened by optogenetic and cybernetic technologies demonstrating gene switch activation through consciousness (thoughts), as well as my 'Stem cell and biofield hypothesis', which offers the understanding that what occurs at a stem cell level, when up-scaled, can relate to you.

When we then consider traditional medicine concepts and understandings, such as those of TCM, where it is believed that the lung stores corporeal experiences and the heart stores all emotional, mental and spiritual phenomena (most likely due to the presence of cell surface receptors on the lung and heart), and that the chakra system is believed to act like a memory system, these recent scientific observations therefore offer validation for traditional medicine observations, and the possibility that who you are may possibly come from the interactions between your physical body (your cell receptors/meridian system/chakras) with your environment and your consciousness (mind/brain). When you compare the similarities of modern scientific technology findings with the concepts of traditional medicines in regard to self and non-self-differentiation, you would agree that this is an impressive achievement by these ancient systems. Why? Because 5000 years ago, the technology to observe these microscopic structures such as the MHC was not available! The integration of all of these systems offers us an opportunity to further understand this phenomenon.

Perhaps the integration of traditional and modern concepts, as I suggest, offers a plausible explanation of where your soul lives.

I would like to raise another question with you regarding the immune system's reaction to donor organs. Is the immune system reacting to the physical structure of the donor's organ cell receptors or to something else? Following on from the above train of thought opens up the possibility that the immune system may be stimulated, not by the actual organ itself, but by the emotions or memories of the donor that are stored, not in the donor organ, but outside the donor organ, that is, their bio-electric signals and cues within the environment (universe). These emotions and memories (unique bio-electric signals and cues — frequencies) are then picked up by the cell receptors of the donor's organs, which are then received by the recipient's consciousness from those organs.

Let me extrapolate this thought a little further. When you do, it becomes possible to realise that bio-electric signals and cues, such as energy, emotions, intention and memories, may all have the potential capacity to stimulate your cell's receptors and the subsequent cellular processes initiated by these receptor stimulations. When you realise that this is possible, then it would make sense that you interact with the energies of 'things' *before* the 'thing'; for example, your arm moves after the energy field around the arm changes! This possibility has been shown to exist by using a monkey's brain to move a robotic arm, as demonstrated by Miguel Nicolelis: 'A monkey that controls a robot with its thoughts'[3], which may offer validity to the idea that matter (robotic arm) follows energy (thoughts generated from the monkey's brain). Furthermore, various people and websites have reported that Professor Bundzen from St Petersburg, Russia, found that 'the response in Kirlian aura seems to precede (appear as soon as or earlier than) electric processes in the brain during a decision-making process'.[4] When interpreting his research, one could confidently say that a thought (energy) appears in the aura (biofield) before any electrical activity can be detected in the brain (matter), hence matter follows energy.

Identity is now being shown by science to be found in stranger places than ourselves. For example, an article in *Science Daily* titled 'New light shed on cell division' states that the authors believe 'the centromere is a very special epigenetic element, in which identity itself is carried outside the DNA'.[5] Although this is not on the actual cell surface, it is another step demonstrating that your identity is not just carried within your DNA, as once thought, nor the organ, nor your body for that matter. Although the centromere is within your body, it is not the only construct within you that seems to have an identity. As previously mentioned, traditional medicines have associated the heart and lung with having identities as well. Knowing this information exists, I suggest that it would make more sense than holding on to the past belief that DNA was the foundation of identity, and therefore we were all doomed to live out whatever was programmed in our genes, or assuming that all the individual organs, endocrines and body parts have a separate identity, or that identity is associated with the chakra system and so on. Let us instead consider following Occam's razor ('all things being equal, the simplest explanation is usually correct'). The simple understanding would be that you (the entire you) are in fact a receiver of information.

Being open to this understanding would therefore lead you to the possible acceptance that you are not really inside your body in the first place, albeit until now, you may have perceived that you were. The information contained in this book suggests that you are not in your body, but are instead in the interactions between you (your BodyMind complex and biofield) and your environment (the universe; Uni-code). These interactions are then recognised (received) by both the energies of your cell surface receptors and the energies within your biofield, such as the energetic pathways of the meridians (i.e. meridians acting as filters based on Professor Ćosić's work[6] and the understanding of TCM) and the chakra system, and your conscious mind (as suggested by Lanza's biocentrism[7]). Once these bio-electric signals and cues are received, they are interpreted as your perception of yourself! Of course, more testing and research needs to be conducted to validate my theory.

Bruce Lipton, in his observations of cellular biology[8], does offer some support for this theory based on his reporting of a similar insight in relation to cell surface receptors, albeit he does not refer to the meridian system or chakras as receptors, nor to the idea of biocentrism and the 'Stem cell and biofield hypothesis'. For now, however, the information that I have presented to you does offer a possible mechanism that demonstrates that you are in the environment; in the universe (as referred to in FlameTree: *the personal development & healing system* — the interactions between the Uni-code and your biofield).

I will explain this theory with an analogy. Picture a radio with an antenna, and the radio is tuned to receive one station only. That station is radio station 'identity FM'. So, if you are sitting there and listening to radio station identity FM's music and the radio stops working, you could say the radio stopped working. Although the radio is not functioning, the actual broadcast did not stop being transmitted. The broadcast/environment is still there, that is, radio station identity FM continues to transmit. All you need now is a working radio to receive it! This is what I believe may be occurring, based on the information that I have presented here, and is what may be potentially occurring with organ transplants. That is, the organ's cell receptors are part of a collective group of receptors that receive the information about you. It would not be too hard to imagine that if the 'self' receptors, say of your lung, could be removed and transplanted onto someone else's cells, then the receiver of your receptors has the potential to start recognising your perceptions, because they now have your receptors, which are tuned into your station and identify 'you'!

The more cell receptors you have of your donor, the greater portion of their perceived reality would be received, which would then have to be integrated with your own cell receptors and the information of you. I point out that this theory is open to the possibility that this is what occurs when a donor's organ, which is inclusive of the cell surface receptors, is transplanted into another person. The recipient recognises the donor's perceptions despite the donor being deceased. This understanding adds credence to the saying, 'the spirit persists whether the body is here or not'. It also adds further depth to the understanding of my 'Stem cell and biofield hypothesis', that your unique frequency of you is already being transmitted within your biofield, and that healthy bio-electric signals and cues influence a healthy biofield, which through resonance may allow you to tune into a healthy version of you, which becomes expressed as your physical self (the healthy receiver) through the activation of your bio-electric code. The healthier your bio-electric signals and cues and your biofield are, the clearer the reception is to the transmission of 'you', which means the more likely it is that you will live your life optimally and purposefully.

The take-home message — your transformation from eternal *worrier* to eternal *warrior*

The *eternal worrier smiles* because they believe that their existence is based on genetics and that they have no control over what they receive from their parents, and as such can blame others for their lot in life. They believe that when they die, they are gone forever because their physical form has perished and there is no energetic connection to the universe.

The *eternal warrior smiles* because they know that their existence is not based on just genetics, and that they can take responsibility over what they receive and transmit (healthy bio-electric signals and cues) into the universe, and as such, they do not blame others for their lot in life. The eternal warrior knows how to create and maintain their own healthy bio-electric signals and cues and maintain a healthy biofield, which allows them to tune in to their life's purpose optimally. They know that their transmission of their bio-electric code continues even when their unique representation of consciousness (URC), which is the fractal representation of the bio-electric code physically expressed, perishes. They realise that, even though some things in our universe may never be explained, they are inspired knowing that there is more 'out there' to experience. The eternal warrior knows that keeping a childlike amazement and wonder at the endless possibilities contained in this universe makes them receptive to these endless possibilities. They know that they can only ever limit themselves by not making the choices, so they choose not to limit themselves and to be open to all the endless possibilities in life!

CHAPTER 8

The redefining of you

Why consider going through the process of redefining you? Because when you stop to *truly* re-evaluate your life, the chances are you are not authentically living your life of purpose optimally. Today is the day where the opportunity has been created for you to understand that redefining you is about who you are *Being*. I remind you that, at the beginning of this book, I stated that it is not about who you *think* you are or want other people to think you should be; it's all about who you are *Being*. Your ability to think is only a part of the equation, albeit a necessary part of the process as will be explained below, and although your thoughts and who you are *Being* are similar in that they can both change every single second that you are alive, *Being* not only allows you to actively change, it actively encourages change. Thinking, however, doesn't actively encourage change. For example, you most probably don't think twice about it, but you already have a belief that you have a personality of some description, but the reality is you are not your personality, or simply put, you are not who you think you are!

Who you think you are at present is based on a faulty belief that encourages rigidity and stagnation in you as a person, and ultimately impacts negatively on your health, wellbeing and ability to live your life optimally with purpose. Who you think you are is your 'routine you', and according to neuroplasticity, routine negatively impacts on your right hemisphere.[1] To actively encourage positive neuroplastic change in your right hemisphere, you need to continue to have novel experiences as often as possible. If your 'routine you' routinely thinks you are being a good person or you are already achieving your purpose in life, then the chances are that the right hemisphere is unhappy. If however, you are *Being* (as defined in more detail below), then you are able to unstick your thinking and create a more healthily functioning right hemisphere and positive neuroplastic changes in your brain — a whole new you![2] I already know that what you are currently thinking is influenced by the filters you are using to navigate your life (filters are discussed later in this book), and they are creating, without you truly thinking about it, unhealthy bio-electric signals and cues, as previously discussed. I already know that you are transmitting unhealthy bio-electric signals and cues without realising you are actually doing this, and they are currently impacting directly on your biofield and keeping you stuck in your current definition of you! As previously discussed, an unhealthy biofield will result in the unhealthy expression of your bio-electric code, which then results in an unhealthy expression of your genes, and as discussed in chapter 7, this interferes with your cell membrane receptors' ability to receive a clear reception of the transmission of 'you', which means it is more likely that you will not be living your life optimally and purposefully.

Now that I have made these assertions that you are stuck in your thinking, which means that you are being an eternal worrier (as you determined at the start of this book), if you don't agree, or if you are not who you previously thought you were (before you started reading this book), then who are you 'being'? This is where I need you to revisit in more detail the definition *Being*. *Being* is inclusive of alignment, synergy, authenticity and synergism, where you are ***actively*** existing in a reality where all possibilities are achievable and available to you, where everything in your life flows with the energies of the universe (which I refer to as the Uni-code) harmoniously and peacefully. This may contrast with the current idea of who you think you are 'being' based on your current definition of you! All you need to do now to understand the difference between *Being* and how you currently think who you are being is — to consider how many limitations you already have self-imposed on your life because of who you think your personality is or who you think you are being. Unlike the process that resulted in the currently defined 'you', the process of *Being* is reflected in a life of endless possibilities, harmony and peace. Although the words 'being' (the noun) and 'be' (the verb) essentially refer to the same thing (existence), I point out that I make a clear distinction between the words 'being' and '*Being*'. *Being* is an active process where you are ***actively involved*** in every aspect of your life, and you are in alignment, synergy, authenticity and synergism. I emphasise ***actively*** because you can still 'be' (exist) without actively doing anything. Simply existing, which you are currently doing is what I call *passively* 'being'. Passively being is void of alignment, synergy, authenticity and synergism, where you are not actively participating in your own life and you are stuck in routine thinking, or more appropriately, you are living your life without consciously feeling your life! This is a very different state of 'being' to what I call '*Being*'. The outcome of *passively* 'being' (the absence of alignment, synergy, authenticity and synergism) is a life not lived with purpose to its optimal potential, with a rapid return to the Uni-code (which in this case refers to premature death), unless, that is, you consciously make the choice of Being (not just thinking about 'being') the eternal warrior.

Understanding the difference between 'being' and 'Being' is essential, because when you are Being, you are also open to all the steps that allow you to create, that is, the steps I refer to as the Law of Creation, as outlined below in figure 8.1. I highlight that this is very different to *passively* being or just existing.

To further illustrate this difference, I would like you to consider the act of listening. The act of listening requires no physical activity as such, but to actively listen requires you to 'Be', rather than just 'be' (exist). You need to actively participate (Being) in not only listening, but hearing, feeling, responding and acting on what you have heard. I know that you probably value your ability to listen to other people, and although this is important and active listening is essential for healthy communication, the act of listening not only refers to listening to other people, but listening to and feeling *you*. Being is actively listening to your own innate wisdom (discussed in more detail in chapter 13) and to the Uni-code (all that is, where all frequencies, possibilities, ideas, thoughts and everything else infinitely co-exist — the 'universal plan' or the Beginning) so that you can express your unique representation of consciousness (URC), which is the fractal representation of the bio-electric code physically expressed, freely and abundantly.

I again assert that your current definition of you, who you think you are, is more likely associated with 'being' and not 'Being'! You are most likely not actively listening to your innate wisdom and the Uni-code. If you were, you would be on your way to living your life of purpose optimally and abundantly, and the chances of you reading this book would be very low because you would already be living from a place where you are Being the eternal warrior who is immune to the 'something for nothing' disease, actively Being the inspired go-getter paddler who takes responsibility for your life, so that you are consciously making the choice to actively create healthy bio-electric signals and cues, a healthy biofield, the healthy expression of your bio-electric code and genes, thereby allowing your cell receptors to receive the healthy transmission of you, which is reflected in you living an optimal life with purpose and flexibility. This, however, may not be your current reality because you may have not yet reached this state of Being. Instead, you are navigating your life (surviving, not thriving) by using the eighteen different filters (discussed later in this book). Living in this reality obstructs you from Being, and as such only contributes to you creating unhealthy bio-electric signals and cues without you even thinking about it, because you are currently stuck in the state of being the eternal worrier.

The good news here is that this can change! I know that you can change from surviving (being) to thriving (Being) if you decide to make the decision to redefine you. To illustrate the consequences of not changing, what do you think would happen to you if all you did was lie in bed, day and night, every day and every night, and that is all you did? You may be existing (being), but all you are doing is passively being, and without a doubt, lying there will lead to the development of bed sores. Once they occur, they would become infected because you are not doing anything to remedy them with some sort of intervention, and so they will inevitably lead to your premature death (going back to the Uni-code). This is the result of passively being, a heavily exaggerated outcome, but an outcome nonetheless! Not Being (actively doing) results in a truncated life every time, unless you act to change your state of passively 'being' to 'Being' by redefining you.

Recall from above that Being is always an active process, and it involves you participating in all the steps that allow you to Be and to create your reality by actively listening to your innate wisdom and the Uni-code. You now know that Being is very different to your current understanding of being (and the dictionary definition). You may have read books such as the The Law of Attraction, which have also used the term 'Being', but their meaning is poorly defined, and is blurred between Wellbeing, Inner-being and Human beings. Unlike the Law of Attraction, I have a clear and concise definition for Being, and for the practising of each of the steps that allow you to achieve Being and to create by using the Law of Creation, as defined below. Before this discussion, I ask you to take a moment now to stop and imagine a plant growing in nature.

A growing plant occurs actively (Being) and precisely (listening to and responding to the Uni-code) without any waste or limitations of thinking (living its life of purpose optimally), and as such creates its reality (Law of Creation). Although plants are not humans, they demonstrate ways of being able to take in the sensory data (bio-electric signals and cues) they gather in their everyday lives, integrate it (healthy bio-electric signals and cues) and then 'behave' in a way that is appropriate in response (healthy expression of their bio-electric code and gene expression, which allows them to receive their transmission from the Uni-code of Being) so that they live optimally and with purpose. This is an example of Being and creating (Law of Creation), albeit using plants as the example. You may argue here that plants cannot feel or think, or have brains like humans, so how can you use them as an example? I agree with you to the extent that plants achieve Being and the Law of Creation without a classically defined brain (i.e. a mammalian brain)! You, on the other hand, have a brain, and unlike plants, it is automatically assumed that you are able to process information, yet you have not yet achieved this state of

Being and created your optimal life purpose, as plants do without brains! This reminds me of an old joke about plants: How do you make a 100- metre-tall acorn tree only grow to six feet? Give it a human brain and ego!

It is incredible to consider how plants can process their environment without brains, based on the assumption that processing information requires a brain; however, when comparing ourselves to plants, maybe having a brain is the problem! Said another way, your brain at present is your problem in that it hinders your ability to achieve *Being*. Unlike plants (although it is a topic of debate) you think, and as previously discussed, most of your thinking (consciously or not) is creating unhealthy bio-electric signals and cues, unless that is you are *Being* and actively listening (to your innate wisdom and the Uni-code), actively feeling, actively breathing, actively giving, actively receiving, actively thinking, actively being conscious and so on. *Being* can only result in healthy bio-electric signals and cues, a healthy biofield and the healthy expression of your bio-electric code and genes, which allows for your cell receptors to receive the healthy transmission of you. When you are *Being* and are actively involved in creating (Law of Creation), then through the laws of brain neuroplasticity, this creates a new pathway that your brain cells (neurons) will use, thereby creating the possibility for you to be consistently, actively listening to your innate wisdom and to the Uni-code (*Being*), a reality that allows you to *Be* and create your reality consistently. This would then allow you to reconnect to the Uni-code and the healthy transmission of your unique representation of conscious (URC). Brain neuroplasticity makes it possible for you to change from being and surviving to *Being* and thriving with a higher level of consciousness. I discuss a higher level of consciousness in greater detail in my book *The golden ring*.

Now that you have a clearer understanding of the distinction between 'being' and '*Being*', I will guide you through implementing the various steps involved with creating the Law of Creation so that you may create and bring your optimal life's purpose into your reality, just like the plant. Firstly, I need to clarify here that, like *Being*, I use the Law of Creation in a very specific way, unlike those advocating Creationism or the proponents of the Law of Attraction who advocate that 'you get what you are thinking about, whether you want it or not'. Unlike these other incomplete understandings, I specifically and purposefully state that the necessary elements for Law of Creation are the synergistic interactions of four key elements: resonance, coherence, consonance and respect, while following the six steps in figure 8.1 and *Being* the eternal warrior. At this point, it may sound easier to be a plant, but it only sounds easier because you were never taught to *Be*, and the neurons in your brain have not yet travelled this route. For this to occur, you need to not only make the choice, but you need the above-mentioned key elements, because without them, you are unable to create and manifest your optimal life of purpose, as directed by the Uni-code through your URC. Before discussing the Law of Creation steps, I first need to explain each of the above elements for the Law of Creation.

In physics, resonance is defined as a phenomenon occurring when a vibrating system drives another system to oscillate with greater amplitude at a specific preferential frequency. You can associate this with playing music very loudly, that is, the loud music blasting out of the speaker resonates with you — you can feel the vibration of the music through your body. In biological systems, resonance is described as occurring at a cellular level, as previously discussed in chapter 6 where I made reference to Professor Ćosić's discussion on cell membrane resonance.[3] Why is cell membrane resonance important in the Law of Creation? Firstly, consider that you are a multicellular organism made of several trillion cells. Each cell in your body has a cell membrane (otherwise it would die), and as such, cell membrane resonance is a phenomenon allowing for cell-to-cell communication, which is occurring within you now. Cell membrane resonance includes many types of molecular processes such as electronic excitation, polarisation, field-generated force effects, heat, and resonant processes such as dipoles vibration.

Resonant processes were first proposed back in 1968 by Froehlich (Froehlich theory) in order to explain the extraordinarily high sensitivity of certain biological systems to extremely weak electromagnetic signals.[4] In Froehlich's model, long-range collective interactions within cell membranes may lead to oscillatory biochemical reactions, for example, enzyme-substrate interactions in the greater membrane of the brain. The resulting slow chemical oscillation is connected to a corresponding electric vibration by means of the large dipole moments of reaction-activated enzymes. Thus, a macroscopic oscillating polarisation is built up, causing large regions to oscillate coherently in the 10 to 100 Hz region, which is responsible for EEG activity. Froehlich theory may explain resonance processes associated with cell-to-cell signalling, brainwaves and enzymatic chemical reactions, particularly with cancer.[5]

Although the discussion on cell membrane resonance contains numerous jargonistic terms, I want to draw your attention to cell-to-cell signalling and brainwaves. Your brain controls the cells in your body. One of the ways that your brain does this is through brainwaves, as explained by Froehlich theory in resonance processes. I would also point out that your feelings, thoughts and perceptions (belief systems) influence your brainwaves[6], which may then influence your state of *Being* as indicated by the second step in Figure 8.1 (the first step is to listen!). Recall above that physics defines resonance as a phenomenon occurring when a vibrating system drives another system to oscillate. I make the association here that your brain may be considered like a vibrating system, because brainwaves, which are influenced by thoughts and perceptions, will cause your cells (another vibrating system) to vibrate. This collectively influences cell-to-cell communication via cell membrane resonance. This then impacts on what you are *Being* and the transmission of you; what your cell membrane receptors are receiving.

It is interesting to note that the relaying of information through resonance, as bio-physicist CWF McClare from Oxford University published on 'resonance in bio-energetics', is reported to be one hundred times more efficient in relaying environmental information than physical signals such as hormones, neurotransmitters and growth factors.[7] When you consider this in the context of the Law of Creation, your feelings, perceptions and thoughts, the process of resonance is an efficient way of communicating who you are *Being* and creating and manifesting your reality, provided you are actively listening.

The next element of the Law of Creation is coherence. This is defined as the quality of being logical and consistent, as well as the quality of forming a unified whole. I point out here that your feelings, perceptions and thoughts, if they are not coherent with who you are *Being* and what you want to have, will impact on your ability to create and manifest anything that is logical and consistent to you. This will then affect who you are *Being* because you are unable to be in alignment, synergy, authenticity and synergism when you are being incoherent, and from this state you are unable to actively listen, which is the first step in the Law of Creation.

The next element is consonance. I will use music again to assist in explaining this element's role in the Law of Creation. In music, consonance refers to a combination of notes that are in harmony with each other due to the relationship between their frequencies. Your feelings, perceptions and thoughts, like musical notes, are frequencies that also need to be in agreement or be compatible with each other. For example, the various opinions and beliefs you have and the various actions that you take need to be in consonance (harmony), as this influences what you have (create and manifest), as well as who you are *Being*. Without consonance, you are unable to *Be* in alignment, synergy, authenticity or synergism.

The final element of the Law of Creation is respect. Without respect, as with coherence and consonance, it is not possible to *Be* in alignment, synergy, authenticity or synergism with yourself and with those in your environment. When you are not *Being* respectful, listening to your innate wisdom becomes much harder to achieve. Said differently disrespecting yourself diminishes your ability to tune into your own innate wisdom and creates downward spirals according to neuroplasticity.[8]

As listening (actively) to the Uni-code is the starting point for the six steps of Creation, anything that impacts on your ability to actively listen — such as unhealthy bio-electric signals and cues, an unhealthy biofield, incoherence,

THE ETERNAL WARRIOR'S SMILE

dissonance, the actions of being disrespectful and not *Being* in alignment, synergy, authenticity and synergism with yourself within your environment — will impact on your ability to effectively, consciously feel, *Be* and consequently have. As illustrated in figure 8.1, actively listening and feeling comes before thinking, thoughts and interpretation, but the issue that most people face, and that may include you, is that you do not actively listen and feel before you think. Not listening and feeling is influenced by the eighteen filters you are currently using without thinking to interpret your thinking, thoughts and other stimuli. It may sound paradoxical, you do not think about thinking, but the issues you are facing in your life right now prevent you from living your life's purpose optimally because you are not actively listening to your innate wisdom and Uni-code! Instead, you are navigating surviving your life by using filters that distort your feelings, thinking, thoughts and interpretation of all other stimuli within you and your environment, which leads to unhealthy bio-electric signals and cues and the sequalae that this causes unless you are making the choice to consciously change and redefine you.

I can make this statement because I created a personal development and healing system that enables people to reconnect with their innate wisdom and Uni-code so that they are able to actively listen and feel before thinking, using thoughts and making interpretations. From what I have observed in those individuals who have experienced the **FlameTree** effect (discussed in more detail in the book *The science and achievements of FlameTree: the personal development & healing system*), it is essential to identify and clear the eighteen filters that you are currently viewing your life through. This is imperative because those eighteen filters influence the four key elements discussed above, the six steps outlined in Figure 8.1, and your ability to establish healthy bio-electric signals and cues, a healthy biofield and expression of your bio-electric code and genes so that your cell receptors are receiving a clear transmission of who you are *Being* so that you are creating your reality where you are actively listening, feeling and living your life of purpose optimally!

The reality is that you are living your life through your filters without consciously being aware of it, and this inhibits your ability to actively listen to your innate wisdom or the Uni-code, thereby resulting in you living your life sub-optimally and sub-purposefully. As you continue to follow figure 8.1, you will see that each step can and does feedback on itself, as well as on all other steps. Each step must resonate with the next, and all must be coherent and in consonance with each other in order for something to be created. This means that, even before you reach the *Be* step, the elements discussed above continue to shape and influence your ability to *actively listen*, *feel* and then *think* before getting to *Be*. Once you reach the *Be* step, the next step is naturally *say*, that is, self-talk and saying to other people. When this is in flow, you are able to *do*, which involves the actions required in the physical world and the actions to feel and emotionally respond so that you are able to maintain resonance, coherence, consonance and respect, while being aware of the filters that may distort your thinking. In so doing, the opportunity is created for the creation and manifestation step, that is, to *have*.

If, however, you are not actively listening and feeling, the reality is that you are still thinking (or not consciously thinking), having thoughts (albeit unconsciously), perceiving and believing through the eighteen different filters and being the eternal worrier. This all contributes to your unhealthy bio-electric signals and cues, your unhealthy biofield and the unhealthy expression of your bio-electric code and genes. This state of being reinforces your brain's neurons to keep this pathway of being your reality, and as such, your cell receptors are not receiving the healthy transmission of you and you are no longer in a state to apply the Law of Creation because you are not actively listening (the first step to the Law of Creation)! Your ability to create and manifest your life of optimal purpose is impeded.

I would highlight to you here that, whether you are being the eternal worrier or *Being* the eternal warrior, you are still creating your reality, but as the worrier at this present moment, it is not the inspiring optimal life of purpose version. The good news here is that by understanding how the Law of Creation and the 'Stem cell and biofield hypothesis' work, by *Being* and making choices, you are now able to dynamically, with consciousness, make the choice to create your optimal life purposefully by actively listening, which not only benefits you, it benefits those around you and ultimately the world!

The understanding of the Law of Creation above may also explain why the Law of Attraction worked for some people, but not others. As you can now see, the proponents of the Law of Attraction offered an incomplete picture of how to attract and manifest.

What this means is that the Law of Attraction will work for those people who are manifesting something that they, by chance, already had the necessary elements (from the Law of creation) for the Law of Attraction to be successfully implemented in their life. Said another way, if a person did not have all the elements from the Law of Creation to be successfully implemented in their lives, it could not possibly work for them to attract what they wanted or desired whether applying the Law of Attraction or the Law of Creation.

Figure 8.1 The elements of the Law of Creation

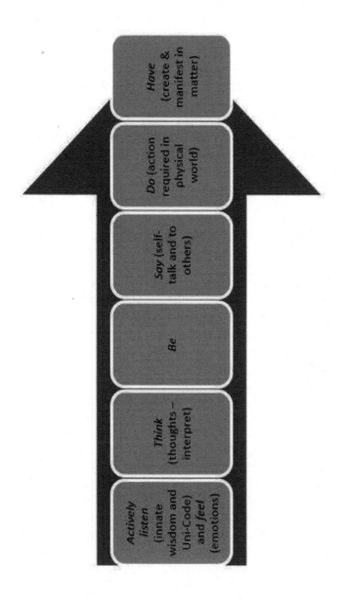

I want to caution you regarding the Law of Creation. Although it is possible to create and manifest 'things' using the Law of Creation, a rigid belief that most people have is that you need that 'thing' to feel happy and fulfilled. I need to raise to your consciousness the reality that whatever 'thing' you have in life will *never* make you feel happy or fulfilled. Happiness and fulfillment (bio-electric signals and cues) do not come from having a 'thing', but rather the experiences and feelings (the unique bio-electric signals and cues) that you *create* and *manifest* from having the 'thing'. You can immediately and directly relate to the experience of feeling good when you acquire a new 'thing' or achieve a goal. For example, you were most probably told to go and do 'something' positive with your life, such as get a job or earn a degree, either of which was supposed to provide you with the opportunity to acquire a 'thing' that would make you feel happy. That 'thing' could be a better standing in society, education, job prospects, quality of life and so on. A 'thing' could also be something material, such as a new item of clothing that might make you feel sexy or a new piece of jewellery that makes you feel funky, or a new toy that makes you feel young.

However, these 'happy' feelings that you acquired from having 'things' are usually short-lived! Why? Because you were not actively listening to the bio-electric signal and cue of you *Being* sexy, funky or young. Said another way, you did not actively listen and feel, then think you were happy, sexy, funky or young in the first place, and therefore you are now relying on the 'things' you acquired to make you feel this way.

The more you rely on 'things', the more 'things' you need to keep you feeling happy, sexy, funky or young. Just as I encourage you to begin redefining you, I also encourage you here that, in your redefining of you, you need to consider redefining and updating your thoughts and thinking about needing to acquire 'things' to feel good, happy, sexy, funky or young, and that you need to be open to active listening first to your innate wisdom and Unicode. There are no 'things', or in fact, any other people, that can bring you happiness or any other emotion as such. Instead, it's the feeling you choose to have in your present moment. This is essential to understand as you begin the process of redefining you, but knowing this does not stop you from making the conscious choice, when actively listening to your innate wisdom and the Uni-code, to have (create and manifest) what you want. As shown above in Figure 8.1, you need to first *actively listen and feel*, *think* it, *Be* it, *say* or speak it and *do* it, and then it will be created and manifested by you and show up in your life, that is, you will *have* it. This will occur provided all the elements (resonance, coherence, consonance and respect) of the Law of Creation are there in harmony and you are consciously *Being* (alignment, synergy, authenticity and synergism), while free of the eighteen filters that previously distorted your thinking, so that you are immersed in healthy bio-electric signals and cues, a healthy biofield with the healthy expression of your bio-electric code and genes, and as such you are consciously *Being* the eternal warrior. In this state, your cell receptors are receiving the healthy transmission of you from the Uni-code, which is observed as your URC, and living your life optimally and purposefully.

It is essential to actively listen to your innate wisdom and feel your way through life because if you don't, inevitably your thoughts and perceptions become your rigid beliefs, which is essentially where you are at now, and if you are not actively listening, then your beliefs transmit unhealthy bio-electric signals and cues arising out of unhealthy thoughts. Please complete the following statement to assist you in understanding this point:

'I do not think I am .... <u>(fill in blank)</u> ...'

In the testing phase of the information contained in this book, this question was asked of many clients, who predominantly (but not exclusively) inserted a negative response, for example, 'I do not think I am good enough' or 'I do not think I am confident enough'. The interesting observation I made when asking this question was that many people also had a belief that they were deficient in some way. This makes sense when you recall Maslow's hierarchy of needs, which states that your deficiency needs must be met first before you concern yourself with self-actualisation/transcendence and the Law of Creation. Furthermore, these same people didn't want to feel that way (not good enough or confident enough and so on), so they kept looking for ways to make them feel better, for example, by 'buying a house (or some other acquisition) that they believed would make them feel good and confident'. This acquisition would only be a temporary fix because, although they thought this would fix the issue, the issue was created through not actively listening! The reality was that these people had not yet redefined themselves, nor were they thinking of their rigid beliefs because they were being eternal worriers, not realising they were blaming everything for their feelings. I advocate FlameTree: *the personal development & healing system* as the system to not only reconnect with active listening and feeling, as discussed above, but to also redefine you, your thoughts and beliefs.

If you do not actively listen, but automatically think and falsely associate a need of 'things' to not feeling '.... <u>(fill in blank)</u> ...', this results in unhealthy bio-electric signals and cues which, through brain neuroplasticity, will become your default belief without you consciously making the choice to have this belief, and this is only one example!

How many of these unhealthy beliefs (unhealthy bio-electric signals and cues) could you have? One thing is for certain, there is more than just one, and for the majority of them, you would not consciously realise you are feeling, thinking, being, saying, or doing, yet alone having (creating or manifesting)! They are your automatic, unconscious, default beliefs that are operating now as you read, with many of these beliefs being someone else's that you have adopted and accepted to be true and valid! Without realising it you are surrounding yourself with unhealthy bio-electric signals and cues, which as previously discussed leads to an unhealthy biofield and the unhealthy expression of your bio-electric code and genes. This makes it so much harder for you to actively listen, feel and regain resonance, coherence, consonance and respect so that you can clearly receive the transmission of you, so that you can then think, *Be*, say, do and then have a reality where you are optimally living your life's purpose.

As previously discussed, to create change, you need to firstly actively listen and be conscious of your feelings and then of your thoughts (which are bio-electric signals and cues). It is imperative that you realise that it is not about acquiring a 'thing' or 'receiving approval', 'acceptance' or 'love' from someone else that brings about change! You are personally responsible for that change. Being responsible means following the steps of the Law of Creation where you are *actively listening* and consciously *feeling*, then *thinking*, where you are actively changing your pre-existing unhealthy bio-electric signals and cues that are currently automatically playing, to healthy bio-electric signals and cues so that you resume *Being* (in alignment, synergy, authenticity and synergism) based on what you are listening to from your innate wisdom and the Uni-code. This immediately initiates healthy bio-electric signals and cues and will be in harmony with the Law of Creation elements, that is, it will resonate with healthy bio-electric signals and cues, be coherent, have a healthy consonance, and there will be an inherent respect for who you are *Being* and what you are creating.

Before moving on to the next steps of the Law of Creation, I will use a previous example from above about feeling happy, sexy, funky and young. Based on the Law of Creation, this cannot occur by acquiring 'things'! It can only truly occur by *listening* to your innate wisdom, and then *feeling*, then *thinking*, and then *Being* happy, sexy, funky and young. Then you need to *say*, which involves what you are saying to yourself and also what you say to others, and then *do* — actions required in physical world so that you can *Be* happy, sexy, funky and young in your present moment, as if it has already happened, which may then, based on the idea that matter follows energy, create and manifest 'things' into your reality (*have*) that are happy, sexy, funky and young.

Prior to FlameTree: *the personal development & healing system*, I recall a method where a therapist, to assist you to change and redefine you, would suggest that you consciously practise self-talk. This is where you needed to say to yourself what you thought you wanted to be (as opposed to listening to what your innate wisdom is telling you) and use this as your own self-talk. For example, you may say to yourself 'I am happy, sexy, funky, and young' as your self-talk, and it was believed that, the more you repeated this to yourself, the more you were likely to increase the possibility that your actions would inevitably change and you would not need, or want, those 'things' to make you feel happy, sexy, funky, and young. As you will recall, self-talk without active listening, feeling and then thinking is like the yellow paint, and your thoughts here are the black ball. You can therefore immediately see how the self-talk method used on its own is hopelessly outdated.

I recognised that self-talk alone did work for some people, but the only way it worked was if the person using self-talk already had a very strong belief that they could create change by self-talking, or they also believed in what was chosen for the self-talk (e.g. I am strong), as self-talk works exceedingly well in someone who already believes that they are strong in that area of their life. So, combining this self-talk with an already existing strongly held belief did not change the black ball's programming, it only reinforced what was already there! FlameTree, however, overcomes this problem with self-talk because it directly reconnects you to listening to your innate wisdom and the Uni-code, and promotes *Being*. Unlike self-talk, FlameTree aims to rectify your inability to actively listen and feel, and to assist you to rectify faulty thinking (unhealthy bio-electric signals and cues). Once you have rectified your faulty thinking, for example, regarding buying stuff to make you feel a certain way, and you are actively listening, feeling and *Being* (e.g. happy, sexy, funky and young), the outcome of this change is that you may still buy 'things' that will 'enhance' your feeling of *Being* happy, sexy, funky, and young, but you are no longer relying on these 'things' to feel this way.

I will use another example to demonstrate this point. Have you ever had that friend, or know of someone, who continually chooses the wrong type of partner? It's OK if you don't, but the scenario plays out that the partners they choose are always the same, with each relationship ending in the same way, and everyone else can see it except for them. When yet another relationship fails due to that individual not listening to their innate wisdom and the Uni-code, coupled with the eighteen different filters they are using and their faulty belief systems, they swear off relationships and vow to only try again when they find and can have the 'right one'. You know now there is no 'right one'! The reason why they never find the 'right one' is because they are not listening, and they are still thinking with the same faulty beliefs, using the same filters, and without realising it, through resonance, they are transmitting unhealthy bio-electric signals and cues by passively being the type of person who attracts the wrong type of person. This will be explored in more detail in the next chapter, but for the moment, I encourage you to focus on what it is that you are waiting for in order to *allow* yourself to *Be* a certain way.

I appreciate that currently you are most probably walking around doing the best you can with what you have, while most probably insisting on doing it your way (remember self-help?) because everyone and their dog is telling you how to live your life! For example, you have been told to be good, grow up, get a haircut, get a good job, get married, get some kids, think good thoughts, live in peace, remember to breathe, eat well, exercise, and the list goes on and on. Everyone keeps telling you what to do, but no one really tells you where or how to start. For most people, it usually starts with a deficiency need, that is, the 'problem'. Something like, 'I don't have my freedom (the deficiency needs) because I have to live at home with my parents'. A 'solution' may be to move out. Moving out, however, creates a new problem of 'But I do not have enough money (another deficiency need)!' You now need a new solution to solve the money issue, which might be to get a job. Getting a job creates a problem because you need to have skills or experience to get a job (another deficiency needs)! This means another solution must be found to address your first deficiency need of not feeling free. During this process, a recurring pattern may be seen that could be interpreted as, 'My life is full of problems; living is solving them'. Your life is then driven by this faulty interpretation of your life (unhealthy bio-electric signal and cue), and as such you become a slave to this belief!

Another example to demonstrate this is associated with acquiring a new car. You may want to purchase a new car for transportation or to make you feel good, but you realise that you do not have enough money (the problem). What's your solution? Get more money, but this then creates a new problem of how to get more money. So, you now need to find a solution to this new problem, as discussed in the previous example. As you may now appreciate, this cycle goes on and on and on. However, I would bring the following question to your attention: Why is it that you think you want 'something' in the first place, like the new place to live, a new car or whatever? The above two examples did state you wanted freedom for a new place to live, and transportation or wanting to feel good for the car. Although these suggestions may appear as valid reasons for wanting something in the first place, they do not tell you where to start, and in fact are causing more issues for you! So, what's the answer?

You may have worked out the answer from our discussion above about the Law of Creation. You need to start at Law of Creation step 1, which is the easy solution to all your problems, and that is to actively *listen* to your innate wisdom and then feel the emotion as if it ('the thing') has already occurred. The issue that's occurring here when *you think* you want that 'something' before you listen and feel, is that *you think* you want it because you have thought first, *you think* you will be a certain way once you have acquired it! That certain way is the complete opposite to the way you felt when you first decided to find a solution for your deficiency need or problem. Although *thinking* is the second step of the Law of Creation, there is no way you can get to this step before implementing step 1, that is *listening* and then *feeling* before you think! What you are doing instead is not listening to your innate wisdom, and the outcome is an unhealthy bio-electric signal and cue, which is most probably occurring as you read without your awareness, albeit having read this far I would like to believe that you are now more aware that this is occurring. When you are not listening, you are no longer Being in alignment, synergy, authenticity or synergism, and without these four elements Being in harmony, all that you will achieve is transmitting and resonating unhealthy bio-electric signals and cues, and as such you are lacking the basic ingredients for the Being, which impacts on your ability to use the Law of Creation.

You cannot continue to live in this way! Why? Let's say, for example, one of the purposes for reading this book is that you want to feel happy, content, satiated, satisfied, fulfilled, and so on, because you believe that you need to fill an empty feeling inside you. Now, prior to reading this book you would have been looking to fill this empty feeling with a 'thing', whether that is a material 'thing' or a person 'thing' — both are associated with unhealthy bio-electric signals and cues. In order to fill this perceived empty feeling (your deficiency need), you set about achieving that 'thing', whatever it is. The day comes in your future when you attain your desired 'thing', and for that first week or month, your need to feel happy, content, satiated and so on has been met and your perceived empty feeling is no longer felt. The reality, however, is that it is still present, but it cannot be felt because you now are feeling that you are whole and complete. I would ask you to briefly reflect on this perceived belief and ask yourself the following questions: Now that you have this 'thing', are you really Being happy, content, satisfied, whole and complete? Do you want more? Is this what you really wanted now that you have it?

Everyone thinks they know *how* to be happy, content, satisfied or healthy. You know what to do, right? Wrong! If you did, you wouldn't be reading this book, because you would be already living your life of purpose optimally without relying on any 'thing' or 'person' or 'book'. You have already established that this is not the case because you identified with being an eternal worrier, and you have not yet worked out how to be eternally happy, healthy and content without having that 'thing', whatever that 'thing' may be, that you feel will make you feel something else apart from empty! You may get motivated or enthused to change something once you get that 'thing', but it is usually short-lived and that is as far as it goes. Motivation is great as it makes you create the action for change, but unless you convert that motivation into inspiration or *Being*, where you are actively listening, feeling and then thinking, all that will occur with motivation is a fading away into nothingness, only for the deficiency need or problem to soon re-emerge.

I will use weight loss as an example to further illustrate this. Although you may not have a weight problem, you possibly know someone who does, and if you are like most people, you will look down one day and say, 'I'd better lose some kilos'! What would you do? Again, if you are like most people, you would go on a diet and buy a gym membership. You may also change the food in your fridge and pantry, buy yourself a fancy set of scales, and set out to lose that unwanted weight. After a few weeks/months (depending on your goals) of motivated action, you are now a few kilos lighter. You celebrate because you have done what you set out to do, so you take your foot of the weight loss accelerator and your previous habits start to creep in again. What happens then over the next few months? You put all the weight back on, and then what do you start to think? Maybe you start thinking you are a failure or not good enough, which is what you most probably thought before you decided to reduce your weight (albeit unconsciously)! You now get stuck in this thinking (unhealthy bio-electric signals and cues) that you had before becoming motivated to make these changes in the first place!

The reason why this situation occurs for you is that although you did the weight loss 'things', you were not listening to your innate wisdom, you were not feeling before thinking and you were certainly not *Being* 'weight loss'. You may have done the healthy 'things', but you were not making a choice of listening to *Being* healthy. As discussed above with the steps to the Law of Creation, you must first *listen, feel* and then *think* so that you can start to *Be*. It is more important to focus your choice on *Being* rather than on acquiring one 'thing' that is perceived by you to make you feel happy. These 'things' are in fact distractions from listening and *Being*. Acquiring 'things' based on your faulty perceptions of life will never get you permanent results! To truly create eternal change, you need to start listening, as per the steps of the Law of Creation, and *Being* the eternal warrior (both are healthy bio-electric signals and cues), as these will determine what you do and what you will have.

Having read to this point, you are now aware of the three big reasons why most people don't change — fear of change, fear of failure and being lazy. I have helped you to remove the excuse of genetics and have now demonstrated how listening and Being is more important than thinking (e.g. you need to acquire something to feel a certain way). I would now ask you to identify the **one** common factor throughout all of the issues you currently face in your life at present? Did you immediately work it out? It is you! Recall what was previously discussed, where it was highlighted that no one can change you apart from you! Only you can redefine you! The issue as it stands is that the current 'you' can't help you because it was 'you' that got you into this mess in the first place! As you have read to this point, I know that you are more open to the possibility of accepting this, as well as to finding your solutions. So, what do you do? The solution is simple.

This book offers you the opportunity to create change by teaching you how to redefine you. It does so by assisting you to remove false truths and excuses and by demonstrating that, by listening and showing you how your feelings, thoughts and perceptions influence you, your environment, your life and those around you, you can change and redefine you. How can this help you? Recall that it is not only your feelings, thoughts and perceptions that are a source of bio-electric signals and cues (healthy or unhealthy), so too is your environment, which will influence your biofield and the expression of your bio-electric code and genes.

Now that you know this, I want you to recall the flea and glass jar story. Why? Because a major limiting perception that you cast over yourself (most people do this unknowingly), which is probably the key issue that limits your progress in life, is that 'you think there is something wrong within you or your environment'. This thinking prevents you, like the flea's glass lid, from reaching your optimal potential and living your life's purpose. It really doesn't matter what that 'something' is or where it is coming from, because what truly matters is that you are thinking and perceiving it to be the case, that is, until someone demonstrates that you too can 'jump out of your glass jar'! The problem you currently face is that you are 'stuck' in this perception of something being wrong, and as such, you automatically create your own unhealthy bio-electric signals and cues. This then acts like static interfering with your ability to listen, feel, then think, say, Be, do and have (create and manifest).

To further understand how you are stuck in this self-limiting perception of something being wrong, I want you to consider the following scenario. Let's say, for example, that this perception of something being wrong comes to you at home as you sit to dinner with your family. You feel uneasy, but as this thinking is occurring within your home environment, you think all is okay because you believe that you are safe and loved, and you think that you belong, therefore your physiological needs, according to Maslow, are being met (i.e.

eating, shelter and belonging). If this was not the case, then this perception of something wrong would be more intense for you, but because this is not your situation, you don't really think much of this peculiar feeling.

Let's continue with this example, and say that later that night after dinner, you decide to go out dancing with your family and friends. On your way to the venue, there is that peculiar thinking again that something is wrong; however, although you are no longer in your home, you still believe you are safe and loved, and believe you belong because you are in a car driving there with your family and friends, so again you think it must be okay, and so you continue to not listen or pay it attention. This thinking then happens again on the dance floor, and although it may make you feel nervous, you continue to not pay it attention, but you know it's still there. The next day when you are at work, you notice that same thinking of something being wrong again! At this point, your mind kicks in and starts to really search for what is wrong (thinking), and you then make a connection — the something wrong was associated with that work-related issue, and you then think that you have solved the mystery to this feeling, but have you? Driving home from work, sitting in peak hour traffic, that mysterious thinking strikes again! But you thought you had worked it out! Your mind kicks in again and starts where it left off. It begins to look high, low and all around, but still nothing can be detected for this perception that something is wrong!

What you had done initially in identifying your work as the cause was due to your desperation to find the answer for it, you confused 'causation' with 'correlation'. What does this mean? You ended up accusing your work-related issue of causing you this perception of something being wrong in an attempt to satisfy yourself that you had found the cause, but now you are still searching for it! The problem here is that, when you blame something or someone else for how you are thinking, you are mistakenly associating this as the cause (causation), but in fact it is only a correlation. This example highlights that you have not listened to your innate wisdom, nor are you *Being* the eternal warrior, and as such you continue to suffer the consequences of your self-imposed glass lid.

If you are still unsure where I am heading with this scenario, and if you have confused causation and correlation, I will explore it in a little more detail with the following example. Imagine that crime goes up on a hot day, as do ice-cream sales. Therefore, it might be easy to blame the increase of crime on the sale of ice-cream. This may appear to be causation, as both go up simultaneously on hot days, right? Wrong. Although it would be easy to assume this is true, just as you did in the above example, blaming work as the cause of your perception that something is wrong, something inside you says,

'Hey, wait a minute, something is wrong here with this association! That logic does not add up.' And that is because a hot day causes ice-cream sales to increase as well as more crime, but the increase in ice-cream sales and the increase in crime are correlated, not causative. So, you are right to challenge your initial logic here, where blame was placed on the ice-cream sales for the increase in crime, which did not make sense. Similarly, blaming the work-related issue for your perception of something being wrong in the previous example is also a correlation and not a causation. What does this mean for you?

I am steering you to the understanding that the only common factor in the above examples is *you*! It was you who perceived something was wrong in each of your different environments (at home, in the car, on the dance floor and at work). Why? Because it's *your* perception that something is wrong and no one else's! It is also your perception that you think you are safe because you believe you need to belong (Maslow's third need in the hierarchy of needs), because if you think you don't belong, you would feel unwanted, alone and unsafe! If you think this, you would then become stuck in this thinking pattern, and you would then start to believe that you are the only one experiencing it, so you may mistakenly conclude, 'I don't belong'. You may even then take action by removing yourself from certain social outings. By believing these faulty and disempowering belief systems (unhealthy bio-electric signals and cues), you may have convinced yourself that you are the problem, and that if you don't belong, how can you be accepted by others.

Once you are in this state, your biofield is being bombarded by your own unhealthy bio-electric signals and cues, which then creates an unhealthy biofield. You are now passively being, you have stopped listening to your innate wisdom and the Uni-code, and you are no longer coherent, you lack consonance and respect (the necessary elements for the Law of Creation). You are now transmitting and resonating these unhealthy bio-electric signals and cues, and paradoxically, you continue to create this, which is most probably how you have arrived at this faulty conclusion, confusing causation with correlation, in the first place. This may also explain why you are where you are at now in your life. You may be thinking that you are, for example, discontented, you don't have all the answers, disempowered, a void that tells you during quiet times that something is missing or wrong in your life, you are not good enough, you will never make it big and so on.

As previously indicated, there is zero chance for you to create your reality, where you are optimally living your life of purpose, when you are stuck in this worrier mind state. When you are passively being the worrier, all you get is just more of the same unhealthy bio-electric signals and cues, yet somehow you know deep down that, although your faulty perceptions of being the eternal worrier are dominating and you think you don't belong, this is not your true state! Somehow you know that you still have the ability to create change in your life, and so you begin to make changes to cope with your reality of your life's situation, but instead of creating healthy bio-electric signals and cues and following the Law of Creation, you inadvertently manufacture more unhealthy bio-electric signals and cues in the form of masks.

The problem that you are now creating is that wearing a mask gives you something to hide behind, so you may think you are being strong, superior, right or justified, but this only hides who you really are, and you know you are still feeling the exact opposite of how you feel with the mask on. James Clavell described this in his book *Shogun*: Volume 1:

> *It's a saying they have, that a man has a false heart in his mouth for the world to see, another in his breast to show to his special friends and his family, and the real one, the true one, the secret one, which is never known to anyone except to himself alone, hidden only God knows where.*[9]

Said another way, when you are being the eternal worrier, you inevitably create at least two masks for yourself to wear. The first mask you show to the world. The second mask you show to your close friends and your family. However, your true face, you never show anyone, and it is this face that is the truest reflection of who you are. The two masks you wear cover up your deficiency beliefs about yourself. The question I ask you here is: Why do you need to hold on to these deficiency belief systems and your two masks in the first place? I will be bold here and state to you that there is one very simple reason: It's called your 'payoff'. It is easier for you to cover yourself up and *say* and *do* what everyone else around you wants to *hear* and *see*, than for you to feel vulnerable by showing the *real* you! The main reason you do this is because you want to stop yourself feeling emotional pain and fear, for example, the emotional pain and fear of rejection, not being accepted or loved. This is the same reason why many people bow to peer pressure. It is, however, also true that you cannot get anyone to agree with anything that they don't already agree with; it is impossible. So, what is a payoff?

Payoffs are unhealthy bio-electric signals and cues that come in a variety of forms, but they usually serve to make you (the person who is receiving the payoff) feel better about yourself. If it did not make you feel any better about yourself, you would not desire the payoff! The reality is that the masks you need to wear to achieve your payoff only add to your already unhealthy bio-electric signals and cues, which is contributing to your now self-sustaining unhealthy biofield. Add this to cognitive dissonance and you get to continue being the eternal worrier. This is reinforced by perceived basic human values that we *all* want, that is, we want to feel respected, be liked, be loved, feel validated, appear to others as what your society presents as desirable (e.g. strong, dominant), or being right about something (we all know how good that feels — you are wrong, I am right!), or to feel justified about your position or to maintain your current comfort position. A couple of examples here might include not giving charitably to Third World countries and looking away when advertisements for giving to starving children come on the television. These are all examples of unhealthy signals and cues that continue to impact on your now unhealthy biofield, and once you get into this state (being the eternal worrier), it then also impacts on your ability to listen, which collectively serves to limit your optimal potential for living your life's purpose.

The question here is: Why aren't you making the choice to 'feel good' and to start listening again to your innate wisdom and Uni-code, so that you can generate healthy bio-electric signals and cues and regain *Being* the eternal warrior? The answer again is you! You are the problem, because it is your mind that created the problem, and as such, your mind cannot see past your problem, unless that is, you begin implementing the activities referred to in this book, as well as implement the various ROAs, in particular FlameTree: *the personal development & healing system*, which, along with other ROAs, has been purposefully created to support these changes.

Now that your awareness has been raised, I ask you to be mindful of others around you. If you are aware, for example, of your partner or friends demonstrating these habits or traits, I encourage you to consider making the choice to share this knowledge with them. Why? Because the chances are that they would not be aware that they are behaving in this way, so without this information, they will continue being the eternal worrier in an unconscious and destructive manner. If you say nothing, you are enabling your family or friends, who are in your immediate environment, to continue being the eternal worrier, which not only makes them 'small', but may be another factor holding you back from reaching your optimal potential and life's purpose. By not taking action and allowing others to continue being the eternal worrier, you are also choosing to continue being an eternal worrier! Why? Because you are not choosing to control your environment by placing powerful, happy and amazing individuals (family and friends), who are also a source of healthy bio-electric signals and cues, into your environment, as an eternal warrior would! Let's face it — not only do you want to be mindful of yourself, you also need to consider the people you have in your life who may all also require a helping, loving and understanding hand with honest, caring and healthy feedback to assist then in achieving their goal of living optimally, living purposefully.

We all require someone who will dare to hold us in a position of empowerment, and who cares enough about us to actually be honest with us and not just pad our ego. I encourage you to take on the warrior roll and pass on this book to your 'perceived' normal or troubled family member, friend, colleague or any one you see that needs help. Why? Because this is the key purpose for the existence of this book, and it's the right thing to do. Assist people to regain their ability to listen, feel and then think so that they can return to Being the eternal warrior in their life. Imagine the change in consciousness that could occur if everyone were Being the eternal warrior, optimally living their life of purpose in harmony with everyone else. However, by not making the choice to redefine you, you remain being the eternal worrier who wants to avoid feeling like an idiot, being belittled, disrespected, small or wrong. You may argue or defend yourself so that you are seen to be right so as to avoid these feelings. The point I am making here is that, in redefining you, you must let go of the story that you are telling yourself about yourself right now! You need to let go of the need to be right and to understand the impact of each of these things on your life. For every payoff you receive, there is a cost. For example, the payoff of having to be right is that you cost yourself understanding and love from others (no one really wants to associate with a know-it-all!). The cost for each of your payoffs is potentially huge, and can deeply affect your current life, whether you are aware of it or not. So, in order to assist you in redefining you, you may consider now as a good time to ask your close friends and family to start being honest with you!

Another way of interpreting the unhealthy impact that payoffs have in your life is by understanding that when you say 'yes' to your payoff, you are also by default simultaneously saying 'no' to its opposite. For example, when you say 'yes' to a relationship that does not meet all of your needs, you are also by default simultaneously saying 'no' to a relationship that meets all of your needs. If you are saying yes to not making the choice of redefining you, then you are saying no to Being the eternal warrior! All you will then do is continue wearing your masks to hide your true face from the world, believing you will make it in your world! It may sound ridiculous that you actually wear masks to make it in your world, but I reinforce the point here that you do in fact wear them. Why? Because there is obviously a payoff for wearing your masks and, as said earlier, it is usually to 'make it' or 'survive' in life without having to confront your emotional pain and fear. There are, however, costs to wearing these masks, and many of these costs are insidious and possibly impact on your long-term health and wellbeing due to their transmission of unhealthy bio-electric signals and cues.

Wearing masks immediately prevents people from seeing the real you. You may not really care about hiding your real self for now, but at some point, you are going to want to share your life with someone special or develop a close friendship with someone (recall that this refers to Maslow's need number three — belonging). This is potentially a point of conflict for you, as it is for most people — do you wear your mask and lose a close friend by refusing to open up and make the connection deeper, or do you let them see your true face and risk them mocking, rejecting, judging you and so on? Sadly, the fear of failure (one of the big three reasons why you don't try) prevents you from ever allowing those close to you to really be close to you! 'What if I show them my true face and I fail to impress them?' To make it worse, the masks you wear to 'make it' result in making you more alienated. The more alienated you become, the harder it is to ever really allow someone to see the *real* you. You can see how this may become a vicious cycle that feeds off itself, and you are then forced to continually create new masks and switch between wearing the appropriate one around the people who expect to see the mask that they know as you! As previously stated, all this does is sustain your unhealthy biofield and reduces your possibilities of listening and Being the eternal warrior.

You may be pleased to know that these issues are relatively easy to address once you understand why they occur in your life. A behaviour that is not an issue or a theme (that is, a healthy bio-electric signal and cue) is one that results in what I refer to as the four wins:

1. You win and you feel good.

     Based on all the scientific research I have presented to you; you have the potential to do whatever you need to do! For you, this could be the potential for better health, reduced pain, an abundance of joy, calmness, contentment, inspiration, freedom, energy and health, or a zest for life, a state of enlightenment, where you are living your authentic life and being your optimal self. The choice is yours! As the ROA motto says: Live optimally. Live purposefully.

2. I win.

     By 'I', I mean not only myself, but any eternal warrior who shines a light to inspire worriers to transition living optimally and purposefully.

3. The other person/people in the interaction win and they feel good.

    Any worrier who you assist by making them big and strong, who you hold accountable and who you assist with your training and by giving them this book may improve their health, wellbeing and personal development, as well as move toward achieving enlightenment and the other possible benefits listed above under 'You win'.

4. Our community wins and they feel good.

    Imagine a world where every single person is living their life from a place of abundant joy, calmness, contentment, inspiration, freedom, energy and health, a state of enlightenment and having a zest for life because they are doing exactly what they are meant to be doing with their life; living optimally and living their life of purpose. This is what I refer to as our sentient caretaker society!

As the old adage goes, 'A rising tide raises all boats'.

A behaviour that is an issue (an unhealthy bio-electric signal and cue) arises when you begin behaving in a way that only makes **you** feel good; that is, you default back into primary and secondary behaviours that keep you in the worrier state. Take as an example a mother becoming overly assertive and angry at her son who is attempting to do his homework, but is in need of her help. The mother, in her attempt to assist the son, behaves by raising her voice, her default reactive behaviour. The mother behaves like this based on the combination of her past conditioning, and the payoff is that she gets to wear a mask of feeling strong (the mother has a win) and gets to avoid feeling like a failure for her inability to assist her son in understanding and comprehending the homework, so the mother's need of educating her son goes unmet! The behaviour of being overly assertive and raising her voice could be labelled by her as pathetic, that is, once she accepted her own self-labelling!

Any issue that recurs in your life — for example, the mother described above — could be considered a theme and will continue to be so until you come to understand why the issue/theme occurs in the first place. While a theme exists, it will be an ongoing source of unhealthy bio-electric signals and cues, which will continually arise in your life to create disturbances until it is resolved. For example, if you find yourself in a series of failed relationships, the recurring theme would be the failed relationships. Within that theme could be one or more subthemes; for example, my relationships fail because the other person does not take me seriously, or I keep meeting the wrong person and so on. This is where you need to be authentic with yourself and acknowledge that you are the common factor in all your relationships, and as such you have the problem (the recurring theme) that continues to plague you! Irrespective of the theme and whatever the problem is, it is coming from within you, until you resolve it.

As you begin making your choice to interrupt being the eternal worrier by choosing to feel good, this is where I would like to introduce you to the 'Three steps for effectively communicating your needs', and reinforce here that this form of listening and acceptance is the first step for you in dealing with any issue that recurs in your life, provided, that is, you are conscious of the recurring theme and taking responsibility for it. This is where FlameTree can assist you to identify the priority theme or issue (which then makes the following step obsolete). However, in the absence of FlameTree, once you identify (via acceptance and listening) your perceived issue or theme, the second step is to label your identified default reactive behaviour and actions that occur when your perceived needs are not being met. Whether you are conscious of it or not, you are always trying to meet your needs. In order to meet your needs, you behave in a certain way and undertake certain actions. Should your primary attempt fail and your need goes unmet, you often then behave in a default secondary manner in an attempt to have your needs met, and this is where the issue may intensify. That is, by defaulting from the primary to secondary way of behaving to have your needs met, you actually decrease the probability of having your needs met. The third and final step is to enhance your communication based on your new understanding that more effectively meets your needs. As this is an important process in redefining you, I will explain this in more detail below.

Step 1. Listen: what is your issue(s)/theme(s)?

If you have FlameTree, you can skip this step and go to step 2, if not, you need to firstly accept that you are the common factor for all your issues and themes and then listen so you can identify your perceived issue or theme. Once you do this, you need to also recognise that you have needs (as outlined by Maslow — see chapter 2), and whether you are conscious of it or not, you are always trying to meet your needs. To have your needs met, you create goals. Goals are the steps you use in order to reach your needs in life.

To assist you in this step, I suggest that you may want to ask yourself several questions, such as:

- What need is your recurring theme/issue associated with?
- Why do you believe you have this need?
- Why has it become a recurring theme/issue for you?

- Is your reaction to your identified need not being achieved a 'fallback' position that you revert to? That is, is your behaviour a pre-set one that you immediately and unconsciously do?
- Does this fallback position actually aid you anymore in reaching your need?
- Is your reaction something that you can let go of?
- What belief of yours is being violated?
- What emotion is coming up for you when you think about your belief not being met?

To be able to successfully complete step 1, you need to do this from a place of *Being* the eternal warrior where you are actively listening to your innate wisdom before you feel and then think, as outlined in the steps for the Law of Creation (refer to Figure 8.1 above), while integrating the four elements necessary for the Law of Creation without the eighteen filters, which creates a self-sustaining healthy biofield. This process is assisted when you already know and understand your life's purpose. Not knowing your life's purpose may be the source of your issues/themes occurring in the first place. This is where receiving FlameTree can assist you here, but in the absence of FlameTree, start with one issue or theme. For example, an issue could be not getting enough intimacy in your relationship, not earning enough money from your work, not having enough free time and so on. By asking the above questions and accepting that you are the common factor here, you can then move onto step 2.

Step 2. Label the behaviour

The second step of this process is to understand that you have previously behaved in a way that pushed your desired need further away from you because you were not actively listening. In order to change this, you must realise that you have previously committed this behaviour and this was influenced by your past conditioning (part of the reason why you behave the way you do). Once you are aware that you do indeed behave in this way, you now need to label the behaviour. For example, you may label your behaviour 'childish', 'spiteful', 'immature', 'irresponsible' and so on. By labelling your reactive behaviour, you are doing something different so that you are now better able to create change.

Once you have labelled your reactive behaviour, you must now also be on the constant look out for this behaviour recurring. That is, you must realise immediately when you are reacting or about to react to life situations using your labelled behaviour. This labelled behaviour then becomes a sign (bio-electric signal and cue) for you that reawakens you to your issue/theme where your needs are not being met. If you don't do this and you continue behaving in the same way, it diverts you from actively listening and *Being* the eternal warrior, which takes you further away from your goals (your need that you want met). Now that you understand that this behaviour is pushing your need further away from you, it stands to reason (usually) that you will want to quickly let go of this labelled behaviour and behave differently.

What I need you to understand here is that it is *your behaviour* (how you act when you don't achieve your goal to satisfy your need) that we are labelling. It is *not you*, that is, you are not insulting yourself. You are merely labelling the behaviour that forms your fallback position openly and honestly with no judgements. For example, although you may label your behaviour as being pathetic and childish, you are still, however, a worthwhile person who is open to the possibility of choosing to behave as an eternal warrior.

To further assist you in step 2, I recommend that you work out what your payoff is while understanding that by behaving in that pre-set way is not helping you meet your need. As previously discussed, you also need to understand that there is a cost to you and your life in using the payoff, and usually the cost is exactly the need that you wanted met not being met! What you were after in the first place, you end up sacrificing by not redefining you and making these changes! Being aware of your actions and behaviour and being able to play it through your mind *before* you engage and display the behaviour will contribute to achieving your needs. Once you can see and possibly predict the outcome of your anticipated behaviour — that is, it will create chaos because when it is labelled by you, it appears negative (an unhealthy signal and cue that you have just identified) — you may then choose not to do that behaviour!

Some other examples of what labelling a behaviour could be include silly, pathetic, unintelligent, or short-sighted and so on.

Step 3. Understand and communicate your needs

The third step in this process is to understand the reason why your need was not met and that your past conditioned behaviour drove that need further away from you. As previously explained, the main reason why your need was not met is because you failed to effectively listen, understand and then express your need optimally and purposefully in the first place! This could be considered an 'undelivered' communication because you may have sent a message, but the person who was meant to receive it did not understand it. To understand why they did not understand it, you need to ask yourself this question: What was it that you were really trying to get across that got lost? Once you find this understanding, you can practise a new philosophy and modify your actions/behaviour so that you can communicate your needs more effectively and be better able to implement your goals to achieve them.

An interesting point that I want to bring to your consciousness here is that this process is assisted when you already know and understand your life's purpose. If you are *Being* the eternal warrior, where you are listening to your innate wisdom before you feel and then think, as outlined in the steps for the Law of Creation, while integrating the four elements necessary for Law of Creation without the eighteen filters, then you would be living your life optimally and purposefully, and as such your needs and goals would have already been met! This is a possible outcome from receiving FlameTree (the **FlameTree effect**) as observed by myself and all the certified FlameTree healers and students and as experienced by those having received FlameTree. In the absence of FlameTree, following the processes outlined in this book may also assist you in reaching this place.

An example to demonstrate the 'Three steps for effectively communicating your needs' would be the theme of not receiving love from your spouse. Your perceived need is to be loved. I will flag here for you that this perceived need to be loved is in fact your core faulty belief. For now, let's continue with the example that your need to be loved is not being met, so one of your goals is to receive love from your spouse, and one action that you require from your spouse that demonstrates their love for you is for them to pay attention to you. Once you believe that they are not paying enough attention to you, your immediate reaction, for example, may be to demand from them that they spend more time with you. This demand arises firstly because your need for love is not being met, and secondly, spending time with you is what you perceive your spouse needs to do to show you love. You believe that your behaviour here is justified because your need is not being met and your action to rectify this, based on your past conditioning, is the only way that you know how to communicate your feelings when your need for love is not met.

What you need to understand here is that, although your past conditioned behaviour and the way you initially communicate your message is a major problem, your faulty belief about requiring attention to feel loved is the root cause of this issue/theme. Your reactive behaviour is not entirely your fault, as this was the way you were taught to react based on your past conditioning which stems for your faulty belief about needing love expressed as attention from others, such as your spouse, to feel loved. If you are not aware of this core issue/theme and if you are not familiar with any other options, then how else are you expected to react? In this example, you are trying to communicate your needs to your spouse; however, the way that you communicate this message is deleterious to your desired outcome, albeit you have not yet addressed your core faulty belief, which we will park here and continue on with the above example. Your message could be possibly interpreted by your spouse as you are behaving like a needy child seeking attention, or wanting to control and dominate the relationship, or something else equally negative. This could be the possible interpretation by your spouse based on *their* perceptions about how things are communicated and their faulty beliefs about love.

I would point out here the importance of sharing this information, because if you didn't have their faulty belief about love, then your interaction with your spouse would be very different! In any event, not actively listening, and the subsequent failed communication, has a cost to it, to you and to your life. The cost of your perceived reactive behaviour is that your spouse could possibly be annoyed with you and does not want to spend more time with you because they have judged your behaviour in a negative way. The paradox here is that you probably already knew and could predict the outcome of your past conditioned behaviour before you acted on it. Why? Because your past experience of behaving this way always results in the same outcome! The end result is that you don't have the very thing you wanted (your need for love with your goal of receiving attention from your spouse), and your spouse is now more distant from you than when you started expressing your felt need. This means that you now need to heal this rift in your relationship, as well as attempt to get your original need met. The point here is that you can avoid all of this chaos; as the adage says, prevention is better than cure. How can you do this? With the 'Three steps for effectively communicating your needs'! Staying with our example above, the theme that you're not receiving love from your spouse due to your core faulty belief that makes you needy for attention.

Firstly, you need to actively listen to yourself and recognise the issue/theme that you feel that your need to be loved is not being met, this is the exact point where you need to stop and be *completely honest* with yourself and acknowledge that this feeling is *not* something created outside of you (i.e. caused by your spouse not paying attention to you), but is in fact coming from within you based on where you are at within yourself. What does this mean? It means that you are not actually upset at your spouse for what you perceive as not loving you due to inattention; you are in fact upset with yourself for not loving yourself unconditionally, and for relying on someone else (your spouse) to make you feel loved. This is being completely honest with yourself and allows you to take responsibility and accountability for your actions in life. Listening and then taking responsibility is one of the hallmarks of *Being* an eternal warrior.

Secondly, from the moment you identified your issue(s)/theme(s), and are completely honest with yourself, and have accepted that these feelings come from within you, you now need to label the behaviour (e.g. immature). This was the same behaviour that pushed your desired need further away from you.

For example, you may label your behaviour 'childish', 'spiteful', 'immature', 'irresponsible' and so on. By labelling your reactive behaviour, you are doing something different so that you are now better able to create change.

Once you have labelled your reactive behaviour, you must now also be on the constant look out for this recurring behaviour, for the times that you miss step 1. That is, you must realise immediately when you are reacting or about to react to life situations using your labelled behaviour.

Also, work out what your payoff is from behaving in your default reactive manner, that is, your labelled behaviour as well as the cost (pushing your desire away). Possibly, behaving in this immature way makes you feel strong and special. In your mind's eye, play out the scenario acting out your immature behaviour *before* you engage your spouse and see in your mind how it doesn't work.

Being the eternal warrior, you are listening to your innate wisdom before you feel and then think, as outlined in the steps for the Law of Creation, which then places you in a position where you can predict and choose your future behaviour and free yourself from chaos, beginning to create the you that you want. That is, you can choose to feel good (in the above example, loved) within yourself independent of your spouse (or any other thing or person, for that matter) and by doing so, what are you feeling? Good!

Because you made that choice to feel good in your present moment, and this creates a healthy bio-electric signal and cue, which automatically influences your biofield in a healthy way. If you make the choice to feel good in your present moment, you can predict how you will be feeling in the future ... that is feeling good! When you continue to feel good, you continue to immerse yourself in healthy bio-electric signals and cues and a healthy biofield, you're also more open to listening to your innate wisdom and the Uni-code, and *Being* the eternal warrior creating your own reality.

Living from this place allows you to have more clarity and peace, which makes it easier for you to follow the steps for the Law of Creation; *actively listen* and *feel*, then *think, Be, say* (self-talk), *do* (make choices) and thereby *have* (creating your reality), while integrating the four elements necessary for the Law of Creation (resonance, coherence, consonance and respect).

Thirdly, understand and communicate your needs. Understand that the reason why your need for attention was not met could be due to your partner expressing love a different way. Understand that your past conditioned behaviour of demanding attention drove that need further away from you. Understand that the main reason your need for attention, and hence love, was not met is because you failed to actively listen. Finally, understand and then express your need optimally and purposefully!

Your desire for attention to feel loved was your 'undelivered' communication because you sent a message (immature behaviour to get your spouse to pay attention to you), but your spouse, who was meant to receive it, did not understand it.

What you were really trying to get across, which got lost, was the fact that you wanted to be closer to your spouse and feel loved because you did not love yourself. Once you find this understanding, you can practise a new philosophy and modify your actions/behaviour so that you can communicate your needs more effectively and be better able to implement your goals to achieve them.

This will be easier than ever before, because you can now be open to finding as many alternative ways of communicating your need or goal by knowing that your need to be loved has already been met by changing your core faulty belief about love, from an unhealthy signal and cue to a healthy one. Once you have made this choice, you will instead be seeking how to possibly enhance your feeling of love by *interacting* more with your spouse rather than *demanding* they love you (immature behaviour to get attention) so that you can feel loved. This is one of the ultimate outcomes of redefining you! Living your life from this place means that you now have the choice to better communicate with your spouse. You begin to express your needs in a way that does not create a potential for conflict because you are meeting your own needs and are now emotionally responding (not reacting) to yourself and your spouse. This new behaviour becomes a healthy bio-electric signal and cue, so the chances are your spouse will not react to you in the way that they might have previously (as described in the example above) because you are no longer blaming them for not feeling loved (attention)!

If you have not reached this point of *Being* the eternal warrior where you are listening to your innate wisdom before you feel and then think, as outlined in the steps for the Law of Creation, which assists in creating a self-sustaining healthy biofield as yet, then in the absence of receiving FlameTree, one possible way that you could choose to create change is to remove your mask(s) and take the chance of expressing your true self. Following on from the above example, you might express yourself to your spouse in this way:

> *I am feeling unloved, and I know this is my issue and what I need from you is your help to assist me to overcome this. What I feel I need is to spend more time together. A thirty-minute walk together would be great, or if you have any other suggestions, I would be more than happy to hear them.*

This response would be seen as a step towards improved communication and delivering your message in a healthy way, where you are listening and taking responsibility.

Once you complete this three-step process, you need to choose the one way that you believe will work best when you deliver this message. For example, when I asked my friend to share with me what she does when she thinks she is unloved and requires more love from her husband, her response was that she requests that he take her out for dinner. She, however, predicted his reaction would be to not go out for dinner because they do not have enough money. The issue here is that my friend would begin arguing about money; however, we know this is a waste of time because it is not addressing the issue. The underlying and unsaid issue is that my friend does not consciously and actively feel loved.

The fact that my friend, after following this three-step process, can now label her behaviour as being 'demanding' and now knows that if she continued with that behaviour it would produce conflict in her relationship, she is therefore free to identify a solution. The solution in her case was for her to own all that is occurring to her, as it is coming from within her. This allowed her to find another way to communicate her feelings to her husband by saying, for example, 'I am feeling unloved because we haven't gone for dinner for ages and all I feel I do is cook and clean. The way you can show me love is to take me out for a nice dinner. It doesn't have to be a fancy expensive dinner, just somewhere nice that gets me out of the house and us having a meal together that I haven't had to prepare.' Not surprisingly, her partner heard this communication and was able to meet her needs with no chaos, but although this is a solution to her felt need being met, unless she redefines herself, her faulty belief about love will continue, and her need to work out ways to delivery this message to her spouse will be an ongoing issue.

The take-home message — your transformation from eternal *worrier* to eternal *warrior*

The *eternal worrier smiles* because they do not understand the way we create our world via the Law of Creation. They believe they are powerless victims who have to suffer what the world throws at them. The eternal worrier believes that happiness and contentment come from things, which forever locks them into the 'must have' trap where they continue to buy new things in order to feel good. They passively listen and accept that 'I don't belong' is valid and confuse causation and correlation. Then in an effort to cover up their insecurities, they create masks to obtain the payoff, for example, 'fitting in'. The cost of behaving in this way is wearing many different masks to be able to 'fit in', which becomes exhausting and confusing, and creates unhealthy bio-electric signals and cues that sustain an unhealthy biofield, which creates an unhealthy expression of their bio-electric code and gene expression. This outcome limits them from actively listening to their innate wisdom and keeps them being the eternal worrier, oblivious to the Law of Creation and the elements necessary to achieve creating, and as such they cannot *Be* their real self. They are unable to show their true face and are therefore unable to live their life purposefully and optimally.

Eternal worriers must hold on to their stories and their need to be right by blaming things and others for their life so that they feel good about themselves. They do not understand the concept of when they say no, it is the opposite of their yes, and therefore the universe chooses for them. The worrier does not understand that by not labelling their behaviour, not knowing the payoff of that behaviour, and not knowing their unmet need or goal, they become stuck in a very destructive cycle (unhealthy bio-electric signal and cue) of doing the exact behaviour that costs them exactly what they wanted in the first place. They blame others for the disappointments and bad luck that manifests in their life and are unaware of the Law of Creation and the elements necessary to create their healthy reality, resulting in an eternal unhealthy biofield.

The *eternal warrior smiles* because they understand that they must actively listen to their innate wisdom and to the Uni-code so that they can create their own world. The eternal warrior understands that happiness and contentment come from within, and any happiness or contentment obtained by things or people will be transient, and therefore they escape the 'must have' trap. The eternal warrior accepts that 'I don't belong' is a false belief system that was induced by misunderstanding causation and correlation. They know that masks are worn for a payoff, but the payoff is not worth the cost of who they truly are. They show their true face and choose to live their life purposefully and optimally. They let go of their stories, their need to be right, and understand when they say no, it is they who are choosing the opposite of their yes. The eternal warrior acknowledges the need to label their behaviour and they know the payoff of their behaviour and the cost of their unmet need or goal. They understand the destruction of this cycle and, as such, cease doing the behaviour that costs them what they wanted in the first place, thereby avoiding this negative cycle, which becomes a healthy bio-electric signal and cue. They know that by *Being* (alignment, synergy, authenticity and synergism) the eternal warrior, they are able to listen to their innate wisdom before they feel and then think, as outlined in the steps for the Law of Creation, while being able to integrate the four elements necessary for the Law of Creation without the eighteen filters, which creates a self-sustaining healthy biofield.

CHAPTER 9

The effect of you and your thoughts on your life (and what they attract to you via resonance)

Have you ever wondered where your thoughts come from?

Maybe you have, but if you haven't, do you believe that they come from your brain? Have you ever wondered why it is that, when your friend says, 'Let's go out', you say, 'I was just about to say that'? Or why it is that you had a feeling about a friend, and then suddenly the phone rang and it was that friend you had that feeling about? Well, thanks to a device called a *magnetoencelphograph,* which contains a probe known as a 'super quantum induction device' (or 'squid' for short), we now have a means of finding the answer to that question.

The 'squid', using non-contact sensing electrodes, reads the action of the brain without the need to sick probes directly into the brain! The 'squid' has no parts that actually come in contact with the head, and its main function is to read magnetic fields (another example of bio-electric signals and cues).

The reason we are speaking about this device and what it reads is because of what it actually tells us, which is, in short, that the neurological activity that we call 'thought processing' is not limited to the locality of brain (head)! Brainwaves (bio-electric signals and cues) are transmitted from your brain (head) into the environment, that is, you emit them. The same is true for atoms and molecules, which constantly emit energy. Said another way, your thoughts are constantly being transmitted from within you to the outside world, and as such, when something is being transmitted, it is by default seeking a receiver. There have been numerous studies that are still ongoing into this phenomenon. For example, researchers are investigating why it is that a Qi Gong master can transmit their signal, which then exerts a physical effect that is received and observed on their students, even though the individuals involved are in completely separate rooms!

The significance of bringing this to your attention is twofold. Firstly, it demonstrates the fact that we are all interconnected; that is, we are both transmitters as well as receivers of information (thoughts) in a shared energy field (environment). This explanation follows Occam's razor (that is, the simplest explanation is usually the best explanation), and it would serve to explain how it is that we can have a thought that a friend has just verbalised without that friend knowing we had just had that thought, or can be thinking about a friend and that friend rings on the phone, or how a Qi Gong master is able to create a physical effect on their students, even though they are in different rooms.

Secondly, although thoughts (bio-electric signals and cues), as emphasised by American neurobiologist William Calvin, do not reside in particular places in the brain, but are shifting patterns of activity over the brain's surface, and the brain is believed to emit this activity (which can be detected by the 'squid'), what if, however, this actual activity (feelings and thoughts) already exists within the ether or environment around you, and was not generated by the brain at all? What if this activity was in fact being received by the brain, which then becomes interpreted as thought? The possibility that the information is already in the environment reinforces my receptor theory described in chapter 7, that is, we receive information from the environment that determines how 'you' were formed, including your thoughts and beliefs. But what does this have to do with beliefs?

Beliefs, all beliefs, everything we hold as true (all of which are bio-electric signals and cues, whether healthy or unhealthy), are all received and transmitted by the receptors on your cells, with the central place for interpretation for all these messages being your brain. Your body will align with your beliefs and vice versa because all your cells have receptors that receive information. What you are feeling and thinking is transmitted quite clearly via your brainwaves directly into the environment, but what is in the environment is also received by your brain, which influences your feelings and thoughts and who you are Being. We are energy, and so are our thoughts; these energetic patterns (thoughts) are transmitted into and received from your environment, and can therefore directly impact on the environment, on you and the people in your environment, as well as on your thoughts and who you are Being.

I already know that it is occurring in your present moment, and this should provide you with the impetus to look more closely at what you are feeling and thinking. Said another way, what you think directly impacts on your environment and on the people close to you, and the closer they are to you, the greater the impact. Needless to say, that this is true of people thinking about you — you are also a receiver to their feelings and thoughts. However, this is not limited to people, but to the transmissions available to us generated by the environment. I would point out here that if you want to use this information, you must firstly realise how important knowing this information is, not only for you, but also for everyone in your environment. This information is based on my understanding of what is currently being reported in the world, and I have brought all this information together into the one place (this book) so that this may create a pathway that may reveal how you can have complete power over your life.

Simply put, once you are aware of what you think, and that you are thinking AFTER actively listening and feeling, you can begin changing your beliefs and therefore alter the path of your life. You must therefore also *'be careful of what you say to yourself, about yourself when you are by yourself.'* The Law of Creation exists as a multidirectional flow, with each step dynamically influencing another. Step 1 can influence step 3 (i.e. the flow is linear and not linear). For example, have you ever taken an action without actively listening, and then immediately after that action stopped and thought to yourself, 'Now why did I do that?' Each step in the Law of Creation is like a synthesiser and balance between all steps and their interactions is key. A simple change in your perception or belief really can change your life! Recall I took you through the example of adapting your perception around money earlier in this book? If not, go back and read over it because now would be the time to strengthen that perception and add feeling to create a new, powerful and healthy belief (a healthy bio-electric signal and cue). To further demonstrate this point, I would like you to consider an experience you might have on a night out if, for the entire week before the night out, you told yourself you were going to have a terrible time and meet nothing but boring people and waste your night. What kind of night do you think you would have? Exactly. You would have a terrible night and meet boring people! What you therefore perceive (your thoughts) or believe or think will happen, *will* happen. If you manage to change your perceptions and beliefs, you will change your life. If something is therefore happening in your world that is not the way you want it to be, *you* now realise that you *have* the power to change it. After all, *you* created it in the first place! What you focus on in your thoughts, whether they are healthy or unhealthy bio-electric signals and cues, is what is attracted to you based on the Law of Creation. Making a conscious choice to actively listen and feel and then change the way you think (what you are transmitting as bio-electric signals and cues) changes what you will create (receiving bio-electric signals and cues) in your world.

I expect that, having read to this point, you would now better understand the power of your conscious mind, but if you still haven't caught on to what I'm suggesting, stop for a moment, breathe and focus. Now take on board the following:

> You are more powerful in your world than any other individual could ever be! You have the complete and utter power to instantaneously change your world and everything in it.

There are two key things that can aid you in your understanding of this. One, your perception and what you are currently creating (consciously or not) can be instantaneously changed; and two, you are powerful beyond measure, and someone that powerful simply cannot be a victim, nor can you ride in the blame vehicle, which will be discussed in greater detail below and in chapter 11. I state here that the worst possible thing that could ever occur in your life is that you would be a victim of a belief, that is, an unhealthy bio-electric signal and cue, that is *your* own belief without even realising you are its victim, and that is completely okay! Why? Because I have established that you are powerful beyond measure and can instantaneously change your beliefs. Remember that your beliefs both *already* exist within your environment (which is shared with everyone else) and are based on your perceptions, which are clouded by the eighteen filters (refer to figure 9.1 below).

Figure 9.1. How we see/observe/perceive the world.

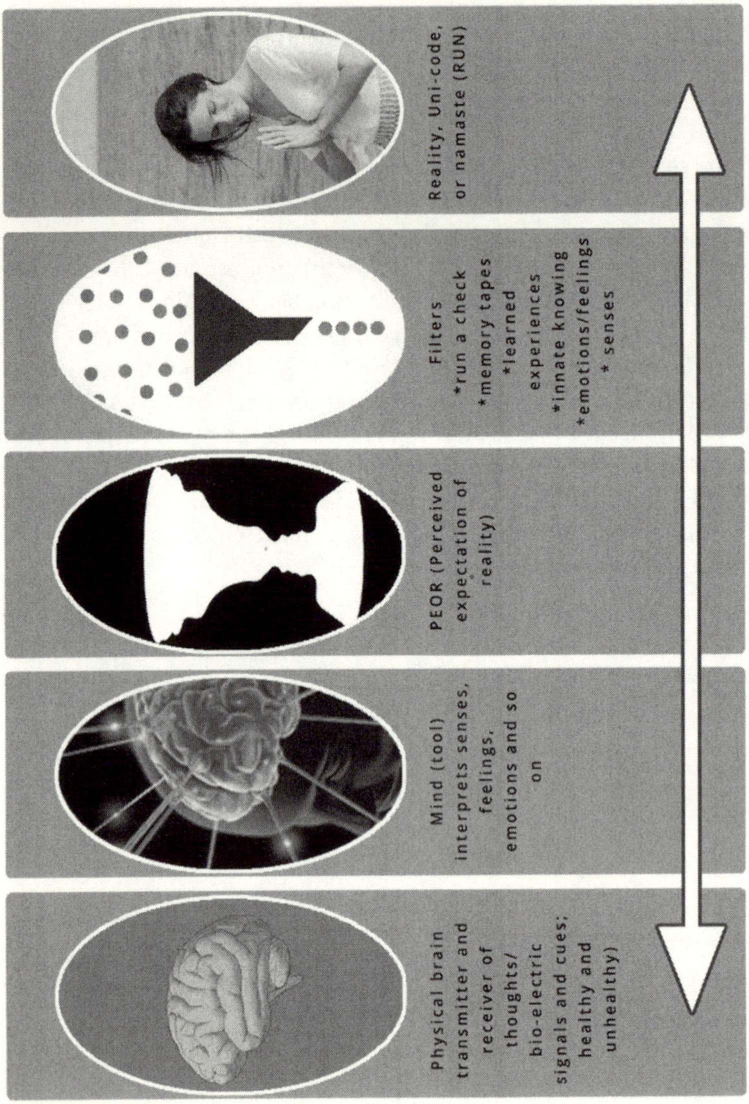

One way to explain figure 9.1 is with an example. What needs to be firstly explained here is that 'Reality, Uni-code or namaste' (RUN) is unchangeable; that is, the physical brain and cell receptors are changeable via neuroplasticity and represent an electrical circuit that flows from A to B (electricity through the axon to the dendrites), and this is what occurs unless it is short-circuited. But RUN already exists within the environment and is unchangeable. What is changeable is everything from the physical brain and cell receptors to filters, which are further elaborated on in figure 9.2. An example that can be used to highlight this changeability in relation to mind, perceptions and filters (all examples of bio-electric signals and cues) is the reaction you may have when you hear the phrase, 'The boss wants to see you in his office'.

The mind receives the information (a bio-electric signal and cue) about seeing the boss, and it has to make sense of why the boss wants to see you. In searching for the 'why', the mind will investigate all avenues of information (both healthy and unhealthy bio-electric signals and cues), and as such, perceptions about the 'why' are created. The question you could ask here is: why create scenarios in your head in the first place?

The answer is survival! To be forewarned is to be forearmed, so as soon as you perceive a threat to you, your wellbeing, your life and so on, you take evasive action. The mind, during this process, also 'stacks information', which is how memory works, and this is why it is thought that remembering isolated facts does not work. What many of us are not familiar with is that, during this process of receiving information, part of your mind runs through your eighteen filters, for example, searching for your past experiences similar to that 'why'. Again, the reason why the mind does this is to be prepared for what happens next and to ensure your survival. In this example, where the mind automatically (without being conscious of it) processes the 'why' through your filters associated with past experiences, this creates a problem, and that problem is that your past begins to dictate, not only your future, but your present moment! So you can see the potential problem here if you are being the eternal worrier — unhealthy bio-electric signals and cues associated with all your past experiences of being in this mind state will increase the possibility that your reactions to processing information, such as 'why', will result in unhealthy perceptions of both your present moment and future experiences, hence the emphasis on eternal!

I want you to return to the above phrase, 'The boss wants you in his office' and consider what you will feel when you are using your eternal worrier mindset, and its filters and past experiences. The chances are that you will feel like the eternal worrier and have perceived a negative feeling (unhealthy bio-electric signal and cue)! That is, as the eternal worrier, your past experiences would have been most probably negative interactions with 'bosses' or with that specific boss, or what you may perceive as authority figures, while possibly also having the eternal worrier filter of 'Oh no, what have I done wrong?' Then, like magic, you immediately have thoughts of what you might have done wrong, and those thoughts assail and plague you! This scenario is an example of receiving and transmitting unhealthy bio-electric signals and cues from the mindset of being the eternal worrier.

Now consider how you would feel if you interpreted that phrase with the mindset of *Being* the eternal warrior. It would be the complete opposite to the example above! I am aware that you may not be there yet, but you are not alone in being the eternal worrier. This statement is reinforced by the feedback I received from many people who I asked to respond to the above phrase. The majority of respondents conveyed that they began to invent reasons and excuses for any behaviour they thought may have been unsatisfactory to the boss involved (in order to work out how to survive by not losing their job/income, the perceived threat). If you extend this example to when you are actually sitting in front of the boss in their office, and even before the boss starts talking to you, the probability is that, in the eternal worrier mindset, your thoughts would have already convinced you of predicting a negative outcome of this meeting. Said in another way, you are already having thoughts about trying to make up excuses to counteract what you perceive your boss is going to tell you. However, the reality of the situation was that your boss wanted to see you for the purpose of telling you in person what an amazing job you have been doing lately and a promotion was on the cards.

The point of this example is to illustrate how much time, energy and effort can be wasted on trying to explain away an imaginary situation/outcome, which I refer to as your perceived expectation of reality, that hasn't even occurred! While doing so, you are creating unnecessary negative thoughts (unhealthy bio-electric signal and cues) that only serve, through resonance, to attract negative things (unhealthy bio-electric signals and cues) to you as you also create this reality!

With the above boss example, although the outcome was related to the boss wanting to personally tell you what an amazing job you are doing and an upcoming promotion (a healthy bio-electric signal and cue), it is true that the opposite possibility to this would be that they may have wanted to 'haul you over the coals' for something they thought you were responsible for (an unhealthy bio-electric signal and cue). If this was the outcome, it would have then validated the energy you were transmitting worrying about how to answer your boss. Both of these outcomes (good job/promotion or the coals) are, however, valid options and exist on the opposite ends of the spectrum of duality occurring within your environment, and are also reinforced by your beliefs and perceptions. You believing the worst may have been based on the belief that bosses have traditionally been known to haul employees over the coals more than reward their behaviour.

The concept of duality and how the mind creates and rationalises our world is illustrated below in figure 9.2.

Figure 9.2 Duality and the split mind - understanding the world and making it make sense

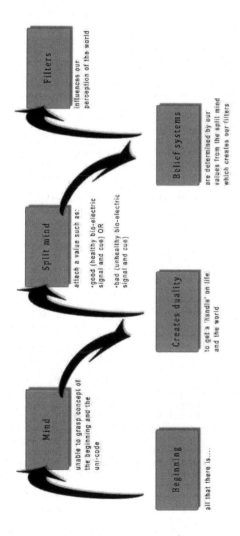

What needs to be explained here about the mind is that, in order to try and comprehend the environment around you (referred to as the Beginning or Unicode in figure 9.2), the mind automatically begins to break down the enormity of the Beginning into smaller, more manageable pieces of information. In doing so, duality is created, that is, the minute you label something, the polar opposite of what you just labelled will also be generated. For example, if you label something as 'good' (a healthy bio-electric signal and cue) then you have simultaneously created its polar opposite, something 'not good/bad' (unhealthy bio-electric signal and cue). This is referred to as a split mind, that is, you now attach a value to things based on what was created by the duality. When you judge these to be true and valid and you feel a certain and predictable way about them, they are now referred to as a belief system. The meaning you therefore attach to these smaller, more manageable pieces of information is responsible for generating the tension between the split mind duality that has created the beliefs, or the two poles, that result in creating dis-ease. This occurs because the split mind tension disrupts communication and functionality within you, as demonstrated in the above boss example. This negative perception (unhealthy bio-electric signal and cue) is therefore transmitted by you, which affects your biofield, which surrounds you in your environment, and the expression of your bio-electric code and genes.

The interesting part about duality, which you may have already started to understand now, is where *you* focus your bio-electric signals and cues (intention/thoughts/beliefs) is more important than the duality itself. Using the example above, the two possible outcomes are both valid (good job/promotion or the coals), but if you are being the eternal worrier, then your mindset is focused only on being hauled over the coals (the unhealthy bio-electric signal and cue). Not only are you expending unnecessary energy on an event that has not occurred yet, you actually increase the probability of that exact experience occurring for all the reasons discussed in the last chapter. Living from this place would take the shine off the actual positive comments your boss may have had for you.

Although filters appear on the last part of figure 9.2, they are by no means the least significant, as they too contribute to our bio-electric signals and cues. It is therefore important to highlight and understand what constitutes a filter and how they influence your bio-electric signals and cues. Below is a list of eighteen filters that are commonly used, often without realising you are using them, to navigate your world:

1. triggers
2. thrown to
3. add-ins

4. deletions
5. memories
6. internal rules
7. distortions
8. generalisations
9. threshold (i.e. screaming children)
10. feelings/emotions
11. experienced-based story (EBS)
12. tickles an EBS ('I can't quite put my finger on it')
13. projected emotionally charged memories (ECMs)
14. self-talk/internal dialogue
15. universal truths
16. cause and effect (if … then)
17. framing and reframing
18. magical thinking.

I would reinforce here that, when you are being the eternal worrier, you will be using one or more of these filters to navigate your life. As you have not reached *Being* the eternal warrior yet, it is important that you become familiar with these filters so that you can consciously make changes to them as you redefine yourself. Let's now look at some examples for each of these filters to explain how they act as unhealthy bio-electric signals and cues:

1. **Triggers:** These are past memories or events that you have not processed efficiently and they still carry a 'charge' for you, and as such are unhealthy bio-electric signals and cues. For example, if a relationship ended badly for you and two weeks later your best friend was talking about your ex-partner in a positive manner, you might be *triggered* by the emotion of anger, as you may have interpreted what your best friend said as being hurtful. This anger, however, is not in your present moment — that is, in your RUN. Instead, the anger is actually a projection from your past being experienced in your current reality. This creates the illusion that it is your reality, and thus makes it your reality because you were triggered by an emotion (anger in this example) that takes you back to the past hurt. If, however, you had processed the emotions from the past relationship break-up, and it was no longer an unhealthy bio-electric signal and cue (now only a past bio-electric signal and cue), then you may have not have interpreted the words about your ex-partner as being hurtful (another unhealthy bio-electric signal and cue). Without that trigger present, the chances are the emotion of anger would not have been felt — that is, you would not have been

triggered as there was no residual unhealthy bio-electric signal and cue present about your past relationship!

2. **Thrown to:** This is when a bio-electric signal and cue powerfully occurs in your current reality (this is usually an unhealthy one) and reminds you of a past event or feeling (usually a past unhealthy bio-electric signal and cue). Your brain is 'hijacked' and you are thrown into that past reality. You often feel helpless when it happens! It is as if you have no control over your brain — but you do! The perception that you don't means that you start to project your past feelings onto your present reality and future possibilities, and the unhealthy bio-electric signals and cues mutually reinforce each other. For example, if you experienced a break-up in the past where your then (but soon to be ex) partner was extremely kind to you, buying you flowers and chocolates, booking a nice room at a hotel and buying you a beautiful dinner, only to later break up with you that night (shock/disbelief!) — this becomes a learned experience of life (e.g. your unhealthy bio-electric signal and cue history) that your mind now has access to.

   Let's now move forward three years to a new romance. You are about to celebrate your first year anniversary, and your new partner, being a loving, caring and sharing type of person, decides to plan a beautiful day by sending you flowers and chocolates, informs you that you will be spending the night in a nice room at a hotel and going out for a beautiful dinner — these are all bio-electric signals and cues that are usually interpreted as healthy ones, but where does your mind go? What is coming next? Correct! The impending breakup! Even though this was in your previous experience, not your current relationship, your mind cannot help but go there! This is what is called a 'thrown to', where you would be emotionally reacting to the past event during dinner, and you might be seen to be unsettled, and accuse your current loving partner of one year that they were going to end the relationship with you, much to their surprise!

3. **Add-ins:** An 'add in' occurs when you extend what you are hearing from another person. These are considered very dangerous. What do I mean by dangerous? I will use an example. Let's say you invite someone to your party, and the person replies with, 'No, I can't come to your party.' However, what you end up hearing is the 'add-in', that is, 'No I can't come to your party *because you stood me up last week and we are no longer friends*'. Obviously, the other person did not actually say the words in italics, but your mind added them in (based on your past unhealthy bio-electric

signals and cues) to create your reality, which only serves to intensify your existing unhealthy bio-electric signals and cues. In this scenario, you would become really upset and offended that you were rejected by your friend. You believed your 'add in', based on a past situation where, beyond your control, you had to cancel without notice an important meeting with your friend, and as such you might be seeing their non-attendance as a possible payback! In your 'add-in' reality, you might end up reacting to their response by not caring that they didn't come to your party, and you don't call them again — that is, until you heard from a mutual friend that this person was very ill and was going through a course of chemotherapy to treat cancer. The reason why your friend couldn't make it to your party was because they had just found out they were diagnosed with cancer, and based on their fears and filters, they could not ask for help nor did they want to discuss what was occurring for them, so they just said 'no'. You can now see how dangerous 'add-ins' can be!

4. **Deletions:** Like 'add-ins', these can also be very dangerous, and they operate in a similar, but opposite, way. For example, you might ask your new partner of about three weeks if they wanted to come to your friend's birthday party and they respond with 'I would love to come to your friend's birthday party to meet your friends, but on this occasion I can't be with you as I have a pre-arranged work function that I must attend, and which I am unable to cancel. Can we organise to meet up with your friends on a different day?' Instead of hearing what was communicated to you, you filter it with the following 'deletions': '... I have a work function ... no I can't be with you ... I am unable to cancel ...' You deleted all the nice things (bio-electric signals and cues that are usually interpreted as healthy) that were said, leaving you with a distorted meaning (bio-electric signals and cues that are being automatically interpreted as unhealthy). For example, you could interpret this as meaning your new partner puts work ahead of you, which may arise because of issues you have about, for example, being loved and valued! This deleted filtered meaning can become even more complicated if you join it with an add-in, for example, 'Because I am not worthy of love' or 'I don't really want to meet your friends because they are not my type!', thereby synergistically reinforcing unhealthy bio-electric signals and cues.

The possible reason for the 'deletions' (and the associated 'add-ins' in this example) may be associated with your own past unhealthy bio-electric signals and cues about not being loved and valued.

Having these unhealthy bio-electric signals and cues coupled with these filters, when your partner does something or acts in a particular way that you believe reinforces your unhealthy bio-electric signal and cue of not being worthy of love and valued, you will react to it, possibly by stating, for example, that they do nothing to make your relationship work and that they value work over you!

This reaction may come as a surprise to your partner, as they believe they have been only supportive of you and have been looking for ways to get closer to you, like meeting your friends! Due to your existing unhealthy signals and cues, coupled with your filters, you have not observed their efforts because your mind had been deleting them via the deletion filter!

5. **Memories:** The filter of 'memories' usually occurs when a current event is happening that reminds you of a past event (a bio-electric signal and cue). You then project your previous experience or memory onto your current event, which then impacts on how you react to your current reality. For example, if your friends were surprising you with a birthday party, and you suddenly remembered a past surprise party with a different group of friends who made you feel totally embarrassed (an unhealthy bio-electric signal and cue), ruining your special day (further reinforcement of this unhealthy bio-electric signal and cue), you might start to experience feelings of worry and anxiety (unhealthy bio-electric signals and cues) at the hint of another surprise, even though you now have a new friendship group who have created a happy environment, as they are loving and caring friends who have not done anything that has placed you in any embarrassing situations. In this example, your past memory (an unresolved unhealthy bio-electric signal and cue) is like a video in your head that is as clear as the day it occurred, so you end up reacting to this unhealthy bio-electric signal and cue, which is not what's actually happening in your immediate environment.

6. **Internal rules:** Internal rules (bio-electric signals and cues) are the belief systems you have that form the framework you base your life on, and you find it extremely hard to go against them. For example, if you have an internal rule that you must always be truthful, when you realise that someone is not being truthful (including yourself), this 'internal rule' is activated and you immediately enter into an emotional state, which is usually an emotional reaction of rage (an unhealthy bio-electric signal and cue caused by unprocessed anger).

Another example could be if you have the 'internal rule' that your spouse should not interact with ex-partners because you have the belief that an 'ex' is in the past, and your past should not interfere with your present and future. This 'internal rule' was made clear to your spouse before they become your spouse, and although this was not an issue for them, you both agreed on a solution that worked for you both, which was that, if either of you should encounter an 'ex', you would immediately inform the other. Although this was made clear and agreed to, you are then placed in a situation where your spouse, beyond their control, encounters an ex-partner at an event you both attended, and for whatever reason, did not inform you until much later after the event. When you are finally told of the encounter, this is where your 'internal rules' filter activates and you immediately enter into an emotional state, in this example, it's the emotional reaction of rage. However, the fact that a solution had also been mutually discussed now creates another potential problem — that is, the 'internal rules' you have about keeping your word; or what you believe must occur when you do not keep your word; or spouses should be honest and honour their word, as you have more than one 'internal rule' that you use to base your life on. In this scenario, you now have several 'internal rules' (bio-electric signal and cues) being violated (which are now interpreted as unhealthy signals and cues), which therefore synergistically reinforce the other unhealthy signals and cues, aggravating the situation and the emotional reactions experienced by you and your spouse that stemmed from the initial internal rule, the ex-partner issue!

Why the emotional reactions in both examples? Because a boundary of yours had been crossed in both scenarios, and in both scenarios, they were your 'internal rules' that had been broken. The issue here, however, is not with your personal 'internal rules' per se, but whether or not your 'internal rules' match other people's 'internal rules', such as your spouse's in the example above. What you consider inappropriate, based on your 'internal rules', may be seen by others as not an issue based on their internal rules.

Finding the balance between being able to modify your own 'internal rules' through recognising your own beliefs and perceptions in life, and identifying what is appropriate and inappropriate with others, such as your spouse, becomes the art and challenge of creating a successful life, for example, living together with your spouse. In any event, you need to be aware of your 'internal rules' and effectively communicate them for any relationship to work.

7. **Distortions:** This refers to 'distortions' of any reality or present truth (RUN). This, however, is different to your 'internal rules'. For example, let's say you arrived at a birthday party and saw the host (the birthday person) looking in your direction, but instead of walking to greet you, they stopped short of you and walked to the table full of presents, which was about a metre and a half in front of you. In this example, a possible distortion of the reality could be that you assumed the host was looking at you, but ignored you in favour of the presents, and as such, you create a distorted meaning of what just occurred, such as 'They looked right at me but ignored me and walked to the table full of presents, how rude!' You then have an emotional reaction and do not enjoy being at the party. The reality of the situation in this example (the present truth), however, was that the room was crowded and the host didn't actually see you in the crowd, was not looking directly at you as you had thought, but instead had already intended heading to the table full of presents at the request of another friend at the party, which was their focus. The emotional reaction you had was based on the 'distortions' of your reality (the present truth), which was most probably based on past unresolved unhealthy signals and cues.

8. **Generalisations:** The 'generalisations' filter is easily identified when you use terms such as 'everything', 'always' and 'never' in your speech. Although these terms are bio-electric signals and cues, they are often interpreted as unhealthy ones. For example, 'I *never* meet the right person'; or 'Everything *always* goes wrong for me'; or 'You *never* help out with the housework!'; or 'You *always* think you are right and *everything* I say is wrong!' Generalisations only reinforce unresolved unhealthy bio-electric signals and cues, closing you off to any other possibility for anything else to occur, such as healthy bio-electric signals and cues. For example, if you use the generalisation filter of never meeting the right person, how can you be open to actually meeting the right person? You can't, because it never happens to you, and as such you emotionally react to your life and reinforce your unhealthy bio-electric signals and cues.

9. **Threshold:** A 'threshold' filter is associated with the personal stress level that you are currently set to. For example, new parents may not be able to stand their screaming baby, but by their second child, they do not even notice the baby screaming, despite in the past, before they had children, becoming very upset with other parents who would not pacify their screaming babies! The 'threshold' filter in the above example is the 'how long' and 'how much' of the crying they can stand. The issue with 'threshold' filters, however, is not about how long and how much, but rather the emotional reactions you experience when you begin to approach

them. Every situation in life has a threshold (a bio-electric signal and cue) which, when reached, will become an unhealthy bio-electric signal and cue. Why? Because you begin to feel that you are no longer in control of the situation you are in, and as such, when your 'threshold' limit is reached, your emotional reactions take over in the belief (falsely) that emotionally reacting will in some way offer you some feeling of regaining control of the situation.

10. **Feelings/emotions:** Whenever feelings or emotions (bio-electric signals and cues) predominate the mind, as demonstrated with many of the filters mentioned above, it is more often than not associated with a reaction (an unhealthy bio-electric signal and cue), which usually originates from an 'internal rule' being violated or from some past unresolved experience (another unhealthy bio-electric signals and cues). These unhealthy bio-electric signals and cues synergistically reinforce each other and may then interfere with how we interact with the stimuli in our current environment, thereby influencing how we see our present reality.

    The predominating belief ('internal rule') or past unresolved experience will dictate your feeling or emotional reaction, which is quite often a 'knee-jerk reaction' based on the prevailing 'internal rule' being violated or previous unresolved experiences where that feeling or emotion had been in control. For example, on Valentine's Day, let's say your spouse has a beautiful date planned for you and begins the night by saying, 'My darling, I love you and I want to be with you forever...' However, before they can finish, your mind accesses the feeling or emotion of the last time you heard those words, which may have been when a past partner shared those words (or something to that effect) with you, but tragically died in a car accident the next day! The meaning you may have attached to this was that, when someone tells you they will love you forever, they are lying because forever is only one day. We then experience the predominating feeling or emotion associated with the loss of a loved one, even though it is not happening in your current reality. When your life's situations are processed through the 'feelings/emotions' filter, instead of responding to your spouse's loving comments (healthy bio-electric signals and cues), you react to it in a negative way (unhealthy bio-electric signal and cue) because your past feelings or emotions cloud your ability to respond in a healthy way, and you react in a very different way to what your spouse was anticipating!

11. **Experienced-based story (EBS):** The 'EBS' filter comes directly from your life experiences, often those that have created unhealthy bio-electric

signals and cues, which usually dictates your life's direction without you ever really being conscious of this filter being used. For example, when a relationship ends, your 'EBS' filter may be 'My relationships fail because I am better off alone' or 'Maybe I am meant to be alone'. Recall when something didn't go your way, such as a relationship, and you will most probably have made these assertions, not only to yourself, but often to those around you. It is not unusual for this filter to be used even when you are in a relationship, which is then a source of unhealthy bio-electric signal and cues that are created in the background by having these thoughts or feelings, and through resonance (as previously discussed), you will be unconsciously projecting them into your current relationship. Without consciously modifying this 'EBS' filter, it attracts, creates and manifests other unhealthy bio-electric signals and cues, such as arguments and emotional reactions, which reinforce the 'EBS' filter.

Now that you realise that these 'EBS' filters exist, and when you consider that you can add other filters to this, such as the 'add-ins', 'deletions' or 'internal rules' filters, it is not unusual to reflect back on your own current or past relationships and begin to wonder what actually came first in your past arguments — the person in your relationship, such as your spouse/partner, or the filters, such as the 'EBS', that you unconsciously are running your life through? This could be considered as an equivalent question to 'Which came first: the chicken or egg?'

12. **Tickles – I can't quite put my finger on it!** This filter is exactly like the 'EBS' filter, but with the 'tickles' filter, you are not quite sure what the experience was, and it continues to elude you. You experience a felt sense of something familiar, kind of like déjà vu, and something that you did not like (bio-electric signals and cues interpreted as unhealthy), but you can't quite put your finger on it. Irrespective of what created this tickles filter, the issue here is that you are distracted from your current moment in life and are (for as long as it takes to recall) stuck in your past, which only serves to reinforce this unhealthy bio-electric signal and cue and distort your reality in your current moment. Tickles are usually persistent and demand your attention, but once you finally recall what the experience was, you now have an EBS, which, unless you clear and resolve this filter by being shown the way, as guided by me or by using one of the ROAs such as FlameTree: *the personal development & healing system*, you will stay stuck in your unhealthy bio-electric signals and cues, such as the emotional reactions you manifest.

13. **Projected emotionally charged memories:** These are similar to the 'memories' filter, but they are projected onto your current reality, as

opposed to being spontaneously encountered. This means that you are validating your unresolved past experiences (unhealthy bio-electric signals and cues) as always being true, and like 'internal rules' filters, they usually dictate how you interact with your life. This is because you are projecting them onto your current reality, which makes your current reality always match your unresolved past! The end result of this filter is that you continue to live in the past and block any opportunity for growth and change (healthy bio-electric signals and cues).

14. **Self-talk/internal dialogue:** This filter is associated with the conversations you have in our own mind about yourself (self-talk), and like most of the filters discussed, you are generally not conscious of yourself using this filter. In most cases, the 'self-talk/internal dialogue' filter is an unhealthy bio-electric signal and cue that, through resonance, attracts, creates and manifests more of the same unhealthy bio-electric signals and cues. For example, if you were in a conversation with someone and they showed an interest in you, and were listening intently to what you had to say, a 'self-talk/internal dialogue' filter that you may have could be triggered, such as 'Why are they listening to me?'; 'They must be wanting something from me!'; or 'They are just being kind to me, they don't really like me.' The issue here is that you never experience the reality of your current situation, let alone what is being said during an interaction with another person, because your 'self-talk/internal dialogue' filter is active. If left unchecked, it will dictate what you believe to be true about yourself.

15. **Universal truths:** These filters, like 'internal rules', will influence how you interact with your environment. 'Universal truths' filters are the truths that you believe operate the universe but apply directly to you. For example, if your current wealth situation is not what you desire and you repeatedly hear that you need to be dishonest to make millions of dollars, and you see on the news that a well-to-do person has been arrested for embezzling money, then, based on these observations and experiences of the world, you might create a universal truth that to make money, you have to be dishonest (an unhealthy bio-electric signal and cue). This 'universal truth' filter, which runs in your mind, may therefore create the universal truth for you that if you are honest, you will never make money! Anyone you meet who does have money, and who might genuinely be able to help you, or any opportunity that arises that could legally and honestly make you money, your 'universal truths' filter will sabotage by immediately taking over. You can only see the person or opportunities for making money as being dishonest. When you couple this with an 'internal rule' about being honest, it is easy to see how these filters, when interpreted as

unhealthy bio-electric signals and cues, synergistically reinforce each other and impact on your ability to grow and evolve, and as such allow other unhealthy bio-electric signals and cues to be created.

16. **Cause and effect (if ... then):** This filter refers to the idea that *if ...*, for example, you had more money and time, *then ...*, for example, you would be happier in your life. This is what I refer to as 'if ... then thinking'. It may start to be obvious to you now what issues would be caused with a 'cause and effect' filter. Like all the filters discussed, cause and effect filters are usually unhealthy bio-electric signals and cues that dictate how you navigate through your life. For example, when we introduce another person to our friends, if we had a cause and effect filter of 'If I introduce you to my friends then it would make the friendship happier', the cause and effect filter could mean that your friendships are not happy unless you introduced people to your friends, and therefore, if you were not introduced to your friend's friends, then you could not be happy, or at least not as happy as you could be. Another example would be, 'I will be happy when I am rich', which could be interpreted as, for all the time that you are not rich, you are unhappy!

17. **Framing and reframing:** This filter affects your reality in an interesting way. How you choose to frame or reframe a situation greatly affects your experience of that situation. For example, if I was to take you into a room full of strangers and framed the experience to you as 'Everyone in this room hates you, they despise you and this experience will be one of the worst experiences of your life' (an unhealthy bio-electric signal and cue framing), the chances are that you will experience this as the worst possible experience in your life (an unhealthy bio-electric signal and cue reaction), because it was framed to you in a way that was interpreted as an unhealthy bio-electric signal and cue. If, however, I reframed the above example as a healthy bio-electric signal and cue, such as 'Everyone in this room loves you, they adore you, and this experience will be one of the best experiences of your life', you would most probably feel a difference in yourself (a healthy bio-electric signal and cue response) in comparison to the initial way this example above was framed. The issue here, however, is not with the person doing the framing or reframing for you, it is, in fact, you. You are the only person in your world responsible for doing the framing and reframing of your own life; no one else! It is your mind interpreting the environment, and it is in control of whether you perceive and feel the bio-electric signals and cues in your life as either healthy or unhealthy. Recall here that what you project, through resonance, you will create, and will then also receive, which influences your biofield, the

expression of your bio-electric code and genes, and being able to clearly receive the transmission of you.

18. **Magical thinking:** The 'magical thinking' filter describes a wide variety of non-scientific and sometimes irrational beliefs that you may use to interact with your environment and with those around you. 'Magical thinking' filters stem from beliefs that are generally centred on correlations between events rather than causations. For example, a belief in the power of spells or rituals could be considered as interpreting your life through 'magical thinking' filters. The issue here is that few people may share the belief that you genuinely have, and as such, you feel that you are alone in your quest to work out how to either avoid being impacted on by these spells, or be able to use spells to change your environment. Either way, you may feel that you are alone in trying to work out how to process your magical thinking.

Regardless of which filter or combinations of filters of the eighteen described above are being used, they are all examples of bio-electric signals and cues being interpreted in an unhealthy way, which are then used to navigate your world, with the end result usually initiating a behaviour or reaction (an unhealthy bio-electric signal and cue) that is either *diffusing* or *arming*, which then impacts on your biofield and the expression of your bio-electric code and genes, as well as receiving the healthy transmission of you. Although the terms diffusing and arming may be new to you, you are constantly diffusing or arming situations, whether you are conscious of doing it or not. For example, *diffusing* the message means that you accept what is as what is, but in a depressive kind of way, which is interpreted as an unhealthy bio-electric signal and cue. That is, although you *diffuse* the message, it still peeves you in some way, but you are not yet bothered enough to do something about it, yet it festers in the background and as such creates another source of unhealthy bio-electric signals and cues. The issue when you *diffuse* messages is that, regardless of what the original message was, *diffused messages are* usually stored 'under your skin', so to speak, until you have enough stored to hit a threshold after which you then explode! This is best expressed by the old saying 'the straw that broke the camel's back'.

Arming the message usually means that you let whoever is the closest to you or the last person you have been in contact with have 'both barrels' immediately! Said another way, you explode immediately, which is another immediate source of an unhealthy bio-electric signal and cue! So, whether you diffuse or arm a message (consciously or not), either way generates unhealthy bio-electric signals and cues, which synergistically reinforce any filters that are present.

The point I would like you to understand here is that it is essential to become aware of and remove as many filters as you can, not only for your own sake, but for those around you. How to achieve this becomes the challenge, particularly if you have not had FlameTree. But I will teach and assist you with the necessary foundational skills through reading this book that will assist you in meeting this challenge. In addition to this book, I would like to reinforce again that the signature ROA, FlameTree: *the personal development & healing system*, is another way that is highly recommended to uncover then eliminate sources of unhealthy bio-electric signals and cues.

Although filters have been associated with creating unhealthy bio-electric signals and cues, they do serve a basic function, and that is to protect you. Even though they may protect us, they are still considered to be unhealthy bio-electric signals and cues as they are designed by you, but designed when you are being the eternal worrier in the false belief that they will protect you in some way, much in the same way discussed previously regarding the perceptions that something is wrong. They are both perceived by you! Who you think you are is based on the values you were taught, such as cultural, social, educational or work values, which then influence your personal values. These values determine your interactions in life within your environment, you believe how safe you feel and how much energy you need to invest in protecting yourself, and as such this influences your physiology through your feelings, emotions, thinking and perceptions. As previously discussed, you are projecting into your environment your 'masks' that you want others to see, and will use filters to support this in order to maintain your level of perceived protection (from, for example, that feeling that something is not right). All these are examples of ongoing transmission of unhealthy bio-electrics signals and cues.

Following on from the previous discussion about masks, the masks that you wear appear as what you are or are not, but they are also a reflection of what your society accepts as normal (as you perceive it). Common masks include being strong, right, dominating, justified and not giving up, which all serve to avoid looking weak, wrong, dominated, failing and unjustified. What you project validates your masks and filters, which then becomes a self-fulfilling and self-perpetuating cycle of being the eternal worrier, which influences the reception of the healthy version of you and your ability to be your optimal self and fulfil your life's purpose.

Masks do, as discussed, fulfil many of your perceived needs, albeit they are usually reactive perceptions that are unhealthy bio-electric signals and cues, for example, the perceived needs of esteem (validation of beliefs), belonging, justification, being right, avoiding conflict, or feeling loved. They also assist in fulfilling needs such as safety, physiological or self-actualising, which can be interpreted as healthy bio-electric signals and cues provided that you are *Being* the eternal warrior, listening to your innate wisdom and applying the Law of Creation. Your masks may derive their strength from how great the initial stimulus (the bio-electric signal and cue) is from your environment. I will use an example here to clarify this point. Consider being placed into an environment where the commonly held perception (the bio-electric signal and cue) of weakness is judged as wrong, and will therefore be punished. Based on this scenario, you now have an unhealthy bio-electric signal and cue in place. In order to protect yourself, you will immediately create a mask of 'toughness' so that, to the outside world, you appear 'tough' and therefore 'not weak'. By doing this, you reinforce your initial unhealthy bio-electric signal and cue. The payoff here is that you manage to avoid being judged as being wrong, and therefore avoid being punished, but this situation still creates unhealthy bio-electric signals and cues. You therefore adapt to the dominating unhealthy bio-electric signals and cues in order to minimise being punished (another unhealthy bio-electric signal and cue), which impacts on your biofield, the expression of your bio-electric code and genes, and your ability to listen to your innate wisdom and receive the healthy transmission of you.

What you need to realise here is that any stimuli will generate a response from you. The response generated will always be a measured response that is both specific and deliberate. All responses are therefore calculated by your belief systems, and as such will influence the masks you create, as well as your bio-electric signals and cues, whether they are healthy or unhealthy. Sometimes when a stimulus (a bio-electric signal and cue) is present, you do not immediately create a mask for it. In this instance, the stimuli can be thought of as being required to overcome a threshold. Said another way, a stimulus may have to occur or be repeated many times to elicit the response of creating a mask in a proportional manner, similar to diffusing a message. Interestingly, your intention, as outlined previously in regards to healthy bio-electric signals and cues, is the key to this process. I will explain what this means.

Let's say your environment dictates what you need to be, for example, a 'caring' person, because the cost of being perceived as an 'uncaring' person will result in you losing out in life, such as in a relationship that you value. If your perception of losing out is a strong enough stimulus, this thought that you may strike out in a relationship you value because you are not seen to be caring by the other person might therefore be enough motivation to influence you into immediately creating a mask of 'caring' to avoid the cost of losing out in the relationship. If you being perceived as 'uncaring' creates only a small discomfort to you, let's say, for example, because your partner is not worried about it and only gets slightly annoyed with you, you may have to experience them being slightly annoyed at you twenty times before you create a mask of 'caring'. If, however, they are very annoyed with you, then it may only take one experience for you to create the 'caring' mask! Either way, this would be seen as creating unhealthier bio-electric signals and cues. Irrespective of this outcome, the reason you create masks in the first place is so that you can assimilate them into your repertoire of being able to respond to your environment in such a way as to present to the world that you are, for example, a 'good' or 'caring' person, so that you meet your need to 'belong' within your environment.

As previously stated, the strength of the stimulus will generate the strength of your reaction. When you have a 'trigger' to an action, it will generate an 'over-reaction', which is an unmeasured, non-specific, disproportionate and non-deliberate reaction. Interestingly, it is not the action that dictates your reaction, but rather your perception of the action, which we will discuss in more detail later in the book. At this point, I would like to introduce this concept to you by comparing the reality and perception of birth as an example.

Birth — reality and perception as a comparison

Reality (what is really occurring)	Perception (what you might believe is occurring)
In utero	In utero
Warm, self-contained, safe	Warm, self-contained, safe
Delivery	Delivery
Light	Light is bright or harsh because it is no longer blocked by mum's womb
Ambient	The environment/outside world is cold because it is a lower temperature than inside mum's womb
Some touch can painful	All touch is painful because the doctor smacked my bottom

This comparison of reality and perception illustrates how a baby in utero is *Being* a baby in utero, but if you add perceptions to it, and that is what you do, then you have the opportunity to get it all wrong without the assistance of anyone! Although you may not know how you, as a newborn, truly perceived your immediate environment, the reality is that you not only have your own opportunity to create erroneous perceptions (such as those in the table above), but you also have the opportunity to take on other people's perceptions. Knowing what you know now, the people that were around you as a newborn will impart their own filters, beliefs and ideas of how to view their world, and as such, you would be getting it 'wrong' from day one.

You then continue to be influenced by your perceived expectation of reality, and create a world around you that matches your perceptions, which reinforces and validates them. Let us now discuss this concept in more detail below.

How do thoughts create, attract, change and influence things?

You now know thoughts are energy, and that they can be transmitted directly into the environment as either healthy or unhealthy bio-electric signals and cues, which then, not only influence your biofield and the expression of your bio-electric code, the expression of your DNA and your ability to receive the transmission of you, can also have an effect on those closest to you. As discussed in chapter 4, thanks to the pioneering research in mammalian synthetic biology, gene switches have been designed to be responsive to traceless cues such as light, gas and radio waves! As explained in chapter 4, the research did not stop there. The merging of the fields of cybernetics and optogenetics demonstrated that mental states, such as thoughts and emotions, which are in themselves bio-electric signals and cues generated by brain activity, could also change genes and therefore cell health. All this is achieved wirelessly, like a laptop computer connecting wirelessly to a modem!

You now know that different frequencies exist, and as such, this also applies with mental states. All your thoughts and emotions have a frequency and a resonance, exactly like a tuning fork, and will therefore resonate with similar things in your environment. Different thoughts and emotions have different frequencies, just as different things in the environment have different frequencies. This may explain how thoughts really create and attract things, that is, all things that have a similar frequency and resonance vibrate at the same frequency and will therefore attract things with the same properties and frequency. Said another way, if you are having fearful thoughts, you are setting your thoughts to the frequency of fear, thereby creating an unhealthy bio-electric signal and cue related to fear. This will not only attract and draw directly to you fearful events (other unhealthy bio-electric signals and cues associated with fear) from your environment, just like a fear magnet, but as you are transmitting those fearful thoughts, as demonstrated by cybernetic and optogenetic research, this could also potentially affect those around you, your genes and the health of your cells! As discussed earlier in this book, this goes beyond the old and outdated law-of-attraction explanation, because as stated by ROAs such as FlameTree: *the personal development & healing system*, thoughts being transmitted must be in alignment, synergy, authenticity and synergism (*Being*) with the person for this to occur in relation to transmitting healthy bio-electric signals and cues. I believe this is best demonstrated by hypnotism. It is believed that a hypnotist may hypnotise a volunteer to voluntarily, for example, harm a member of the crowd when they are commanded to do so with a word, such as 'harm' (negative bio-electric signal and cue). When the person who has been hypnotised hears the word 'harm' they are meant to 'harm' a member of the crowd, but when the prompt is given, they do not and will not harm anyone in the audience. Why? Because the hypnotised person is *Being* in alignment, synergy, authenticity and synergism with their thought of *not* to harm another person (a healthy bio-electric signals and cue). Any further attempts to hypnotise this person to harm another will be unsuccessful, provided, that is, their personal value of not harming others dominates their belief systems, and that they are *Being* honest, conscious and responsive to this thought.

When you consider that psychologists and psychiatrists estimate that approximately 70 per cent of your beliefs/thoughts are negative and redundant (i.e. unhealthy bio-electric signals and cues), this places great importance on you needing to be diligent about being conscious in order to change this! This implies that, unless you are *Being* the eternal warrior, then 70 per cent of what is emanating from your head directly into your environment is resonating at a frequency that will be creating and attracting directly back to you negative and redundant events from your environment, and impacting on you and those around you! Like it or not, you are unconsciously transmitting unhealthy bio-electric signals and cues into your environment without even trying, and therefore attracting 70 per cent of 'rubbish' into your life and possibly that of those around you if you are not being aware (conscious) of what your mind is doing. For example, if you are being the eternal worrier, and somehow you knew that something bad was going to happen to you, then the chances are that something bad will happen to you or someone else you know, then when it does happen, you would most probably say to yourself 'I knew that was going to happen!'

The point I am making here is that it is essential that you make the conscious choice to change your perceptions and beliefs (as encouraged in the chapter to redefine you) so that you can start immersing yourself in healthy bio-electric signals and cues. Based on the science of neuroplasticity, this would be seen as creating a new neural pathway from the well-worn one associated with those unhealthy bio-electric signals and cues (negative thoughts). As I have continued to bring to your consciousness, you need to not only recognise but accept the reality that you are having unhealthy bio-electric signals and cues, such as the perception that 'something bad will happen'. When you finally do take this on board, it is essential that you make the conscious choice to change these thoughts *before* something bad happens. By doing so, the outcome could be the prevention of something negative being created or manifesting into your world, directly impacting on you or those around you. This is a great lesson — in anger, you may want bad things to happen to a particular person, but it will almost always result in bad things happening to you because you are the one with those thoughts (unhealthy bio-electric signals and cues), and transmitting them directly into your environment. Your mind *is* the secret of life. You must be mindful of what you are feeling and thinking because you are continually creating your perceived expectation of reality.

The point you should take on board here is that 'you are personally responsible for everything in your life, once you become aware that you are personally responsible for everything in your life'.[2] I like this quote from Bruce Lipton, because it puts you in the driver's seat and removes you from the blame vehicle previously discussed. So now without fear, laziness, or the reasons or excuse of genetics, you can see that you need to make the choice to be more committed to reaching the place of self-actualisation/transcendence.

Focus on *Being* the eternal warrior in your life so that you may reach your optimal potential and live your life of purpose. Doing so automatically results in self-sustaining healthy bio-electric signals and cues, which maintain a healthy biofield and the healthy expression of the bio-electric code, so that, by the laws of nature, you will create and attract other healthy bio-electric signals and cues into your world. Imagine if we had more than seven billion people in the world expressing healthy bio-electric signals and cues!

The take-home message — your transformation from eternal *worrier* to eternal *warrior*

The *eternal worrier smiles* because they believe that thoughts are persistent and unchangeable. They occur within their brain and have nothing to do with what they think, create and attract into their life. They believe that they are at the mercy of the universe — if something good happens, it was meant to be or God loves them; if something bad happens, it was meant to be or God is testing them. Living this way takes the responsibility from them so that their reality is created by others. This means that eternal worriers are never in charge of creating their own reality and get to blame others if and when their life goes wrong. They are not conscious of the power they have to change their thoughts and therefore their lives, and instead they smile because they waste time, energy or effort indulging in false scenarios that have not yet happened, because sometimes, in these false realities, they may feel powerful. This is based on their beliefs of power rather than the actual power of being free of delusions and masks and living a life of potential, and therefore they focus their outcomes on the lower end of the spectrum of life, immersing themselves in unhealthy bio-electric signals and cues. All this does is result in an unhealthy biofield, which sustains the unhealthy expression of their bio-electric code and gene expression, impacting on their ability to receive the healthy transmission of themselves and resulting in poor health. In this eternal worrier mindset, they are not in alignment, synergy, authenticity or synergism with the Law of Creation, and get to blame others for not being their optimal self or living their life's purpose.

The eternal worrier smiles because they are blissfully unaware of the eighteen filters that commonly affect their life. They are totally blind to the fact that they can influence the outcomes of their own life because they are unaware that they are the only person who can arm or diffuse any message. Instead, they fall victim to the message and are doomed to react in a way that their filters dictate. The eternal worrier smiles because they get to enjoy wearing many masks and believe that the more masks they have, the more successful they will be. They enjoy their perceived expectation of reality based on their filters because they get to be right about how the (their) world works. This allows eternal worriers to enjoy the ability of blaming the world for their 'reality', particularly when it is not going their way, and therefore they get to blame the universe, because they believe that they are powerless to use their thoughts to create and attract the things they want into their life. In this way, they are always the victim and not responsible for any of the outcomes in their life.

The *eternal warrior smiles* because they realise that their thoughts are changeable. They know that thoughts already occur around them and not in their brain, which therefore allows them to create their reality. Eternal warriors know they can make the choice to be in charge of creating their reality because they are conscious of the power, they have to change their thoughts and therefore their lives, because they create and attract to themselves healthy bio-electric signals and cues. The eternal warrior smiles because they do not waste time, energy or effort indulging in false scenarios that have not yet happened. They focus their outcomes on the higher end of the spectrum of life. The eternal warrior smiles because they are aware of the eighteen filters that commonly affect their lives, and how they can change the outcomes by being aware that they are the only person who can arm or diffuse a message. They smile because they realise that all masks are a waste of time, energy and effort, as is switching between them. Instead, the eternal warrior places their focus on working to become the 'real' warrior that they are and enjoying their reality as RUN, not as perception of reality based on filters. This allows eternal warriors to enjoy the ability of creating self-sustaining healthy bio-electric signals and cues, which influences a healthy biofield and the healthy expression of their bio-electric code and gene expression, allowing them to receive the healthy transmission of themselves and resulting in their ability to create and attract (Law of Creation) their world, using their thoughts, through resonance, the things they want. This automatically creates a healthier biofield, which in itself creates self-sustaining healthy bio-electric signals and cues for, not only themselves, but for those in their immediate environment.

CHAPTER 10

Thought vibrations, thought waves and their process of regeneration

If you are like most people who are still in touch with their inner child, you may enjoy picking up a stone or pebble and heaving it out into bodies of water such as ponds, lakes or the ocean just to watch the splash and subsequent ripples and waves, which spread out over the water. Thoughts (bio-electric signals and cues) are very similar. Each thought wave that is created spreads out, but apart from the obvious difference between stones and thoughts, while the waves created on water move in all directions but only on the level plane of the surface, thought waves move in all directions (three-dimensional) from a common centre (that is, from your brain), just like rays from the sun.

On Earth, you are enveloped by a great sea of air; however, you are also surrounded by what Teilhard de Chardin calls 'a great sea of mind or the noosphere'.[1] This great sea could also be called the mental ether. Your thought waves move through this vast mental ether, extending in all directions. Thought waves differ from other waves in that they are self-reproducing, much akin to sound waves and in the same way that a musical note can make a crystal resonate. I propose that a strong thought might make another mind resonate with the same thought, especially if the mind is attuned to the bio-electric signal and cue of that particular thought. For example, if I strongly believe that giving to people in need is a good thing and support this belief with my actions in life, when I am in your presence, and if you also share the same thoughts, you may be inclined to give to people in need, albeit you might not yet have acted on this belief. It would therefore be possible, through resonance by just by being around me, that I have stimulated that thought in you into action without having to use words. We may not have spoken about giving to the needy, but being in each other's biofields is enough to resonate this message, like the musical note on crystal. If, however, you had spoken, your mind would have been more stimulated and the effect potentially greater.

As described in the last chapter, like attracts like. If you have 'stinking thinking and feeling' (unhealthy bio-electric signals and cues), then these will resonate with others and will be attracted to you. If, however, you are feeling and thinking high and great thoughts (healthy bio-electric signals and cues), your mind will then also acquire a certain keynote corresponding to the character of these thoughts. Once this keynote is established, you will be adept at catching the vibrations of other minds that resonate or are keyed to the same high and great thought pattern or frequency. It therefore becomes important to be careful of what your friends are feeling and thinking, and don't forget that you are also a friend!

You are what you have created through that which you have thought into existence. You are the sum of your own thoughts, suggestions from others, and thoughts of others that have reached you either directly by verbal suggestions or energetically by means of thought waves, all of which are bio-electric signals and cues that influence your biofield and the expression of your bio-electric code. Said another way, if you have very strong mental thought waves regarding being successful and determined, you are not likely to be affected by someone else's thought waves of failure and discouragement. The opposite is also true — if you have mental waves that are attuned to failure and discouragement, then adding similar thought waves close to you will add to your negative state and further consume hope, strength, resilience and energy. The principle of 'like attracts like' is at work here. What you attract to you occurs via your own thoughts (resonance) and others with the same order of thought. The person who has actively listened, felt and is thinking they are successful will attune readily with the minds of others who share this thought wave. The person who allows their mind to constantly dwell on thoughts of failure will bring into their world those with the minds of failure.

How can you tell where your thought waves are? Answer: by your emotional guidance system. When your mind is creating thoughts that are interpreted as healthy bio-electric signals and cues, you will feel strong, buoyant, bright, cheerful, happy, confident and courageous. You are enabled to do your work well, carry out our intentions and progress on your road to success. These healthy bio-electric signals and cues synergistically reinforce each other, which creates a healthy biofield that also acts as its own signal and cue. In essence you are *Being* the eternal warrior, which automatically creates healthy bio-electric signals and cues and a self-generating healthy biofield, which you end up transmitting, that is, strong healthy bio-electric signals and cues, such as those in thought. This has the potential to affect others, and provided they are in resonance with these, your mental keynote increases the possibility of having them cooperate with you or follow your lead.

When you are thinking negative thought patterns (unhealthy bio-electric signals and cues that are found on the low end of the mental keyboard), you may feel depressed, weak, passive, dull, fearful and lethargic. These synergistically reinforce each other, creating an unhealthy biofield and an unhealthy bio-electric code expression, where you may find yourself unable to make progress or succeed in life, and your ability to inspire other people is practically nil. In essence, you are being the eternal worrier, and through resonance, you attract others with the same mental frequency, waves, unhealthy bio-electric signals and cues, and biofields. The Nett result of this is you end up being led rather than taking the lead for your life!

For some people, positive thought waves seem to predominate more readily, whereas for others, the negative quality seems to be more evident. There are, of course, widely varying degrees of positivity (healthy bio-electric signals and cues) and negativity (unhealthy bio-electric signals and cues), but the degree of difference will always be relative to something. For example, person B may be negative to person A while being positive to person C. This example highlights that you are both positive (a healthy bio-electric signal and cue) and negative (an unhealthy bio-electric signal and cue) to people, albeit the perceptions around us and each person with whom you have relations will vary. That is, someone will see you as positive, for example, your children, your employees and dependents, yet another person will see you as negative, for example, managers, supervisors or anyone else who you perceive may have some form of power over you.

I encourage you to remember in all of this that you are the *real* power behind what you feel and think. Recall that what you feel and think is up to you. You are the master of your own mind, and the only one who can decide to actively listen and feel. Your mind is a tool to be used effectively, and can be likened to a tractor. A tractor is a useful tool when used to turn over dirt in fields or pull other equipment around a farm, but how useful is a tractor when it is lying on its side? Not very useful indeed! In the same context, what use is a mind that is not consciously regulated or being used to create healthy bio-electric signals and cues? Again, not much use, and will only result in you not reaching your optimal self and life's purpose.

I reinforce the point that it is you alone who possesses the power to consciously raise the resonance of your mind to a level of healthy bio-electric signals and cues by an effort of will. It is, however, equally true that you may also allow yourself to drop into a low, negative note of unhealthy bio-electric signals and cues by carelessness or a weak will, where this occurs without your conscious control. The first step to changing this is to realise that your physical brain is the starting point, and the second step is knowing your mind controls much of the behaviour. This means that being conscious of your thoughts, as per Figure 9.1 in the last chapter, allows you to make the conscious choice to regulate your perceived expectation of reality. When you stop to consider the consequences of doing this, you will soon realise that this is true empowerment, because once you can see past your filters, conditioned beliefs and thoughts that are not regulated by your consciousness, you can experience reality as it is for what it is, that is, RUN.

The modernisation of our civilisation, and the development of cities that have taken the place of the naturally occurring environment, has created an imbalance in our living environments (nature-made and man-made). The probability here is that you are like the emerging majority of humans living within the artificial man-made environment, which is inherent with unhealthy bio-electric signals and cues, unlike living in nature's environment. What does this mean? You determined at the beginning of this book that you were being the eternal worrier who is most probably living in a man-made urban/city environment. How many other people living in your city do you believe are also being eternal worriers? I estimate almost everyone! Now that you know of the possible existence of the noosphere or mental ether, and the concept of resonance, living in the same man-made artificial environment with other eternal worriers with negative-thought-pattern-oriented thinking does not sound like a favourable future for you, let alone for those living in your immediate environment — nor collectively for the human species!

I understand that this may initially come across as a doom and gloom outcome, but what is important to grasp here is that it is the relative power of the 'thought wave' being transmitted as a healthy bio-electric signal and cue (a positive thought) that is the key factor. Although it is possible that there are more negative-thought-pattern-generating people (being eternal worriers) than positive-thought-pattern-generating people (Being eternal warriors), the energetics of healthy bio-electric signals and cues (healthy thoughts) are inherently and infinitely more powerful than the unhealthy bio-electric signals and cues (unhealthy thoughts). It is therefore possible to rise above these unhealthy bio-electric signals and cues that come from negative-thought-pattern- generating people and change your individual and collective vibration pattern! All this can simply occur by you making the choice to change your mental attitudes, redefine you and consciously Be the eternal warrior. This reinforces my quotation stated at the beginning of this book:

The potential of humankind starts with you, especially you!

I need to clarify here what was explained above, as you may confuse what was referred to as negative-thought-pattern-generating people (unhealthy bio-electric signals and cues) with pessimism. There is a difference between 'pessimistic' thinking and 'negative' thinking. You can view negative thinking as the same as what has been discussed here — you are being the eternal worrier and it does not really serve a purpose. You can think of pessimistic thinking as a way of feeling then thinking, while *Being* the eternal warrior exploring the possible outcomes with emotional responsiveness, which includes the negative things that could happen. In so doing, they are creating solutions for them before they actually occur. As Einstein said, 'Clever people solve problems, a genius prevents them.' The point being made here is that you must endeavour to not allow yourself to be affected by the adverse and negative thoughts of those around you, including society, and this can only occur when you become part of the solution. What this means is that you consciously make the choice to become a positive-thought-pattern-generating person (*Being* the eternal warrior who is listening and feeling before thinking), where healthy bio-electric signals and cues create a healthy biofield, which becomes a self-sustaining healthy bio-electric signal and cue, which influences the healthy expression of your bio-electric code and gene expression, so that you receive the healthy transmission of you from your environment, allowing you the possibility of manifesting your optimal self, living your life's purpose where you are always *Being* (in alignment, synergy, authenticity and synergism) the eternal warrior with and within your environment.

I hope, as it is for many like-minded people, that you rise to the upper vibrational frequency of your mental prowess and hold this frequency for as long as you can. You must practise this until it is second nature to you, that is, creating new neural pathways based on brain neuroplasticity so that this becomes the new consciousness (healthy bio-electric signals and cues) replacing the current unhealthy bio-electric signals and cues that you are creating now, as you read this book. By creating this change, not only will you be immune to others' negative thoughts and vibrations, but you will be in touch with a great body of strong positive thoughts coming from those on your own plane of development who are focused on creating a healthy change on Earth where we can raise humanity's level of consciousness to a previously unattained level of peace, abundance and prosperity. Doing this allows every individual to free themselves from their self-imposed limiting beliefs, enabling humanity to belong to a successful global civilisation where we are all equal and responsible custodians of a sustainable and workable world, which benefits all sentient beings.

One of the aims of this book is to assist you to realise that you are creating the world around you. As explained in chapter 9, the transmission of your thoughts, whether consciously or not, will impact on you and your environment, bio-electric signals and cues, biofields, bio-electric code, genes, cells, friends and family. I expect it will now make more sense to you that you need to actively engage with what thoughts you are transmitting in order to create your world around you. However, to do this takes more than just sitting under a Bodhi tree; you need be trained in the proper use of thought and will, that is, you must have your thoughts and vibrations in an ordered fashion (as will be discussed in chapter 16) so that you can immediately effect a state change in yourself at any given moment. This knowledge sets you free from the old automatic, outdated and misunderstood actions of your own mind. Strengthening the will is the same as strengthening a muscle — consistent practice and repetition lead to gradual improvement.

The take-home message — your transformation from eternal *worrier* to eternal *warrior*

The *eternal worrier smiles* because they fail to realise that all thoughts are their own. Instead, they believe that their thoughts occur only in their brain and in no way radiate from them in three-dimensional nature to create and attract things of a like nature. The eternal worrier smiles because they accept their world as it is and do not acknowledge that positive thoughts outrank negative ones. This allows eternal worriers to associate with anyone (and their thoughts and outlooks) without understanding that their thoughts will, in turn, affect other people's thoughts and lives. They smile because, by not knowing all of this, they are able to avoid responsibility in their own lives.

The *eternal warrior smiles* because they realise that all thoughts are their own. They smile because they know that their thoughts radiate from them in a three-dimensional nature to create and attract things of a like nature. The eternal warrior smiles because they know that positive thoughts outrank negative ones, and this allows them to select other people with positive outlooks, reinforcing the positive thought patterns around them. The eternal warrior smiles because they understand that pessimistic thinking is temporary and allows for problems to be solved quickly, efficiently and in a positive manner. They smile because, by knowing all of this, they are able to be the leader in their own lives.

CHAPTER 11

Eliciting change

Before you can change something, you need to first understand its nature. As you read through the previous chapters, I expect that you now know and understand *your* nature a little better than before, and therefore can be open to the possibility that you can change it, that is, redefine you. This now brings you to the 'how to' part of this book — how to elicit change and redefine you?

Become conscious, flexible, and aware (present) – *Being* a transmitter of healthy bio-electric signals and cues

Being conscious is the key to eliciting change

So, what is *Being* conscious? I have already redefined *Being*, so here I will focus on the word 'conscious'. The *Concise Oxford Dictionary* defines *conscious* as (1) awake and aware of one's surroundings and identity, (2) aware or knowing, (3) of actions or emotions realised or recognised by the doer (intentional), (4) aware of, concerned with the conscious mind.

Being (in alignment, synergy, authenticity and synergism) conscious means living your life from an observer's position, where you are consciously creating healthy bio-electric signals and cues that become self-sustaining through influencing a healthy biofield. As previously discussed, a healthy biofield influences the healthy expression of your bio-electric code and gene expression so that you are receptive to the healthy transmission of you, as well as *Being* your optimal self and living your life of purpose. Being in that position means that you are simultaneously aware of how you would look to an observer observing you. When you try doing this as an exercise, it is hard at first, like all new things. However, it does, like all things, become so much easier over time with practice. Being able to observe yourself being present is a great way to enhance your memory and recall events — how you looked, your body stature, what you were saying, how you were *Being*, the tone of your voice, and where you were in the room in relation to other people. All of these are valuable things to know so that you can understand who you are and that you are living a conscious life, where healthy bio-electric signals and cues become the norm rather than the exception!

Before continuing, I have an interesting aside: have you ever noticed that many people (possibly you) are not present in conversations? I would like to make you aware of an interesting dynamic that takes place in human interactions. Most times, the person you are talking to isn't really listening to you (I did say 'most times')! Instead, they may be either remembering something in their past that you have reminded them of, recalling something they have to do (like make a phone call), be too busy to stop and really listen as they are preoccupied worrying about getting to their next task, or simply be waiting for their chance to talk (usually about themselves and their beliefs) and so on. If you want to test whether people are really listening to you or not, when you next speak to someone, simply stop talking halfway through your sentence and watch their response. Usually, the other person will jump straight into the conversation with what they wanted to say, never realising what has just occurred! Those who are listening will ask you to finish your sentence.

Whenever I teach this in the FlameTree student tuition course (for more detail please visit www.theflametreesystem.com or www.rhettogston.com) and ask the students to test it for themselves, they always come back to the course amazed at how quickly the other person they were chatting too jumped into the conversation without ever really listening to what they were saying. These observations reinforce that people you converse with are usually not aware (present) of you or your conversation. This begs the question, 'Are you able to be more conscious or raise your level of consciousness?'

Absolutely yes, you can. This occurs by studying 'you' and by becoming more conscious of 'you' (that is how you work, what you truly feel and then think, or what your 'self-dialogue' has been saying to you and so on). In studying 'you', you may discover some of the eighteen filters, as previously discussed, that up to now have been operating unconsciously and affecting your world in a negative way. A mind is only a beautiful thing when it is being used to create healthy bio-electric signals and cues.

Recall the tractor story from above and the 'The river and the canoe ride' story from the Introduction. These stories demonstrate the power of becoming conscious — so become conscious! That is, observe your thoughts and actions and live from a place of choice that exists in the now, and do not act out of programming (more on this in the 'Respond vs react' section).

Once you make the choice to practise Being conscious, I encourage you to give up having to be right and to start perceiving your life as Being the eternal warrior who is immune to the 'something for nothing' disease, actively Being the inspired go-getter paddler who takes responsibility for their life so that they are living an optimal life with purpose and flexibility, which may also involve Being inspiringly peaceful, exciting and great, living in the present and becoming aware. Living your life from this state contributes to creating healthy bio-electric signals and cues, which, through a healthy biofield, can be self-sustaining. I would like to explain more about you making the choice to 'become flexible'. Flexibility here means that, when you discover how you feel or experience an event or situation or anything else that occurs in your life, you understand that it *is not the only way to experience that event*; it is one of many!

As the master and creator of your universe, you can change which experience you have at any moment in the blink of an eye! Yes, this does sound easy in theory, and I understand that applying it into your current moment of reality may in fact be quite difficult because you have attached your identity to how you react. I will use an example here to explain what attaching your identity to your actions and reactions means. It is very common to hear people say, 'It's who I am, that's why I react in that way.' I would like you to stop here and consider this: what if it wasn't who you are? What if your personality is not you? What is being imparted to you from reading this book is that you can define your own personality in every way, and if you (the master and creator of your universe) cannot change your personality, then who can? All that you are is readily changeable in a heartbeat, at all times! This leads to the choice of becoming aware (present). A good analogy would be that you are similar to a radio station, and changing you is as easy as turning the tuning dial.

Becoming aware (present) means that you are in your current situation, fully experiencing it and participating in it. Awareness is having a true understanding about actively listening to your innate wisdom, what you feel, then think, and believe of your ideas, and of how you are *Being* in your present moment. To become aware, you need to earn a degree in 'you-ology', that is, the science of you. What I am suggesting here is that you need to study you! Begin to create a true awareness of you, what you feel, and how you then think. Become more self-interested — becoming aware means that you are fully switched on to what is happening in your current reality as you are *Being* the eternal warrior. This is about you *Being* conscious about what you are feeling or experiencing as you ask yourself the questions that assist you to become conscious. For example: Who are you? How do you tick? What do you like? Why do you like what you like? How do you react or respond in situations? Are you as loving or kind as you could be? Where do you place blame when things don't work out? All of these questions assist you in becoming aware of you.

So how do we become aware? Simple: quietly, in your own head, ask yourself, 'Am I present?' If the answer is no, you're not. If you are thinking how nice that blouse looks on your friend, then you're not. The mere fact that you are asking yourself this question means you're not present! To become present again, all you need to do is the 'Three-step check-in' (not to be confused with the three steps to effectively communicate your needs or the three steps to change your station).

Three-step check-in

1. *Breathe.*

2. *Ask,* 'Am I present?' If you are asking this question, then the answer is no! What does this answer actually mean? The moment you have to ask yourself the question, the answer has to be no because, at that moment, you realise you are not present! When you are not present, you usually get lost in your thoughts, drift off, daydream and so on. You are actually not aware that you have stopped being present and you normally get away with it. By 'get away with it', I mean, for example, that the other person you are speaking to does not realise that you are not present. The few times you don't get away with it is usually when you are asked a question and you have to 'snap back' to reality and normally ask (embarrassed), 'Sorry, what did you say?' A simple way to stop this drifting off from occurring is to ask yourself the question, 'Am I present?' before someone else does. This allows you to practise the art of being present, and as we all know, practice makes perfect.

3. *Stop thinking about other things,* such as 'Yes, I feel present', or that you have to vacuum and cook when you get home, or you have to listen to your friend or something else. Don't 'freak out' or be concerned when you realise how little you are actually present. It takes time and practice to stay switched on for long periods. As your starting point, I encourage you to be conscious in all that you say, do and think. Don't just breathe; be conscious when you breathe, notice how your body rocks when you breathe, feel the air as it moves into your nose or mouth, and this will therefore initiate breathing full deep breaths. Don't just eat your food, taste it, savour it, chew it and feel it consciously. Don't just drink, swirl it in your mouth, taste it and enjoy it. Be conscious of all you are and all you are *Being*, in as many moments as possible.

What are the payoffs for *Being* conscious? They are huge! You make it easier for your body to operate, easier for internal messages like 'Don't eat/drink that' or 'You really don't want that' to get through to you. Actually, enjoy life in the present moment and become inspired with what you are doing, like enjoying a meal or conversation. *Being* conscious allows you to actually create and manifest your world as you would like to see it, and I encourage you to have fun while you are creating.

Be responsible

Recall that people love holding on to the 'It's not me, it's my genetics' excuse. Well, this excuse is no longer valid; it's gone! The reason they loved that belief was they got to blame something other than themselves for the state of their life, and if it wasn't their genetics that was blamed, it was their parents, work, lack of money, or anything else apart from themselves. However, only mugs play the blame game. I ask these irresponsible individuals (the worriers) who want a free pass for having a poor life and who want to validate their poor belief systems to *stop it now. Look at what it could cost you!* Be absolutely responsible for everything you feel, think, be, say, do, and have – *Be* the eternal warrior and start listening first! In this way, you generate healthy bio-electric signals and cues, which can become self-sustaining, allowing you to become the master and creator of your own life and not a slave to the thing or person that you blame.

Let's use an example to further demonstrate this point. Have you ever had a friend (or maybe it's you) who always chooses the wrong partner or the wrong things in their life, and then whines about it to you and says things like, 'Why me? Everything bad happens to me in life. I have the worst luck!' The answer to 'this always happens to them' is simple:

1. They are not really conscious when they make their choices about who to date or what things to include in their life.
2. They have a generalisations filter, which you easily identified because they used the term 'everything' in their speech.
3. It keeps happening because they refuse to take responsibility for their decisions and, instead of using the Law of Creation, they choose to blame someone or something else, like the world, the universe, God, all of the opposite sex or, as demonstrated in this example, luck.

You are now starting to realise that the universe will keep handing you the same lesson until you learn from that lesson, like a parent who repeats, 'What is 6 x 6?' to a child learning their times tables. The only difference here is this parent (the universe) is not restricted by time and is eternally patient; it will ask for the answer your entire life, and keep presenting the opportunity for you to solve the problem for about the same length of time. So maybe it's time to consider *Being* the eternal warrior who is choosing to *Be* responsible and conscious, and is living in the present moment, then observe to see if something changes. By *Being* responsible, you in fact become — and are — in control of making choices in your life. That means you make changes when something is not working and praise it when it is.

Be introspective (with an active mind)

There is a saying that a life not analysed is a life not lived well. What I suggest is that a life without consciously making a choice of *Being* the eternal warrior is a life not lived well. Now that you have read to this point, have you made the choice to *Be* the eternal warrior, and from this place create the opportunity to see how things are going for you? If not, what is stopping you? In business, people look at how the company is performing on a regular basis; for example, are targets being achieved? Are employees working efficiently? Is marketing being effective? Are employees achieving KPIs? Is the company share price increasing? How many times a year do *you* pay that kind of attention to your *own* life while *Being* in the eternal warrior mindset? I expect that this would be zero times! So, when was the last time you asked yourself where are you going in your life, and made a choice as to what you are feeling and thinking? The majority of people who I have asked this question of usually reply that the only time they really had a good look at their life was right before they left high school. If you were a business, you possibly would have gone out of business by now! I suggest that, once you make the choice of *Being* the eternal warrior of your life, you need to look at your life on a more regular basis to assess how things are working for you. This may be achieved by being introspective.

Now, if you consciously make all the changes advocated in this book, and six months down the track you are still miserable, I suggest that you need to change something else! However, at all times, you are encouraged to question my words and ideas, and never stop doing that. Better still, in your process of redefining you, question *your* own words, thoughts and ideas because, as you would now know, the chances are that these need to be changed by you in order to create the necessary changes in your life so that you can truly become conscious!

How, you may ask? Easy, I say: make a change, any change. Does it matter what the change is? No, it really doesn't matter what it is! The key is to make a change, change anything.

If you are unsure what change to make first, as I recommend to my clients because it consistently creates positive results based on the feedback I receive, follow the 'Three steps to change your station'. This process is not one of those 'you need a specific situation to use' things; rather, it is applicable to every single situation in yours or anyone else's life. A word of caution though: usually, after people start using this and begin to understand the ramifications of what it could have done for them in the past, they often become a little despondent. That is, 'If I had only known of this back then, I wouldn't have done this/said that/the situation would not have been so bad' and so on. If this should end up applying to you, I recommend using one of the ROAs such as pro·m·emo essences (go to www.promemo.com.au for more detail) to assist you in processing your emotions, learn UEFT (available at www.rhettogston.com), have a FlameTree session, or perform 409 Degrees – *Just hold it* — or all of the above. Why? Because all ROAs have been created to assist you to avoid entering into negative thought patterns (being the eternal worrier); they are in the past, negative unhealthy bio-electric signals and cues that do not serve to help you now. Yes, by all means look back at situations and see where you could have done things better. Learn and take the lesson; remember to see it as a lesson and not take it personally — don't beat yourself up over it. If you have already slipped into the old negative beliefs, recall that you are projecting them and potentially doing damage to yourself (your biofield, the expression of our bio-electric code, genes, cells and receiving the healthy transmission of you) and to those around you. So, using ROAs aims to harmonise your emotions and thoughts in the now (present).

I will give you an example before explaining the 'Three steps to change your station'. Ms M was so upset with her parenting skills in the past that she broke down and cried, 'I'm such a bad mother, I'm a failure. I am terrible at this job.' All the while, her seven-year-old was sitting next to her, asking her to help change the eighteen-month-old baby's nappy. In this instance, where she ignored her child's words for help, her actions *were* that of being a bad parent, because both of her children needed her and she was not present. (Keep this example in mind, as I will come back to this concept). I am not saying that you cannot look back at your past, by all means do look at your past, do not forget it, but please remember to remain present (aware) while *Being* the eternal warrior. This is *your* life now, not who you were, what you did, or what you didn't do! This is *you* now and this is who you are working with. Now let's start the 'Three steps to change your station' so you can make the conscious choice to change.

Three steps to change your station

1. *Breathe.*
2. *Ask yourself a question (or two).*
3. *Act on the answer to the question (I'll give you the only two answers).*

Step 1. Breathe

Why? Because no matter how bad it gets, breathing is guaranteed to get you through it. When you lose everything you hold dear, it seems nothing can get you out of the abyss. The more you try to act 'normal', the bigger the hole you dig simply because you don't have the energy for being 'normal' right at that point. In fact, what you do have the energy for is not much at all, and all your mind can do is run down the path of 'all that is wrong with the situation', which results in you feeling even worse based on everything I have discussed above about unhealthy bio-electric signals and cues, the biofield and the bio-electric code and so on. So, what you do is breathe. As previously said, no matter how bad it gets, breathe.

Breathing is better than drugs or alcohol because it does us good (see below). Drugs or alcohol do not solve anything for you, and your problem is still there the next day with the added bonus of feeling terrible due to the after effects of the drugs/alcohol — and you have less money than before! (I am still not sure how people rationalise it to themselves when reaching out for drugs or alcohol to help 'calm' them. How does waking up the next morning feeling like you have licked the fur of a camel, coupled with this ill feeling in your stomach, a headache, and significantly less money in your pocket, make you feel better?)

Let's say you do accept here that breathing can help you out (well, knowing that you will at least give it a try first), I have prepared some different breathing techniques that will be extremely useful for you. So yes, your first action for change is to literally breathe. No matter how bad it seems, if you can manage to draw one breath after another, eventually it gets better. All you do is concentrate on getting that next breath in. Seriously, when it is the difference between responding and reacting (discussed later), no matter what you are exposed to, you are in control of your breathing.

Although you cannot control the external situation, the one aspect that you are the complete master and creator of is your internal world (again discussed later).

Why is breathing important? It all comes down to oxygen. Did you know that you don't breathe to get oxygen? You only breathe to exhale carbon dioxide (the by-product of our metabolism). However, you need oxygen for your system. Why? Oxygen is the most vital ingredient for your body. All your systems depend on it, and without it you die. You can go for weeks without food and even days without water, but oxygen — only minutes! Oxygen deprivation has been linked to a number of diseases over the years. So, oxygen is not only good, it is vital.

Breathing and the lymphatic system

What is the 'lymphatic system?' It is a system in your body that acts as an accessory route by which interstitial fluid can be returned to the blood.

Interstitial fluid is the portion of the extracellular fluid that surrounds and bathes your body's cells.

Extracellular fluid is all of the body's fluid found outside the cells, consisting of interstitial fluid and plasma. Basically, excess fluid from your body is filtered out via the lymphatic system, as it permeates almost every tissue of your body. Due to the stylish and functioning design of the walls of the lymphatic system, large particulates in the interstitial fluid, such as escaped plasma proteins and bacteria, can gain access to initial lymphatic vessels, but are excluded from blood capillaries. All of this collected fluid is delivered to collecting ducts and eventually emptied into the venous system near the point where the blood enters your right atrium (a chamber within your heart). This is because there is no 'lymphatic heart' as such to provide draining pressure; however, lymph flow is accomplished by two mechanisms.

The first mechanism involves your lymph vessels. The initial lymphatics are surrounded by your smooth muscles that contracts rhythmically as a result of myogenic initiation of action potentials. When this muscle is stretched, due to your vessels being distended with lymph, your muscle inherently contracts more forcefully, pushing the lymph through the vessel. This intrinsic 'lymph pump' is the major force of propelling lymph. Further stimulation of your lymphatic smooth muscle occurs through the sympathetic nervous system, increasing the pumping activity of your lymph vessels. The second mechanism occurs via the position of your lymph vessels. Since they lie between your skeletal muscles, the contraction of these muscles squeezes the lymph out of the vessels. The one-way valves spaced at intervals within the lymph vessels direct the flow of lymph in one direction, towards its venous outlet in the chest. At a further glance, the most important functions of the lymphatic system include the return of excess filtered fluid, defence against disease, transport of absorbed fat, and the return of filtered protein.

For various reasons, for many different people, the lymph system is dangerously sluggish, and it is possible that your lymph ducts become blocked and lymph is left to accumulate within your tissues. This means that cellular by-products (waste) are not effectively cleared from your cells as they should be, and if left unchecked, your cells will begin malfunctioning. The stagnant environment that results is also rife for infection and local decay of cells. Irrespective of the reasons why the lymphatic system becomes sluggish, a sluggish lymphatic system can gravely impact on the quality of your health, for all the reasons listed above. What can you do to change and improve your lymphatic system? Breathing! This is one key way of shifting your lymph fluid: exercise being the other.

Breathing not only assists in lymphatic flow but in the oxygenation of your body, sustaining life and 'massaging' the internal organs. Now that you realise how important breathing is, and in particular how essential oxygen is for life, how do you get oxygen? It's easy and free! You breathe, as we all do, oxygen every second of the day because if you don't, you would die! Now, although you breath, do you *really* breathe? Possibly not! Why? Because most people breathe without consciously breathing, and when you are not conscious of your breathing, you do not breathe to your fullest potential. This is evident by the number of breathing exercises available to you that you can learn in order to assist you with breathing to your maximum potential, in order to relax you, shine energy around your body, get in touch with yourself, stimulate your lymphatic system and even prolong your life. It's okay if you don't know how to breathe properly. I don't remember being taught this at school either! The great news is that it is really easy to get the basics. The simplest way to teach someone to breathe is to teach them to be able to breathe from the diaphragm.

The diaphragm breathing exercise is simple and easy to learn. Start by either lying flat on your back on the ground or by sitting up straight in a chair. Place your hands flat on your diaphragm area, just below the chest, where your sternum (breast bone) ends.

Move your hands so that your middle fingers' tips are just touching each other. Make certain your hands are resting lightly on your diaphragm. Now commence to take deep, slow breaths from your diaphragm. You will know if you are conducting the breath correctly because, if you are, your middle finger tips will move slightly apart from one another as you breathe in. Practise this until you are breathing slowly and deeply from your diaphragm with your fingertips moving gently away from one another and then back together again.

What I have found in clinical practice that enhances the above-described diaphragm breathing exercise in assisting people to reduce stress is to repeat the above and add the following to it. Firstly, cease your activity and find a quiet location. Take a normal breath (while holding your diaphragm) and count how long a breath cycle takes (i.e. how long it takes for a complete 'breathe in' and a complete 'breathe out'). If it takes, for example, ten seconds, then go with that. That is, you breathe in for five seconds (or half of your complete breath cycle) and breathe out for a further five seconds while saying 'relax'. Continue this protocol for a few minutes or until you feel relaxed or less anxious. Repeat these five to six times per day. If you really enjoyed doing the breathing exercises, here are some other more advanced techniques.

Deep breathing and creating awareness: lying down is best so that you get as relaxed as you can. Close your eyes and focus on your body, searching out areas of tension. Then pay attention to your breathing (if you are like most people, you will be amazed at how shallow and fast we breathe). To aid in this exercise, place a hand on your chest or abdomen and feel the rise and fall of your chest/abdomen as you breathe. Breathe in through your nose and feel your abdomen rise. As you breathe, this should move first. The second area to move should be your chest expanding and the third is the shoulders rising (using the accessory breathing muscles). Exhale through your mouth, keeping the mouth, tongue, jaw and face relaxed, and keep focus on the sound and feeling of long, slow, natural breaths. The process should be the reverse of the inhalation, and should go shoulders down, chest relax, and abdomen down (including pulling your navel into your spine). The breathing cycle ratio should be 4:7:8 — inhale for four seconds, hold for seven seconds, exhale for eight seconds. If, like most people, you try as you read, then you have just completed the above exercise and you should be feeling mentally less fatigued, clearer in mind, more focused and more relaxed. These are just a few benefits of breathing better.

The 'Zen method' of breathing: This is another technique I enjoy and recommend you try. Simply focus on your breathing by taking in a big deep breath in, holding it for as long as feels comfortable, and then releasing it. You have just completed one breath — count it as one cycle. When you repeat this cycle, you have then completed two cycles. You continue until you reach the count of five cycles. That's it! Sounds simple, doesn't it? Well, it is, but you can't fully experience the breath if you are counting it!

The idea behind the 'Zen method' is to breathe and just be aware of your breath cycle without counting in your head the number of cycles you have completed. Still sounds easy? Try it now *without* consciously tracking the number of breaths. It is a little bit more difficult than it sounds, isn't it? It takes some practice, but it is achievable. If you start to make reference to what number cycle you are at or if you know you have reached five cycles, then you have lost your concentration and you should start again! Yes, I know, it's really testing you in the art and practice of being present, but don't approach this as a failure; instead focus on how much more efficiently your body will be working after repeating this breathing exercise so many times. Remember, delivering more oxygen is exactly what your body wants, as this is associated with better cognitive and brain function and improved metabolism, and the whole process of breathing is doing a massage for your internal organs. Collectively this contributes to healthy bio-electric signals and cues and to a healthy biofield. With the Zen method, I encourage you to make sure you set aside some time to practise it, because once you do get into it, you may not be sure how much time passes, as all you are aware of is your breathing! You could set an alarm for a half hour after you start or for whatever is comfortable for you and your day. How long is good? It's all relative, that is, one minute is better than nothing, five minutes is better than one, fifty minutes is better than five. I'm sure you get the idea, but whatever you do, you will notice a difference for the better.

The tantric sexual breathing exercise: The reason why I recommend this breathing technique is because the exercises in tantra help you to live a happier life by improving your physical body, enhancing expression, improving your sexual energy and enhancing intimacy with your partner. How to perform this: firstly, have an empty stomach (do not eat for two hours before this exercise). You must lie flat on the floor and raise your knees up so that your head and back are flat to the ground. In this position, inhale through the nose. As you inhale, the first half of your breathing in raises the stomach only, and the second half of the breathing in raises your ribs, which takes you to full inhalation.

Once there, hold that breath for at least two seconds or until you feel it's time to 'let go', then make a smiley face (top and bottom teeth showing) and breathe out slightly but forcefully, making an 'ahhh' sound until you have fully exhaled (note, it's not the doctor's office 'aaah', but the sound of air escaping off the roof of your mouth). Repeat this for about twenty minutes. In tantra, it is usually recommended someone being there with you, so if you need someone, ask a loved one to be there with you. They could hold your hand or even perform the exercise with you. When you have completed the exercise, stop, rest and be still. Try not to move abruptly and make all your motions small and gentle. So now you know how important breathing is and have a variety of techniques. This concludes step 1 of the three steps to change your station.

Step 2. Ask yourself a question (or two)

The most important question to ask yourself is, 'Is this working for me?' There are only two possible answers: yes or no, which you must act on (see step 3 below).

Other good questions include: who, why, where, what and how? For example, 'Who am I yelling at? Why am I yelling? What am I upset at? Am I really upset at this person? Am I directing this anger appropriately? Should I be angry? Why am I worrying about this? Can I change it? What value has been violated?' There is no limit to the number of questions you ask, but you must then ask yourself, 'Is this working for me?', and then act on the answer to the questions, which brings us to step 3.

Step 3. Act on the answer to the question (I will give you the only two answers)

Yes — if this is the answer, keep doing whatever it is that you are doing. Why? Because 'if it isn't broken, don't fix it'.

No — if this is the answer, change something! Why? Because 'if you keep doing what you are doing the result will be the same, nothing will change. If you change something, everything else has to change'.

Why learn the 'Three steps to change your station'?

The 'Three steps to change your station' is designed to take you from the sympathetic nervous system stimulation state (reactive actions) to the parasympathetic nervous system state (responsive actions), that is, it interrupts your unhealthy bio-electric signals and cues so that you reclaim *Being* conscious and puts you back in control of your life! How? It *changes* the 'push button response zombie state' that you were stuck in before. Now, don't concern yourself with being called zombie (take pro·m·emo or perform UEFT if you experienced an emotional reaction!). Why? Because it refers to 'zombie consciousness states', which is useful or survival when your environment is one of repetition and you can confidently predict what will happen, the payoff is in saving energy by not using your brain (thinking), hence zombie state. Using the 'Three steps to change your station' allows you to change from a reaction state of unhealthy bio-electric signals and cues to a state of response of healthy bio-electric signals and cues, which we will discuss now.

Response vs reaction

After performing the 'Three steps to change your station', you have the opportunity to truly get back into the driver's seat. I say 'truly get back' because you may believe that you live life based on your choices, but unfortunately, you don't! When you really look at your life and the choices you perceive you make, the fact is that you make very few real choices in everyday life, if at all! For the most part, you have been programmed to react to life, just as a computer, robot or machine does what it has been programmed to do automatically — in your case, the program is called 'you'. The 'you' program was written by all of your past conditioning, habits and beliefs based on those around you within the cultural, societal and religious settings that you were born into. What I would like you to do now is flash back to what was discussed previously about *Being* conscious. If you truly understood those lessons, you would realise that you were on the whole reacting to your life based on the 'you' program. If you now make the choice to implement the recommendations in this book, you increase your possibility of making the choice of *Being* the eternal warrior, so that you improve your opportunities to truly begin living for today, in the day, and you will be truly *responding* to your life and life's situations rather than *reacting* (being the eternal worrier — unhealthy bio-electric signals and cues) to your life, as presented by your 'you' programming based on yesterday's conditioning, habits and beliefs.

I will use a simple example to illustrate this. Let's say Suzy was 'dumped' by boyfriend Greg after a two-year relationship. During those two years, Greg (a romantic) bought chocolates every weekend for Suzy to declare his love for her (sweet, right?). Let's also assume that Suzy, who didn't really like chocolates, ate them dutifully because before she went out with Greg, she dated Tom, and she had spurned a gift of chocolates from Tom. Tom was so mad that his effort to be nice had been spurned that he walked out on Suzy. So, Suzy, not liking chocolates and knowing better than to say anything (so that Greg doesn't walk out), ate the chocolates and subsequently put on a few pounds. After two wonderful years, for whatever reason, Greg decided to leave the relationship. And because he felt like 'sinking the boot in' to Suzy, he cited her weight gain (from the chocolates) as the reason he was leaving!

Now, let's play a game with our hypothetical situation. I want you to predict Suzy's reaction to a colleague who has just offered her a sweet (chocolate) the next day! Do you believe Suzy will react or respond? If she is like the rest of us, she will not be that conscious, and will most probably *react* and decline the offer more forcefully than would be deemed appropriate, or she could possibly have a larger reaction and accuse her colleague of being insensitive, or suspect that her workmate is subtly sabotaging her or making fun of her and the weight she has gained over two years of dutifully eating chocolates in fear of being rejected again. If, however, she was *Being* conscious and could *respond* (the eternal warrior), not only would she be aware that her work colleague is offering the treat to be nice and is sharing something that brings them joy and wants to share their bliss with her, she may have been able to communicate her feelings with her first boyfriend better, where the chocolate issue possibly began. She may have accepted or declined both of their offers, but either way, Suzy would have done this from a place of consciousness, and as such created healthy bio-electric signals and cues, rather than the unhealthy ones that contributed to her weight gain, fears of rejection and her reaction to a friendly gesture from her colleague.

Once you are conscious and making choices of how you choose to feel in your present moment, you can actively see your past programming and your unresolved past experience (all of which are unhealthy bio-electric signals and cues), and possibly for the first time in your life, realise where in your life they were holding you back, and where it was in the past that held you back based on the unhealthy bio-electric signals and cues that you had created. You become aware that the program running is not who you truly are, but the pre-set 'reactions' that were put in place by programming when you were too small to remember. What do I mean by this? Most of what you know you have learned by observation as a child growing up. In addition to what you observe, the family unit and close friends also program much of what you know about life, usually based on their own unconscious programs. Have you ever wondered why family units share similar beliefs? It is because the children observe their idols — their mum and dad, parent, caregiver — and take on their beliefs. Ever disagreed with a friend's beliefs at their family's dinner table? Try it and see what happens, but a word of warning: first, know your argument well prior to attempting this, as you may find that you are not only disagreeing with your friend, but their entire family!

If you have been truly understanding what I have been sharing with you about *Being* the eternal warrior and becoming aware (present), then the beauty is that no one's thoughts, beliefs or ideas are right or wrong. The beauty is that they (beliefs, ideas or choices) are not who you are, and you can choose to accept or reject whichever ones you want (remember, they are not you — they are part of the 'you' programming). In your process of creating change and making choices, what I suggest you can do is to start to make choices to believe something that gives you that 'warm fuzzy feeling' on the inside, something good, something that empowers you as a person — which can be interpreted as a healthy bio-electric signal and cue. What have you got to lose for implementing the recommendations in this book? An old disempowering belief system immersed in unhealthy bio-electric signals and cues! When you sum it up, you really have nothing at all to lose and everything to gain by making this choice!

Regarding making choices, I want to reinforce here that choices usually lead to feelings or emotions that can be divided into either unhealthy or healthy bio-electric signals and cues. Here is a quick list of emotions, and for fun, you can decide which list is unhealthy or healthy:

- boredom, loneliness, pessimism, resentment, frustration, doubt, worry, blame, stress, anger, revenge, hatred, jealousy, guilt and fear/despair
- love, delight, appreciation, pleasure, passion, exhilaration, happiness, enthusiasm, belief, reverence, optimism, hope, awe, contentment, gratitude, and joy.

In deciding which of the above lists were unhealthy or healthy bio-electric signals and cues, which list made you feel good? If you did not note the feeling you get when you read each of the lists, go back and read them again.

Having read over the lists (and here I am not being psychic, just sensible), you would have felt one way or another, or more specifically, you felt either 'good' (healthy bio-electric signal and cue) or 'not good' (unhealthy bio-electric signal and cue). I use the term 'not good' because there is no such thing as feeling bad! This is exactly like life; we either feel 'good' or 'not good' about some things or situations we face in life. If, for example, you read the first list and felt 'not good', then you were triggered by these words. This means that you have a belief system at work here that you need to look at or address. Why? Because you should be able to read the first list, understand it, yet *not* feel 'not good' about it. Said another way, when we make these words mean something to us, rather than reading them as a list of words, we are triggered into memories or situations of unresolved past experiences, or are experiencing them through filters, all of which are synergistically reinforcing unhealthy bio-electric signals and cues! The point here is that you do have choices as to how you read the above first list, or as you travel through your life. As previously stated, maybe you should *make* the choice to not be triggered into feeling 'not good', and choose to have 'good' feelings instead in your present moment, that is right now, as you read this book.

Now that I have made you aware of how to truly make a conscious choice, and more importantly, now that you can *see* that you have a choice to either feel 'good' or 'not good', let's now discuss the reason why you should make this choice. Making a choice is empowering, and making the choice of feeling 'good' (a healthy bio-electric signal and cue) or 'not good' (an unhealthy bio-electric signal and cue) creates thoughts. As previously discussed, thoughts, whether they are healthy or unhealthy bio-electric signals and cues, are both transmitted from you into the environment and received by you from the environment. This not only impacts on your biofield, the expression of your bio-electric code, your cells, DNA and ultimately who you are *Being* (receiving the healthy transmission of you), your optimal self and life's purpose, it also impacts on others in your environment.

Another possible impact from making a choice to change could be illustrated by the possible changes in the structure of water, as documented by Dr Masaru Emoto in his book, *The message from water*. Although Emoto's work has attracted its fair share of critics, recall here that you can always make a choice to be open to the possibility of his findings being true. If you are not familiar with Emoto's work, he suggests that words like 'love' (healthy bio-electric signals and cues) create beautiful water crystals, and words like hate (unhealthy bio-electric signals and cues) disrupt the structure of water and form crystals that are unordered and chaotic. Many of Emoto's critics blindly discredit his work, but what if Emoto's observations were true? Given that you know how it feels in your body when you are making the choice to feel 'good' versus 'not good', and given that the human body is approximately seventy per cent water (as is the Earth), it should make you consider the possible implications your words, thoughts, feelings and emotions have on both your body's health and the environment (the Earth's health).

I advocate here that it would make sense to consciously harness the possible healing power of healthy bio-electric signals and cues by making the choice to consciously perceive words, thoughts, feelings and emotions that create healthy bio-electric signals and cues for you. This would be a pre-requisite for redefining you! You need to make the conscious choice of feeling 'good', *Being*, *Being* responsible and responding (rather than reacting). If you are struggling with implementing these concepts, I recommend making the choice to receive support from ROAs such as using pro·m·emo, UEFT and FlameTree: *the personal development & healing system* so that you are supported as you re-empower yourself to *Being* conscious in your life, creating your own healthy bio-electric signals and cues, healthy biofield, healthy expression of your own bio-electric code, which reinforces the manifestation of healthy cells and genes, as well as attracting, through resonance, healthy bio-electric signals and cues such as positive likeminded people and the healthy transmission of you, as you create your world.

You in the driver's seat – external vs internal

Now that I have brought to your attention that you do get to choose your beliefs, words, thoughts, feelings and emotions, you can now begin *Being* conscious (aware) and choose to be a responder rather than a reactor to life's situations, issues and things. Furthermore, you can begin to also look at your internal and external worlds. Let me elaborate more on what this means. I was taught once that you can predict someone's thoughts (internal world) by the external world around them, that is, what is believed internally is represented externally.

You know that you cannot control what happens in the external world (it would be crazy to believe that you can — can you really control day and night cycles or the seasons?), from the knowledge acquired from what you have read in this book. You also now know that you do have some control over your internal world. I have presented you with information that gives you the opportunity to make choices that support you, that is, you can listen, feel and then think, say, do and have (create and manifest) in ways that make you feel good, and you can choose beliefs that help you feel the emotions of happiness, joy, *Being* successful and enlightened. So, the next time, for example, you receive a remark about how you look or what you did, you can make the choice to feel good about it as if a compliment was made. You cannot stop the person from making these remarks in the first place, but you can make the choice to listen, feel and then think by deciding whether they are complimenting you, being rude in disguise, or actually being rude to you. I personally choose (regardless of what they meant by their remarks) to believe that they are genuine. By making this choice, you feel better, and who cares if they were trying to be mean to you anyway? Be the warrior and make the choice to take it as a compliment.

Now that I have brought you to the stage where you are open to make the choice to no longer be a 'zombie', and you can now see the choice to respond to situations rather than reacting, let's now move onto the next chapter about paving the way to Being conscious (aware) in your present moment. But before you do so, let's look at the take- home messages from this chapter.

The take-home message — your transformation from eternal *worrier* to eternal *warrior*

The *eternal worrier smiles* because they live an unconscious life of rigidity, which allows them to live in ignorant bliss. They do not know when to use the *three-step check-in* and the 'Three steps to change your station' to change their state from reaction to response, which means that they are always in a reactionary space, immersed in unhealthy bio-electric signals and cues impacting negatively on their biofield and the expression of their bio-electric code and genes. This places the eternal worrier in the blame vehicle where they are not Being conscious (aware) and are no longer in the driver's seat. Instead, they blame all the things that happen in their life on everything else, and they react the same way in many situations, making them a slave of their universe.

The *eternal warrior smiles* because they live a conscious life of flexibility and awareness, which allows them to realise when they should use the *three-step check-in* and the 'Three steps to change your station' to change their state from reaction to response, which places the eternal warrior in the driver's seat of their life, immersed in healthy bio-electric signals and cues, a healthy biofield, the healthy expression of their bio-electric code and genes, as well as the healthy reception of the eternal warrior. The eternal warrior knows that they are solely responsible for all the things that happen in their life, and they can change how they respond to anything, instantaneously, making them the master and creator of their universe.

CHAPTER 12

Principles to pave the way

When you have a realisation and you become 'awake', as I know you will while reading this book, it is not uncommon to feel slightly despondent and more than slightly let down. Don't be concerned as this is completely normal. I recommend, if you feel that way, to consider using the ROAs, such as pro·m·emo essences to assist process your emotions, perform UEFT, receive FlameTree, albeit having read to here you already know how you can create change in your present moment! You now know and understand that the 'why you feel this way' is completely under your control and you can make the choice to change right now. Good news, right? You should be jumping with joy and choosing to feel good, but this is not always so. The reason you feel let down by work, people or family is always the same, and that is because someone or something has not met a value or an expectation, or you have made a judgement on others or on yourself (reacting rather than responding). Before we can continue, let's begin at the principle of *Be*ing honest and *Be*ing authentic; this section will make more sense if you are *Be*ing honest and authentic.

Get honest – be authentic (healthy bio-electric signals and cues)

You are most probably aware of the phrase, 'If it isn't broke, don't fix it', but what you may have overlooked is the phrase, 'If it's broken, don't deny it's broken and pretend its fine!' I propose that this may be a viewpoint you have not considered before, but it is logical! When you become conscious about it, how many times in a day do you give yourself 'excuses' about why you don't have to do something, or why it will have to wait until Wednesday, or why you don't get up early in the morning, or why you don't go to gym, or why your life is the way it is? These excuses are what I refer to as 'softeners', which are designed by your brain to 'soften' the reality of your life so that you feel comfortable about how things are. Your life will not change until you become conscious of making these excuses, which will inspire you to make the choice to stop using softeners and start being honest and authentic with yourself!

Softeners are the lies you tell yourself to justify your unhealthy bio-electric signals and cues, so stop lying to yourself! The next time you say to yourself, for example, 'I'll just lie here for five more minutes, it won't hurt', actively listen, feel and then think again! Ask yourself, 'Why would I want to do that?' You may answer with, 'I will feel more rested', 'I need more sleep.' Really? The reality is that you are lying to yourself, so I encourage you once and for all to stop lying to yourself! You may think this is not the case for you but let me take you through the example of being overweight (fat) to further explain this. When you are fat, you cannot be anything else because you have excess body fat! I should know. Why? Because I used to tell myself every day that building my business was more important than exercise and therefore the kilos I was stacking on was not fat, until, that is, I had my body fat measured with skin callipers, which was an awareness-raising moment — I had 35 per cent body fat, and no amount of softeners (excuses) could displace the cold hard truth of not being honest and authentic; I was overweight, obese, large or fat! Irrespective of what you would or could say, if you are fat, then you are fat! You could say to yourself, 'Oh, it's okay, that's not too bad', but this does not change your reality of still being fat! Alternatively, you could be honest and authentic with yourself and say, 'I am fat, and I now need to start exercising and eating better!' Either way, I was fat, possibly initiated because of my own unhealthy bio-electric signals and cues, which were then reinforced by all the softeners I used, resulting in the unhealthy expression of my bio-electric code and genes. But, when I finally made the choice to Be honest and authentic with myself, it was the start of creating change and initiating healthy bio-electric signals and cues, rather than reinforcing the unhealthy ones with another unhealthy bio-electric signal and cues called dishonesty, denial or inauthenticity! As you continue re-empowering yourself by redefining you, get honest and authentic with yourself. In doing so, you automatically create healthy bio-electric signals and cues, which opens you up to feeling inspired to create change in yourself. This is exactly what occurred for me, and I ended up designing 409 Degrees—Just hold it — a natural, energising system that has the added bonus of burning fat, building lean muscle and shrinking waistlines. I now implement it on a daily basis to juice up my energy levels, burn fat and build lean muscle.

The change that I made was to choose to do something different. I didn't deny that I was broken (overweight or fat). Instead I was honest and authentic with myself, which allowed me to find a solution to my reality. I am not suggesting that you also have to create a new system (but fantastic if you do) — instead I am encouraging you to become aware and accept responsibility for where you are at and Be honest and authentic with yourself. This increases your ability of Being in alignment, synergy, authenticity and synergism within your environment, creating more healthy bio-electric signals and cues, which, as previously discussed, leads to a healthy self-sustaining biofield that influences that healthy expression of the bio-electric code and genes, and receiving the healthy transmission of you.

At this stage it's worthwhile for you to have an introspection about where you are at. It's truly amazing how many more things you can change once you start *Being* honest and authentic with yourself. If you are one of the growing numbers of individuals who are in need of more energy and are overweight, or would just like a lifestyle program that fits in with your life as you redefine you, then you might want to consider making the choice to purchase 409 Degrees – *Just hold it* (available from www.rhettogston.com), as it worked for me as well as for the subjects in a pilot study when I wanted to scientifically and statistically validate the changes that I observed in myself when using 409 Degrees – *Just hold it* — and a successful pilot group outcome was achieved!

Values, not expectations, not judgements
What are values?

Values (bio-electric signals and cues) are ideals that guide or qualify your life, personal conduct, interactions with others and involvement in your career. Like morals, they help you to distinguish what is 'good' (healthy bio-electric signals and cues) from what is 'not good' (unhealthy bio-electric signals and cues), and in doing so, they are able to guide you in conducting your life in an honest, authentic and meaningful way (*Being* the eternal warrior) based on any environment you find yourself in, and allow you to be immersed in healthy bio-electric signals and cues.

The bio-electric signals and cues associated with values arise from personal, cultural, social and work. For example:

- *Personal values* are principles that define you as an individual. Personal values, such as honesty, authenticity, reliability and trust, allow you to face the world and relate with people as healthy bio-electric signals and cues.
- *Cultural values*, such as the practice of your faith and customs, are principles that sustain connections with your cultural roots. Cultural values may help you feel connected to a larger community of people with similar backgrounds, albeit cultural values are bio-electric signals and cues that can be either healthy or unhealthy. The main point here is that it is your choice of thoughts, *Being* honest and authentic, that allows you to be immersed in healthy bio-electric signals and cues,

which then attract to you others with a similar background, which may not always be associated with cultural values.

- *Social values* are principles that indicate how you relate meaningfully to others in social situations, including those involving family, friends and co-workers. As discussed with cultural values, it is your choice of thoughts and *Being* honest and authentic with yourself that will determine whether you then interact meaningfully (healthy bio-electric signals and cues) or not (unhealthy bio-electric signals and cues) with others in social settings.
- *Work values* are principles that guide your behaviour in professional contexts. They define how you work and how you relate to your co-workers, bosses and clients. They also reveal your potential for advancement, which, as discussed above, ultimately comes back to what you choose to feel in your present moment — feeling 'good' or 'not good'.

The following table provides examples of each type of values:

Personal values	Cultural values	Social values	Work values
Caring	Celebration of diversity	Altruism	Autonomy
Courage	Ethnic roots	Diversity	Competitiveness
Creativity	Faith	Eco-consciousness	Conscientiousness
Friendliness	Multilingual	Equality	Leadership
Honesty and authenticity	Ethnically diversity	Fairness	Equanimity/ethics
Honour	Strong sense of community	Family closeness	Loyalty
Independence	Tradition	Freedom of speech	Professionalism
Integrity	Keeping your word	Morality	Punctuality
Spirituality	Friendship	Reliability	Remunerative worth
Understanding	A fair go	We are all one	Team player

Values are what our parents and society are meant to have taught us. I say 'meant to have' because they seem to be lacking in many areas of life these days. I have observed that many people want to lay blame somewhere or on something for the 'not good' things that occur in their life, but as previously indicated, blame is a mug's game! All this achieves is the reinforcing of unhealthy bio-electric signals and cues, not only within yourself, but with others as it reinforces the unhealthy bio-electric signals and cues for the something or someone being blamed, and as such worsens the blamer's 'feeling not good'. It certainly does not resolve anything! In order to resolve blame, you need to replace it with the healthy bio-electric signals and cues of enlightenment, love and forgiveness, choosing to be honest and authentic, where you are *Being* the eternal warrior within your environment so that you reinforce and strengthen your own healthy biofield and the subsequent healthy expression of our bio-electric code and genes. All of this then reinforces and contributes to sustaining these healthy bio-electric signals and cues. This collectively creates the opportunity for you to harness the power within you to change anything, and allows you to come from a position of *Being* able to make choices and regain control of your beliefs, thoughts, feelings and emotions. Anything other than this outcome will only manifest blame, and this is what I refer to as the 'victim consciousness'. By ***not*** choosing to feel good or feel 'not-good', you will default to the victim consciousness (being the eternal worrier), and this will leave you powerless and immersed in unhealthy bio-electric signals and cues, allowing your 'you' programming through the eighteen filters to continue to dictate your life!

You may believe changing the 'you' programming and always being able to be in your present moment — making the choice to follow your feeling of 'feeling good' and *Being* honest and authentic with yourself — is difficult to achieve, but here is the good news — it's easy, provided you adopt the belief and thoughts that it is easy to achieve. In addition to this, going with a 'gut feeling' may be something you have already experienced (but may not have always listened to it), and this also acts as a value (feel good or feel not good) detector and monitor. It will guide you towards the values that are associated with you feeling good (healthy bio-electric signals and cues) and steer you away from values that are associated with you feeling not good (unhealthy bio-electric signals and cues).

If you don't believe you have had this feeling, stop now and consider when something of yours was taken away or stolen from you, or you misplaced it, and that something was highly valued by you. Where did you feel that feeling of loss — that not good feeling? If you're honest and authentic with yourself, you will be considering — or even pointing to — your gut. You, like everyone else, feels that sick, upset or cold sensation in your gut. This feeling lets you know you value that thing, whether it is a thing, person, emotion, and is easily identified. Interestingly, researchers are identifying the ability of your gut microbiota to communicate with your brain and modulate your behaviour, which is emerging as an exciting concept in health and disease and is referred to as the microbiome-gut-brain axis.[1] This research adds another dimension to the saying 'listening to your gut', but, as explained in more detail in *The science and achievements of FlameTree*, listening to your gut is only the beginning!

To further explain how gut feeling applies to you in life, I will share with you this story from my own personal experience. This is the story about a girl I met from another country while travelling. I judged this meeting to be a fantastic one based on my values at that time. We had taken a shine to each other and enthusiastically exchanged details and promised to stay in touch with one another, which we did. However, it didn't take long for me to start receiving phone calls, letters and emails informing me that she felt that I no longer cared for her and thought I was a liar, or something else to that effect. Why? Although we shared the value (a bio-electric signal and cue) of being loved, her expectations around what she thought showing love looked like made her feel that I did not love her (an unhealthy bio-electric signal and cue), irrespective of what I was doing based on my values and expectations around love. What may have brought on such a dramatic change in behaviour from a girl that I had judged as beautiful and caring, and to whom I was attracted? Well, quite simply, the girl felt (I am not just speaking for someone else here — I had this conversation with her) that I was not interested in her because I could not reciprocate the effort that she perceived she was putting into the relationship, based on *her* value of love. I am the first to admit here that this was entirely true.

What she knew, but did not fully understand, was at that time I was a full-time student overloaded with subjects, and working up to six jobs in any given week trying to save money to buy a ticket to go and see her. Doing this validated *my* value of showing love and commitment in a relationship. Based on my reality at the time, this literally left me with about two hours per night when I was able to sleep.

You don't have to be Einstein to work out that my workload did not leave enough time to interact with her, let alone anyone else, even though part of my reasoning for taking on this load was to see her again. Despite this, there was an expectation by her that I should have been on the phone, emailing or chatting over the internet prior to going to sleep (even though it was the middle of the night for her or she was at work) so that we could at least have a brief conversation. Paradoxically, I was initially able to do that, but eventually the need for sleep became a priority and I was unable to continue those daily calls. This, as you might expect, created tension because, irrespective of how I communicated this need for sleep, it did not change her expectations around her value of love.

The outcome of my inability to maintain these daily interactions meant that her value of communication in a relationship had been violated, and her expectations were too numerous to keep up with. Unable to make a change in this mindset, she made a judgement that, because I could not keep up with her *expectations*, it meant I didn't care! Based on her filters and values, she concluded that the relationship was over irrespective of my reality, values and expectations around making the relationship work by saving money to see her again by working six jobs, while also completing my double degree, generally living, continuing to work out at the gym, instructing taekwondo (she valued my physical strength and skills in taekwondo) and communicating with her, albeit not every day!

The point of sharing this personal experience with you is to highlight that judgements and expectations in your life in the absence of *Being* in alignment, synergy, authenticity and synergism automatically immerse you in unhealthy bio-electric signals and cues, which are guaranteed to bring on emotional pain, misunderstandings and disappointments. My personal story was also reinforced in clinical practice. I can't begin to tell you the number of times I have sat across the desk from someone who was extremely upset that their spouse, partner, work colleague or employer had not done something that they '*expected*' them to do, and they have judged the 'offending' person on their own expectations. The outcome of this resulted in a fight where the alleged offending person had absolutely no idea what had happened! Then the very next week, the same person would sit across from me and talk about another problem related to their expectations not being met, with them again casting blame on someone or something else! What these people continue to do without realising it is play the blame game (being the eternal worrier). They take no personal responsibility for their own choices, actions, feelings, emotions, beliefs and so on. Pointing this out to you here is not about placing blame or pointing the finger at anyone because you and I would have done our fair share of blaming too. Why? Because that's how we have been conditioned to behave! That is, up until now, after reading this book of course!

To further demonstrate this point, I will share with you another personal experience where I had issues of not *Being* honest, authentic and present, making conscious choices or taking responsibility for my own feelings, emotions and thoughts. The outcome of this served to both create and reinforce unhealthy signals and cues, which then impacted on my ability to transmit and receive clear communication. This story may sound familiar, but in this scenario, the roles were reversed. Again, the story involves a girl from overseas, and again it involved unhealthy bio-electric signals and cues associated with expectations, values and judgements. In this story, I was putting what I believed to be lots of time and effort into the communication between myself and new partner (based on my past experience that I shared with you above — I didn't want to create the same problem). But at some point, I was *expecting* a return for my perceived efforts in maintaining the relationship. The reality here was, instead of entering the relationship with healthy bio-electric signals and cues, it began with unhealthy signals and cues, which created an expectation that some of this energy that I was giving out to my partner should come back to me (the blame game at work)! The return of energy based on my expectations, judgements and values, however, was not being met (sounding familiar?).

Based on my past overseas relationship experience, I stopped, sat and thought about the situation, and then started to make a conscious choice to do something different. I decided to speak to her to voice my concerns, rather than expect or judge. Now I thought that the concern was communicated well, based on my perceived expectations of what 'well' meant, but after having to call on three different occasions to have a similar conversation with her by phone, it was obvious that the message was not getting across! Why was this so? What I now realise is that this girl, just like me in my past overseas relationship, had her own expectations and judgements, and they were as strong as my own, so much so that, instead of acknowledging and understanding my concerns, she would instead justify her own position by responding with, 'Oh, you don't call, it's always me who calls you, man, you're so whiny!' Ironically, this was the same judgement I had been communicating to her, but she was taking it as a 'not good' feeling and was defending herself to shift blame.

At this point in the relationship, no progress in any direction was made, apart from reinforcing unhealthy bio-electric signals and cues, and for most of us this reinforces the expectation of getting hurt from being in a relationship. I have come to realise that it was not about me (let's be honest, it really is rarely about us). I accepted my truth and made a choice to be honest and authentic with myself. I decided to stop the conversations about the issue as I knew that, unless I changed, no girl that came into my life could offer what I could already offer myself — the choice of *Being* the eternal warrior, making the choice to feel 'good', be honest and responsible, and respond to life's situations. The automatic outcome of this was that I was then responsible for self-generating healthy bio-electric signals and cues, a healthy biofield and the healthy expression of my bio-electric code and genes, so that not only am I creating and manifesting a healthier version of my personal 'me' program, through resonance, I will also be attracting a healthier version of other people into my life, and expectations, judgements and the subsequent reactions no longer take precedence.

On reflection, I now realise that my expectation of an energetic return was not being met, and I was becoming upset and emotionally reacting to the other person, which is what occurs when you play the blame game. Similarly, her expectation was that I should call and have deep and meaningful conversations with her. You can see that, in this situation, the expectations for neither party were being met. We were both playing the blame game (at the time) and would react emotionally to each other. Where one of us would want to sort the issue, the other would feel that the first one was creating the issue! You can see here that there was no successful outcome for the relationship, and all these interactions only served to reinforce the unhealthy signals and cues emanating from us both, all because of our perceived expectations!

From this experience, I identified a value of my own (not an expectation) that, when I am in a long-distance relationship with someone, I need to hear from them *at least* once a month (the expectation was a return on the energy), either by air mail, email, post, call, or text with the bare minimum of 'Hi, how are you?' I rationalised to myself that this was not too much to ask, and still believe that this value is fair and just. If it can't be met, then I believe it would be a waste of my time and energy to continue on with that relationship.

As previously discussed, once a value has been identified, and you make the choice to be flexible with your value, and be honest and authentic with yourself, you can then *respond* to the situation by sharing your values openly and establish for yourself, as I finally learned to do, that if the relationship is a good fit for you (that gut feeling of feeling 'good') or not (the 'not good' gut feeling), then go with your gut! The alternative is to be unconscious, inflexible and unaware (not present), and continue *reacting* to unmet expectations, making judgements and placing blame on the other person, which is being the eternal worrier. By now you already know where this pathway will lead you, and that is to create and reinforce unhealthy bio-electric signals and cues!

The main reason you need to consciously know your values is so that you can be aware of them, which offers you the possibility of becoming flexible with them. You are then able to respond rather than react to your environment and place yourself in the position of generating your own healthy bio-electric signals and cues. Knowing this allows you to grow and evolve, and generate a healthy biofield and so on, but I have found two recurring obstacles to this for people. Firstly, most people do not feel justified about why they hold their values in the first place, but most importantly, they do not value *Being* honest and authentic with themselves.

Let's face it — we all have values. How you justify having those values will influence you in what you do and how you interact with life. If you do not feel justified with your values, you will be reacting (unhealthy bio-electric signal and cue) rather than responding (healthy bio-electric signal and cue) to them and hence to your life.

Irrespective of whether you respond or react to your values, I encourage you to ask yourself the following question: Who would you be if no one had told you who you were? The answer is: No one really knows because your values/beliefs have already been conditioned but knowing what your values are gets you more involved and puts you back in the driver's seat of your life. Being back in the driver's seat allows you to choose to respond so feeling 'good' becomes the outcome from what you choose to value. Knowing that values are important to us, how can we tell if a value is right or justified? The answer is if 'it feels right to you' or 'it feels 'good' (recall from the 'Three steps to change your station' in the previous chapter that you can only have two answers, yes or no. So, it either feels yes 'good' or no 'not good'!).

You know in your heart when your value is justified or not, but if you are still struggling with the answer, then I suggest you ask someone you trust and value, such as your friends and family. They will, in the majority of scenarios, assist you in determining if a value you hold is right or justified. It is, however, important to take into consideration here that there are possibilities that your friends and family may have a bias either for or against your value. For example, if you come from a strict ethnic background, you are then expected to marry someone with the same ethnic background; but you end up falling in love with a person who comes from a different background. In this scenario, you know in your heart that your value of 'finding love and being loved' is justified, but you also know if you ask your family to validate and support your value on marrying the one you love, they would most probably get a shock and be against the idea!

Having stated this, however, on the whole, asking those close to you if a value is a good fit for you provides you with a good guide to see if your values are appropriate or not.

In the example above where my value was to hear from my partner in a long-distance relationship at least once a month, I am certain this is an appropriately justified value because it felt good to me. When I asked my family if it was an appropriately justified value, they all agreed. I also asked numerous colleagues, friends and acquaintances while writing this book, and I am yet to find someone who believes that 'Hi, how are you?' in an email or text once a month from a partner in a long-distance relationship is too much to ask for. In other words, this value that I hold has been confirmed by me (it feels good) and by others (who agree with me), and therefore it is a justified value.

The reason I shared with you the above two personal experiences is to reinforce that you need to both have and be aware of clear values, not 'wishy-washy' ones, and it is essential that you *do* get involved with being flexible with your values. You need to be clear with your values so that you can then be clear with your responses to your life. To further reinforce this point, I would like to share with you another personal experience story about being at the wrong end of someone else's faulty values and belief systems, but also demonstrate how to overcome these situations by *Being* the eternal warrior and not being the eternal worrier in your life!

During one of my undergraduate degrees, a young man, based on his filters and values, decided to run, to those around me at the time, what is commonly described as a character assassination against me. Imagine for a moment my feeling when one day I went from being able to walk into a lecture room where everyone was happy to see me to everyone avoiding me. This is how you get your first insight into noticing this odd behaviour. You have to wait a little as you have no idea what is occurring, until someone (hopefully, at least, one 'someone') actually comes and tells you what is going on. In this case, I was lucky because there were two honest and authentic people who told me! Needless to say, I highly respect these two people. Why? Because they did not buy into the character assassination this young man was peddling. Instead of acting on one person's story, they actually stood up for my character in a situation where I was not there to do it for myself, in contrast to another person, who stated to me, 'Oh, I don't care about all that, I just don't get involved.' This attitude of not taking a stand reflects weak values in not questioning the person making the accusations, but what was worse were the people who judged me and took on the words of this young man without asking me about his accusations! These people showed that their values had no backbone. Do you believe anyone respects that?

The reason why I share this experience with you is to offer you two tips. One, if you don't make a stand in life, then nothing ever changes and two, if you don't tell your story, someone else will tell it for you! Look back in history and you will see that the majority of the chaotic times are due to someone not making a choice or decision. All of the great moments of the past are when someone stood up and cried, 'Enough!' This is the stance of someone who is *Being* the eternal warrior; they did not worry about what others thought or the obstacles they faced; they made a choice. The question I am asking you now is: 'Are you ready to be the eternal warrior of your life?' I would like to feel that reading this book has opened you up to the possibility of choosing to *Be* the eternal warrior, and will also assist you in making the transition from worrier to warrior. Why? Because by making the choice of Being the eternal warrior, you are also taking a stand and will fight against evil, which echoes the words of Edmund Burke who stated: 'The only thing necessary for the triumph of evil is for good men to do nothing.' So, in a nutshell, if your values have been violated in a relationship, you must walk away (if you don't, you are signing up for pain, and a whole lot of it too). However, you need to be open to self-evaluation and introspection, that is, make sure that before you walk away, it's because of your values and not your expectations.

If it's broken, acknowledge it and then find a solution to fix it. I encourage you to be aware and avoid having expectations of others so that you are open to accepting any person for who and what they are. Be honest and authentic with yourself and only make changes that are congruent with you. For example, have you ever changed for anyone, such as someone you fell in love with and wanted to be with? If you have made that change, are they changes that you made Being true, honest and authentic with yourself? If not, how long do you believe you can keep up these changes? Ask your gut — does it feel 'good' or 'not good'? However, I reinforce here not to judge or have expectations of your gut's response, because at some point in life we have all, including me and I imagine maybe you, continued on with something when our gut was saying it feels 'not good', so what or who gives us the right to judge someone else?

Realise what has been said (not what you heard)
Question: What was said?
What meaning did you attach to what was said? I will give you an example to clarify this point. Let's say someone complimented you on your hair, but as a teenager, you were mocked in high school for a bad haircut. It is possible that you might think the individual giving you the compliment is insulting you. After all, that's what occurred to you in the past, but you would be wrong! Let's consider it another way. Have you ever had an experience where you met a friend of a friend — let's use an example here going on a blind date - You go through the entire evening being charming and witty, and at the end of the night you go home and play the evening back in your mind, but you perceive that the new person (in your mind's eye) was not actually that into you. You start to see (in your mind's eye) all the tell-tale signs that should have been indicators to be quiet or to ask their opinion, where you should not have told that joke, and where you have just plain embarrassed yourself. So now, having created these unhealthy bio-electric signals and cues, you start feeling not good and believe that the blind date was a disaster, which reinforces unresolved past unhealthy bio-electric signals and cues of similar circumstances.

Now the paradox here is that the next day you get a call from your friend who informs you that your date thought you were incredibly charming, witty, told great jokes, and were the person of the evening, and they would love to meet up with you again. You now have two conflicting and different stories for that same evening: one coming from your mind's eye (your perceptions) and the other from your friend relaying to you what your date (their friend) said about the evening (your date's perceptions). The question here is, which of these perceptions is correct? Well, the interesting outcome here is that, on hearing this news from your friend, you start replaying in your mind's eye the entire evening again, and guess what? You now see all the good things that occurred from the same night, bearing in mind here that nothing changed the night — it was the same night, it was only your perceptions of it that changed! What changed was hearing something different to your initial self-evaluation of the evening, and now you can see all the good things that occurred rather than the not good things. In other words, you had an initial assumption that things would go well, but your initial overview of the night was negative and hence made you feel 'not good' (recall in chapter 11 I stated that you cannot feel 'bad'). Now your original assumption (that things would go well) matches the new perception (the date's perception) and hence you feel 'good' now.

What had to occur so that you could change how you feel? Hearing someone else's words of the situation. What if, however, there are two ways of interpreting everything where one way makes you feel 'good' and the other makes you feel 'not good'? Sound familiar? It should, as we discussed this in chapter 9 when introducing you to the concept of duality. Now, assuming you have understood this concept, and let's say that you accept that having this choice is true, the question that needs to be asked here is, 'Why not choose the way that makes you feel good in the first place?' After all, we tend to look at the way that makes us feel not good without consciously making the choice to feel this way, as illustrated in the example above. Knowing that this choice is possible, how then does that make you feel? If it makes you feel better or 'good' (and it will), why not make this choice and continue to feel better or 'good'?

Once you realise there are better ways to do things, there is no need to blame yourself (*blame consciousness*) for the way you were doing it before, or blame others for what happens to you in your life. Remember that everyone is doing the best they can with what they have and know. For example, our parents raised us in the best way they knew how, you were the best fiancée that you knew how to be, you were the best friend that you knew how to be, and yes, you can look back on past situations after you have had, for example, an insight, and can say, 'I could have done that aspect of the situation better', and then go ahead and make the change rather than waste time blaming and creating a victim consciousness, which leaves you powerless in your life and creates and reinforces unhealthy bio-electric signals and cues. Said another way, do something better, like learn the lesson and move on.

The take-home message — your transformation from eternal *worrier* to eternal *warrior*

The *eternal worrier smiles* because they soften their reality and lie to themselves about their life, thinking that all is good. However, by hiding behind their lie, they are unable to actualise the necessary change that would immediately resolve whatever issue is occurring because they cannot be honest and authentic with themselves and admit that there is a problem. The eternal. worrier smiles because, by not knowing their own values, they can blame others for being put in 'bad' situations while being blissfully ignorant that they themselves are the owners of their values, which can be changed immediately once they recognise this. Unaware, they attract to themselves unsavoury situations that make them uncomfortable (even though they don't know why), which reinforces existing unhealthy bio-electric signals and cues, but they are happy to blame others for their feelings (unhealthy bio-electric signals and cues), and perceive that they keep control by reacting rather than responding to life situations. The worrier smiles because not knowing their boundaries allows them to continue blaming someone or something else for their experiences. They smile because they hear all that is being said through their filters and choose to interpret what they hear in ways that make them feel miserable or put down, which validates their softeners about their world. They experience failure after failure and never see the lesson to move toward success.

The *eternal warrior smiles* because they accept reality as it is, with no softeners. They are honest and authentic with themselves, which means that they can actualise a change immediately when their innate wisdom informs them of situations or things that feel 'not good', and as such they are not pretending or deluding themselves. They smile because they not only know their values, they are flexible with them and understand that their values are appropriate to them. Should that value ever become inappropriate for them, they know that it can be changed immediately. The eternal warrior smiles because knowing their boundaries allows them to attract healthy bio-electric signals and cues in the form of experiences that feel good to them, based on those values and others who share them, leading to a healthy biofield, and the healthy expression of their bio-electric code, which allows them to be open to living optimally and purposefully in a life of bliss and happiness. They smile because they hear what is actually being said without filters and choose to hear things in a way that inspires them and makes them feel 'good'. The eternal warrior smiles because they learn lessons from their failures and move on to create success.

CHAPTER 13

Be unreasonable

To create change in life, you need to be 'unreasonable'. You need to question society's dogma! By this I don't mean create anarchy. Recall from chapter 6 the 'streak of yellow paint on the black ball' analogy — the black ball represented all the pre-programmed values, behaviours, thoughts, ideas and concepts in your head that influence you, and would have been programmed by others, which includes the society you were raised in. Now this programming needs to be analysed to see if it actually works for you now. Why? Because irrespective of which society you find yourself a part of (referring not only to other cultures but also sub-sections of the society in which you were born/live), what is it that the society you are currently a part of is doing that offers you the opportunity to change your beliefs, actions or thoughts in a way that doesn't make you fall back into the 'feeling bad' hole?

Yes, I recall mentioning that there is no 'bad', only 'not good', so what do I mean by the 'feeling bad' hole? I will explain this with another short example. In Western society, there has been a trend of body shaming. Examples include: 'They are so fat it's repulsive'; 'They would be good looking if they were thinner'; 'How do they have a spouse when they are so fat?'; 'If you don't have a six pack, you will not get noticed' and so on. Body shaming is an example of a 'feeling bad' hole. In more detail, it's the hole that, as an adult, you keep falling into and expecting, like a child, to be helped out of. Let me explain this in a little more detail using a street analogy. Imagine walking down a street (represents your society) and you fall into a big hole. Falling into the hole is not really your fault because you had no idea what a hole looked like (for example, did you know you were meant to be ashamed of your extra kilos?), let alone realising that you are in the hole (unconsciously or consciously hating your body because, for example, you don't look like a thin, toned and ripped underwear clad model with a six pack)! Like a child who has fallen for the first time, you cry and cry expecting someone (from society) to come and help you out.

Eventually you realise that no one (from society) is coming to get you out, so you do something different; you stop crying and decide to make your own way out. Eventually you find your way out of the hole and you continue your walk along the street (that is living in your society), albeit now bruised and time poor.

The next day you walk down the same street, and because you are using the same mindset as the day before (your preconditioned programming, in this example, 'My body is something to ashamed of because I am fat'), you once again fall into the same hole. You realise immediately the error you made this time, even though you did not avoid the hole when you saw it. Although you fell into the hole again, you have learned something from your past experience, that is, crying for a long time does not make someone help you. This time you cry for half as long as the day before and you get out twice as quick (based on having to find your way out the first time, and remembering most of the way, you kept at it until you actually got out). On the third day you walk down the same street and this time you see the hole, but you still do not take action quickly enough to avoid falling in (that is, you may have been fearful of falling in the hole, and therefore attracted it to you, or maybe you were too lazy to change direction), and you fell in the hole again! On this occasion, however, you do not cry and you get out of the hole quicker than your last effort.

On day four, you are now thoroughly aware of the hole, but due to the social dogma and other pre-programming that you are conditioned with (for example, 'Don't stand out from the crowd', 'Pain is good', 'You are meant to get hurt to learn lessons', 'Enlightenment comes through sufferance', or 'Who are you to love your body?'), you ignore your innate wisdom telling you to avoid the hole and fall into the same hole again! This may have occurred because, although you are now aware of the hole, you may now be feeling fearful about doing something different (not falling in the hole) and 'not following the crowd' or you are 'too lazy to blaze your own trail' because of the effort involved to go against society's dogma, or you just 'did not want to be the odd one out'. Either way, what you need to understand here is 'going with the crowd' is part of basic human wiring. Technically, it's still not your fault! However, knowing this now means that you cannot use this as an excuse anymore for falling back into the hole again!

On day five, it just so happens that you had finished reading this chapter. You already know that the hole exists as part of your past societal reality (or more precisely, your perceived expectation of reality, as discussed in chapter 9) and that you can see the hole, but this time, before you start walking down that same street again, you choose to perform the 'Three steps to change your station'. You stop and breathe. You ask yourself is following societal beliefs of, for example, 'hurting myself due to a poor body image - my body is something to be ashamed of because I am fat' (falling into the 'feeling bad' hole) working for me? You now realise that it is 'not working for you' anymore, as it is feeling 'not good', and you make the conscious choice, with your newly exhibited confidence and assurance (the initiation of healthy bio-electric signals and cues) to walk around the hole. By following the 'Three steps to change your station', you become more present (aware) and raise your consciousness (you are now questioning society's dogma), and from this point forward you will make the choice to feel 'good' so you are able to see the hole and side-step it, never to fall into it again whenever you walk down this street!

After you have become more conscious, flexible and aware, you might come to the realisation that you **do not** have to walk down that specific street — you have a choice (recall the choice to feel 'good' or 'not good') in selecting a street, that is, choose to feel good by choosing a street that has **no** hole. By doing this, you have questioned, analysed and undone the programming (societal dogma which contributed to the 'you' program) and have made the choice to be present (aware) in choosing to feel 'good' and to create your reality around you! You may ask yourself the question, 'What then took me so long to get to this point?' The most likely answer is fear and laziness, as outlined in chapter 1. It takes effort, energy and inspiration to create change, particularly when the change is in relation to societal and family dogmas. Recall that everything has a frequency fingerprint, as discussed in chapter 6, and this societal dogma is no different. For those who are unaware of this, those who fear to question this dogma and do something different, this only attracts fear (an unhealthy bio-electric signal and cue), which triggers your fight, flight or freeze reaction, as discussed in chapter 5. You either resist feeling good (fight), try to 'run away' from feeling good, for example, by emotionally eating, feeling a dominant emotion that does not feel good, or avoiding the situation from feeling good (flight), or are frozen from feeling good (freeze). Once in this state, knowing that the hole is there and being fearful about falling into it only empowers the hole, and through resonance attracts you to it, like metal to a magnet!

If you have any doubt that you are making a wise decision to perform the 'Three steps to change your station' and live without fear, let me remind you of the inevitable consequence of choosing fear. If you unwisely choose fear, you are, consciously or not, putting energy into sustaining being fearful, as if you are faced with a life or death situation. Your reality is that your current situation is not a matter of life or death, but your body has the same fight, flight or freeze physiological reactions to any perceived life or death situation — real or not — or to any situation that you are fearful of. As you now know, the effects of fear are not only deleterious to your health, you will also keep attracting fearful situations to yourself and those around you based on the resonance of these unhealthy bio-electric signals and cues.

I want to emphasise the point here that fear, however, is not a 'bad' emotion. In fact, there are no 'bad' emotions as such. Fear, for example, keeps you alive, that is, fear may protect you from doing things recklessly or damaging yourself and so on. These fears, as previously stated, are healthy bio-electric signals and cues that preserve life and are hard-wired into you. However, feeling the emotion of fear is still a choice.

Dangers are real, but feeling fear is a choice. Recall from an example above that I used to do taekwondo and initially standing before an opponent where I was in danger caused me fear. Facing that fear every class and effectively processing it allowed me to acknowledge the danger in presence of the choice of fear but not feel fear. Eventually this became second nature and I was even able to instruct others. Back to our street example, by choosing not to feel 'fear' and thereby avoiding the 'feeling bad' hole, you have also chosen not to be lazy or freeze-up! Making this choice also requires effort, but the reward (outcome) here is that you avoid the fall into the 'feeling bad' hole, choose to feel 'good' and re-create your life (RUN). It is also associated with healthy bio-electric signals and cues such as positive situations, events, people and so on that you simultaneously attract to you, as discussed previously with the Law of Creation.

These synergistically reinforce your healthy bio-electric signals and cues, which creates a healthy biofield and the healthy expression of your bio-electric code. If you do not do this, then you receive the 'reward' for being lazy, and that is an unhealthy biofield and the unhealthy expression of our bio-electric code and genes! Not much of a reward, but you do keep the status quo, that is to *not* create change and to remain being where you are at, in the 'feeling bad' hole!

Having fear and being lazy about changing only gets you into the societal dogmatic 'feeling bad' hole so much faster than before. Misery loves company, and if you are not making the choice to change (to feel 'good' at the very least), all you will do is to attract more misery (unhealthy bio-electric signals and cues)! Furthermore, if you also suffer from the 'something for nothing disease' as discussed in the introduction, you are doomed to continue falling into the societal 'feeling bad' hole, and each time you do, you will need to find solutions to get out of that hole, provided you realise you are in a hole to begin with! The problem with taking that approach is you are not using 'Three steps for effectively communicating your needs', the *three-step check in*, let alone the 'Three steps to change your station', and are therefore trying to use the same mindset that got you into the problem in the first place to try and get you out!

This scenario reminds me of Einstein's quote: *'We cannot solve our problems with the same thinking we used when we created them.'* Given that you are reading this book and learning the way to always empower yourself with a choice, you may also enjoy another Einstein quote: *'A clever person solves a problem. A wise person avoids it.'* Dear reader, you are here because you are a wise person who has chosen to avoid the 'feeling bad' holes in your life. You are prepared to question societal dogma and create change so that you enjoy the ongoing choice of feeling good and *Being* that warrior, creating and manifesting your life as you want it to be, moving toward your optimal self and living your purpose.

I encourage you to actively listen so that you can 'let you be you', because everyone else is already taken, and to question societal dogma to discover who you are! I will explain this to you with my own personal experience while living overseas in order to complete my studies in Chinese medicine. As part of this experience, I had to travel to China with a group of young people, who I later discovered were very materialistic and selfish, and believed that they were above everyone else. Yes, I realise that you may read this description as me being judgemental after everything that has been discussed in this book, but I deliberately use these words to describe this group of people to illustrate this point, and the interesting thing here is that some of them freely and proudly acknowledged these traits! This 'set of people' or society wanted me to change my behaviour to 'better fit in' with 'the group' (a sub-section of Western society). I was told bluntly that if I didn't fit in with 'the group' and kept to my ways, I would be walking 'on thin ice' and would very quickly find myself out of 'the group' and alone in China! Now, certain members in this group perceived that being all alone in a foreign country like China would be frightening, and thought that I would yield to their demand out of fear of being alone.

Now at this point, I was bemused. Why? Here was a subset of the population — you could refer to them as a society, or at the very least a sub-section of society — which wanted me to modify my behaviour to better fit in with theirs! Recall my description of this group — completely self-serving, derogatory and materialistic, none of which I would want to associate with. Now, even though the aim of going overseas as a group was the common goal of completing the Chinese medicine degree together, and although at that point in time I knew no one else in China apart from this group, their 'threat' of excluding me was, to me, ridiculous! I immediately chose to perform the *three-step check in*, thereby *Being* conscious of the situation to really be present to it, and then performed the 'Three steps to change your station'. After performing these, it became clear to me that this situation would not work and, without fear, I took the appropriate action based on my gut feeling of feeling 'good'. I walked away from that society that was trying to use fear to control me with a smile on my face!

What this group failed to realise was that I did have choices, like you, including the choice of creating my world by attracting other infinitely better people. China has lots of people, even though I knew no one else, let alone the language, in that country, I knew that there would be people in this country who shared my values and beliefs, were happy, easy-going, respectful, decent, honest and authentic, and even spiritual, that would be attracted, through resonance, into my life (recall the frequency you transmit is what you will receive!) and become a society that shared these traits. Said differently, as I have been sharing with you throughout this book, I did not let fear (being the eternal worrier) of being alone in a foreign country where I did not know the language, the people or landscape of the place make me stay in a society that would have corrupted me as a person! Instead I made the conscious choice of *Being* the eternal warrior.

The point that I would like to make here is that if I had worried about being left on my own in a country where I knew no one, or this group not accepting me, or what this group of other people thought about me or wanted me to think, I would have needed to modify who I was in order to fit in with that group — or at least I would have needed to create and wear a mask. Neither of these options in any way benefited me, and my gut (as discussed in chapter 12) was informing me that modifying myself to fit in with lesser values or ideals was feeling 'not good'. If I didn't listen to my gut, then I would not be *Being* me and would not be able to purposely serve myself or the universe — and that to me is far worse than living in fear of being in a foreign country or excluded from any group. As this book has been guiding you to, it is only through finding your authentic self, free from doubt and fear (*Being* the eternal warrior) and immersing yourself in healthy bio-electric signals and cues and a healthy biofield that you can ever set yourself free. By doing this (finding your freedom), you are then *Being* in alignment, synergy, authenticity and synergism so that you create your optimal self and live your life purposefully, opening yourself up to playing the part that you have been given in this world.

Any pretending, modifying or lying about who you are being limits your ability to be who you need to be in order to bring the universe's/Uni-code's plan together! If you have to modify your behaviour away from your authentic self to fit in with a group, then that group does not really accept *you* for yourself or your unique contribution to the universe. If you worry or are fearful (being the eternal worrier) about things, and you follow others who do not have their or your best interest at heart, then it won't be long before you are back in your 'hole', so *don't* do it. Here is your chance to make the choice from being an eternal worrier to *Being* the eternal warrior, and that's exactly what I chose, not only in China, but in all of my life. I share my personal examples with you, not to impress you, but to better connect with you as well as impress **upon** you the importance of empowering yourself to actively listen and then make choices.

I certainly don't regret not fitting in with, not only that particular society in China, but with society in general, and I choose to feel good with what's occurring in my environment right now. Why? Because my choice to *Be* the eternal warrior who knows I am in control of my destiny, and to apply the Law of Creation so I get to create and spend time in a society that reflects my ideas, thoughts, values and feelings, makes me strive to become a better person. If you have already caught on, my logic has a flow on effect. How? Because, when I chose to feel good and started *Being* that better person, this in itself also encouraged everyone around me to strive to become better people.

Observing this unfold in front of my eyes further encourages me, reinforcing the power of making choices so that I am immersed in healthy bio-electric signals and cues and a healthy biofield. I made the choice of *Being* the eternal warrior as I wanted to stay out of the 'feeling bad' hole. More importantly, I went with my gut feeling and followed the feeling 'good' pathway.

Just as I was able to say 'no thank you' to that society that believed in all the things I didn't, without any feeling of fear of being left on my own, you too may consider a similar path. In fact, what you may feel, as I did at that time, is a feeling of setting yourself free! I was able to float away and find a whole new society — more honest and authentic, more open and certainly more fun. That was exactly what occurred in China and I had an even more amazing experience than if I had conformed to that subset of the population/society! Which would you prefer? It is, after all, your choice. I encourage you to be open to the possibility of becoming the warrior in your life, for you, those around you and the greater good of humanity as previously discussed with the four wins in chapter 8, where everyone is making their choice to feel good!

Choose for yourself

George Bernard Shaw stated: *"The reasonable man adapts himself to the world; the unreasonable one persists in trying to adapt the world to himself. Therefore, all progress depends on the unreasonable man"*.[1] This understanding reflects the point I was making to you in the above example. If I was reasonable, I would have adapted to the 'fear and control' of the group and would have been miserable. Instead, I chose to be unreasonable in a country (my world) where I knew no one except for that group, and persisted in adapting the world (that country) to me! I actually progressed further and personally developed. You really do have a choice and it is *your* choice, no one else's. Only you have the power to control who makes the decision. Others can influence any choice you wish to make, but you must be honest and authentic with yourself and take responsibility for your choices, decisions, actions, values, feelings, emotions and thoughts in your life.

You should always aim to be the one who decides for yourself. As previously stated, I cannot imagine how the rest of my time overseas would have been if I had made the choice to yield my beliefs and accept those of the more materialistic society. I would, however, hazard a guess that I would not have been very happy, which would have led me to the 'feeling bad' hole, attempting to get out again. I know I would not have met the other more spiritual and fun society that I created and manifested into my reality.

The take home point here, from my experience, is to make *your* choice, for *you*, not society, and transform yourself from being the eternal worrier to *Being* the eternal warrior.

Get some new ideas and change your focus

The first new idea that you need to implement is that a different attitude brings about a different result. The second new idea is that you need to change your focus. These are two of the best lessons anyone can learn. I will start this section with a story that I feel is relevant to the point I would like you to understand and take on board! This story goes back many, many years to when I was a young boy learning to ride my first bike (BMX back in the day!).

My family had a particular (or peculiar, depending on how you look at it!) way of teaching children how to ride bikes. Basically, it consisted of either my grandfather or dad running beside me, one hand on the handlebars and one hand on the back of the seat, and at some point shoving me off down the road and yelling, 'Go, pedal, go!', then some laughter as I sat on the ground panting, looking skyward, with some grazes, trying to work out what just happened! You may have been taught to ride a bike like that back in the day! In my experience, the first few attempts at riding were on the side of a quiet country road, but when a few cars passed, the adults thought it best to take my brother and I to the local bike track up the road. The track was basically a paddock with one large red gum tree on the inside of a circular track.

Now, the truly amazing thing about this learning to ride experience was that I went around that track two times without falling off. I stopped for a rest and to quietly revel in the fact that I had just ridden a bike on my own for the first time!

Then my dad, with his sense of humour, said to me, 'Next time around, don't hit the tree!' That tree had not entered my mind until that point, but now you can imagine what my mind did when I started to ride again. Yep, you guessed it. As soon as I got near that magnificent old red gum, my brain kicked in and screamed at me, 'For the love of Gibraltar, don't hit the tree!' and then I proceeded to head directly into the tree, with the resultant spectacular stack that you'd expect. It didn't matter how wide on the track I rode, or how fast or slow. Time and time again I rode straight into that big old red gum! I remember trying so hard not to hit that tree, and everyone else talking like me hitting the tree was some kind of cosmic phenomenon! The difference came for me when I completely released and surrendered all fear of looking stupid or cool or anything else that was in my head (basically all thought) and went with my 'gut feeling' of 'just ride'. This feeling empowered me to make the choice to feel good. This is when I got the new idea of 'stay on track' and shifted my focus from tree to track. Needless to say, you already know the outcome without me having to prompt you; no more riding into that tree!

Chances are that you are already know about that 'gut feeling' — that sensation that tells you to turn left or drive to a certain place or gives you the idea to talk to someone. This underused voice/sensation/feeling is a good guide that we all need to listen to when it communicates with us. I say it is a good guide because the gut is only one-third of the whole picture, but it serves our purposes of understanding for this book. If you would like to know the other two-thirds I advocate you read the extra detail in either *The FlameTree Book (Vol 1)* or *The science & achievements of FlameTree (Vol 2)*. If you must name this anything more than 'gut feeling', you can choose any of the New Age titles like 'expanded self', 'knowing self', or the Freudian term of 'actualised self', or the religious term of 'higher self' or the Daoist 'enlightened self'. Heck, if you're into titles, you can call it 'sleedgy mcgoo piebean' for all I care, but I encourage you to listen to it regardless of what you decide to call it. Why? Imagine a situation in which you are presented with a choice. It doesn't matter what the situation is (you would have faced one at some point in your life,) but let us use the example of making the choice between red or black at a casino.

In this example, you can win $50,000 with one choice (red or black) and it won't cost you a thing. Now, if you had that choice and had the gut feeling of red, but instead put your money on black because you rationalised your choice, you know immediately what you would likely say when red wins. 'Awwwhhh, I should have gone with my gut!' or 'My gut knows' or something to that effect. Now reverse it and say that you went with your gut instinct and still didn't win the money. I am one hundred per cent certain that you would not turn around and say 'Awwwhhh, I should have gone with my head!' Consider it for a moment: have you ever heard that statement? *No!* You haven't simply because if you truly listened to your gut, you only sometimes (two-thirds) miss out on the money or anything else you want for that matter. Your 'gut feeling' tells you what is potentially right for you at that precise moment in time. I say potentially here because, in FlameTree: *the personal development & healing system,* we teach you what is missing here — that you are not only listening to your gut feeling, but to the fuller concept of what I refer to as your innate wisdom, which is discussed in my other books listed above.

Now, back to the main story and that tree! The second I focused on 'track' instead of '*not* hitting the tree', change occurred! You need to picture it clearly in your head; a little kid riding around on a dirt track literally saying to himself, 'Don't hit the tree, don't hit the tree, don't hit the tree. And as you know — *wham, smack, bang* — straight into the tree! Now picture that little kid lying in a heap on the ground, covered in dust, baffled as to what was happening, with his onlookers laughing at his expense, knowing that, as I did at the time, I didn't want to hit the tree. But the more I thought 'Don't hit the tree', smack! I know you have the picture now, even if it sounds ridiculous. Well, have you ever stopped to wonder why it seems to work this way? Seeing that this was a defining moment for me in my life, I certainly have, and let me share with you what I discovered when I researched this phenomenon.

The reticular activating system (RAS) is the name given to the part of your brain (the reticular formation and its connections) believed to be the centre of arousal and motivation in animals, including humans. It is situated at the core of your brain stem between the myelencephalon (medulla) and metencephalon (midbrain).

Physiologically, RAS is a structure in your brain stem that is responsible for arousal and sleep, that is, it is responsible for getting you up in the morning and putting you to sleep at night, which is commonly referred to as the 'sleep–wake cycle'. The reticular formation is also vital in controlling respiratory, cardiac rhythms and other essential bodily functions. Damage to the RAS can lead to permanent coma.

The RAS is also the area thought to be affected by many psychotropic drugs and where general anaesthetics are believed to work their effect on inducing you into a sleep. As the RAS is a bundle of cells you have in the back of your brain, which also serves as the filter for what enters your conscious and unconscious mind, it is known as the 'control centre'.

According to Mihaly Csikszentmihalyi in his book, *Flow: The psychology of optimal experience,* 'We filter around 2 million bits of information per second down to 7 +/- 2 chunks of information.'[2] Said another way, all of the available data that comes into your body, everything you see, hear, smell, taste and touch, is a message entering your brain via your central nervous system and going through filters (such as the RAS filter).

This can be likened to the process of filtering discussed in chapter 9. The process of filtering is used to make sense of the incoming information that we know as life. The RAS system oversees the sorting of all that information. It is considered to be a self- filtering system that chooses what you accept or reject based on your beliefs, values and prejudices. The RAS decides which one of the thoughts, ideas, stimuli or any other of the millions of impulses to pay attention to, that is, which one gets to be elevated to the conscious mind. It is much akin to the Law of Creation — what you pay attention to or what is important to you at the time is what you notice as you create it. Said another way, if your primary thoughts were about creating a new business, you would probably begin to see new businesses and ideas. You would hear conversations about new businesses being discussed by other like-minded individuals. In other words, the RAS will reject or ignore anything unrelated to your focus and will highlight anything that is even remotely related to the important issue.

From a pragmatic and practical viewpoint, the take home message here is that if you want to solve a particular problem or achieve a specific goal, then you have to keep it at the forefront of your mind, any way you can (e.g. think about it, talk about it, write about it, blog about it, imagine it completed). Place specific indicators on what you are focusing on, measure it visibly, frequently and attentively, let your RAS create and manifest what you need to you, and you will likely observe an improvement in what you desire. Knowing the functions of the RAS, it makes sense that if your RAS is what awakens you, alerts you like an alarm to those things that are in the forefront of your consciousness, it would also be the part of your brain that will most likely be useful in creating and manifesting things and experiences into your life. This is where you must ask yourself: 'What would you like to create and manifest into your life?'

If you still struggle to work out what you would like to create and manifest, or believe that creation or manifestation is not possible, then I would like you to consider this — what if there was a way to learn how to program your RAS for this to occur? Well, there is! I call it 'FlameTree self-talk'.

Self-talk is not a new concept! It is used in neuro-linguistic programming (NLP) and simply put; the aim is that you tell yourself what you want to believe. So, what is FlameTree self-talk? It is self-talk that is in alignment, synergy, authenticity and synergism (Being) with your optimal self and your life's purpose, where you are purposefully creating healthy bio-electric signals and cues and a healthy biofield effortlessly. Now, about choices, it would make sense that you would choose our FlameTree self-talk to be focused on you being about your purpose. Recall my learning to ride a bike story above, where my self-talk was in fact an unhealthy bio-electric signal and cue that attracted that tree into my pathway, and not focused on my purpose (which was to ride the bike). This should sound a little familiar to you. If it doesn't, then try, for example, replacing 'bike riding' with 'dating', 'job interview' or 'presenting at an important meeting', and replacing 'tree' with 'don't stuff this up'. Let's say, for example, you know that you have just found who you believe to be the perfect spouse. You are floating on air, as high as a kite, the world feels like it is your oyster; your friends and family notice the changes in you, even to the point where they notice that glow in your face and the new shine to your skin. Then out of the blue, someone decides to (and that could be even you) say, 'Well, don't lose them', or something to that effect. I don't have to tell you what happens next. Your focus has now been shifted from *Being* the eternal warrior — that is, 'Oh, I'm so happy I found this person and it's so great hanging out with them and I'm so falling for them, I can do anything', to being the eternal worrier — that is, 'Oh my god, I don't want to make a mistake that will make them leave me, don't let me sound stupid, trip over, spill my coffee, talk about exes and so on!' Just like that gum tree, guaranteed the next date you will say something dumb, while tripping over your own feet and spilling coffee right before you tell your perfect match about all of your exes! Don't focus on the gum tree and you will avoid slamming into it.

Why? I hear you ask. Look at your focus! Where you focus your energy, is what you get. Some may call this the law of attraction, like attracts like, or the law of intent; again, call it whatever you want, but know that it exists! I, however, call it part of the Law of Creation as discussed in chapter 8, where it begins with actively listening.

A brief side note here regarding the publicity about the 'law of attraction'. Although it may help change your life, it is not the complete story. What does not get emphasised is that, once you have used the focus of your energy or the law of attraction, *you* now have to *do* something! That's correct — you need to act. This is exactly what I have said from the start of this book: it all comes down to *you*. I am not saying here that you can't believe in the law of attraction — please feel free to — but I encourage you to be real about it. If the law truly works on its own, then all you would have to do is sit in your lounge room and think positively, then wham, there is that brand-new Mercedes and yacht with your favourite celebrity in the front, right? Right? Wrong! It still all comes down to **you**. That is, using your focus/intention puts you into the mindset that creates the opportunity to create what you want (Law of Creation). You need to be honest and authentic, make choices about following your gut towards the feel 'good' things and away from the feeling 'not good' things, where you are in alignment, synergy, authenticity and synergism, *Being* your optimal self, immersed in self-sustaining healthy bio-electric signals and cues, a healthy biofield and the healthy expression of your bio-electric code, all of which requires you to take action.

For example, if you want to win money, you need to first start focusing on winning money, like the lottery. However, do you believe that you will win the lottery if you don't take the action of buying a ticket in that lottery draw? Before I offer you another example that supports the point being made, I would like you right now to reflect on what has been shared with you and take notice of your state. By state, I mean your thoughts, your emotions, and what you are feeling right now. If you are *Being* honest and authentic with yourself, I believe they would go one of two ways and be something like:

1. 'What my coach is saying makes sense to me. All the things I focus on <u>not</u> wanting to happen always seem to happen! I feel like I have been wasting time in my life and I can't wait until my coach tells me how to change this one! This was a huge realisation for me and I can already see the implications of this in my life.'
2. 'I get it and that totally makes sense to me and I have been using it (consciously or unconsciously)'.

You might not want to change the second option, but you may want to know how to improve on it.

Before I share with you how to improve the second option, I want you to stop again and gauge what your state is now, and then I would like you to notice the change in that state with the next (and easiest) example, the example of money. I am almost one hundred per cent certain the second you read that word 'money' and begin to focus on it, you will notice a change in your state. That is, you may have tightened up (even subconsciously) and that your state went downhill, and possibly fast. Would you like to know why? Firstly, if you have money and are comfortable with where you are at and have peace in your financial life, then this may or may not apply to you. If, however, you don't have much money or you come from a low socio-economic background, then the chances are that at some point in your life you were indoctrinated with beliefs like: 'If you have money, you can be happy and live a better life'. Which is okay, but by default the opposite (its duality) is also being reinforced, even if it is not directly verbalised: 'If you don't have money, you can't have happiness and a better life'.

Now, most people like going to the movies, and we all would have seen those movies that tell you that you can live happily without money, and there are even those movies that portray characters who shun money and its influences on life. These, however, are just the movies, and chances are that money is an issue for you. Thus the reason why your state changed when you focused on 'money', may be because you automatically link 'money' to 'lack of money' and you focus on your lack of wealth, your debt, not being paid fairly for your efforts, or all the money wasted on fines, bills and so on that you have had to pay out. This way of thinking is actually found in monetary terms such as in the word *mortgage*, which when you divide this word up you get *mort-* from the Latin word for death and *-gage* from the sense of that word meaning a pledge to forfeit something of value if a debt is not repaid. It has been found in Old French as *gage mort* as early as 1267. The more common use of the form *mortgage* appears in Old French by 1283. Its use in the English language dates back to 1390, when it appears in John Gower's *Confessio Amantis*. That is, mortgage is literally a 'dead pledge'.

I ask you to again consider this point: you have been conditioned to believe that; 'I've just got to get out of debt then I'll be okay'. Lack, deficiency or vacuity, call it what you want, if that is where you are focused, then that is what you will get and where you will stay. Said simply, you will keep hitting that tree (lack of money)! Now, here is the key to stopping this very negative and destructive cycle (being the eternal worrier) or improving what you have been using.

Firstly, as I have done, stop listening to society and challenge the societal dogma, as discussed above at the beginning of this chapter. If other people want to live in that negative and deficient state (unhealthy bio-electric signals and cues that contribute to creating the 'feeling bad' hole, they can, but it doesn't mean you have to. This is where we have a *choice* and I suggest you go with your gut (gut-brain axis/gut mind) and choose something that will make you feel 'good' (recall we always have two choices: to feel 'good' or 'not good'!). I encourage you to give it a try, so that rather than focusing on the deficient state, focus on the abundant state.

For example, if you are entering a new job, you need to focus on what you will do right, such as learn quickly, recall people's names and be efficient in your role, rather than focusing on what you don't know and worrying about getting it wrong. Let's use another example of money. Your focus here could be you will have an abundance of money (associated with *Being* the eternal warrior) instead of you just needing to make enough to get you out of debt (associated with being the eternal worrier). When you begin to make the choice to start doing this, even if it doesn't work immediately (but it does), note your state. Do it now and note what your state is like. I can say that you will at least begin to feel lighter and better in yourself, and guess what? You did not have to put money into your account, pay your bills or say affirmations to achieve this state change. Nothing may have physically changed around you yet, but your energetic frequency and your state of mind has increased, and soon you will start seeing the benefits of what you have created and manifested appearing physically. To increase the speed of your creation, the next step after being focused is to take action.

If you do, however, get stuck with finding words for your focus, which may then influence your ability to take action, you may need more information or assistance. In this case, you could look for people who have walked the walk. For example, if it is financial advice, go to the resources section at the library and check some of the financial books out, ensuring that the authors are financially successful (e.g. a book on how to become an entrepreneur by Richard Branson). Once you have read that book or discussed it with the appropriate person, then with your new focus you are open to the possibility of new ideas. Now that you are in the mindset of being specific with your focus, it's time to put things into action.

Get some new ideas and rules — what rules?

Before you can put things into action, let's first address rules. Rules? Yes, rules. Hey, let's be serious for a minute. What rules are we adhering to? This is where you need to ask some questions again of your society. How about these questions for example:

- What does it do for me?
- Why do they want me to conform/play by the rules?
- What will conforming/playing by the rules do for me?
- Will it conflict with my interests?
- Why be reasonable?
- Is being reasonable being inauthentic? If so, what has the impact on my life been to date?

Don't accept all rules at face value as such. You need to question many of society's dogmas as these influence the rules that you follow. For example, why should I accept that to have a best-seller, I should keep back from you all the things you paid to read about just to entice you to purchase my next book? Why should you accept that you can't have a better and deeper friendship than what society tells you? Why? Why can't you have it all? Why can't you be unreasonable? Obviously, you do not **need** to abide by society's rules about not hurting or killing another person, but it's the authentic thing to do for a loving and compassionate person! The point here is that we need to make rules that work for you and this involves questioning current societal dogmas, which you already abide by and which have contributed to your 'feeling bad' hole!

The take-home message — your transformation from eternal *worrier* to eternal *warrior*

The *eternal worrier smiles* because they do not question anything! This means that they are therefore not responsible for what happens to them in their life. They smile because they get to blame their family, culture, society and the universe for what they do not have, and as such they fail to engage their RAS to assist them in the creation and manifestation of their dreams. The eternal worrier smiles because they bend themselves to fit people, places and societies, perceiving that they then fit in, despite their 'not good' gut feeling which they ignore. As such, they are not listening and instead conform to societal dogma, but conforming does not benefit them and they can then blame everything else except themselves for their misfortunes, and lack of wealth, happiness and love in life.

The *eternal warrior smiles* because they know to question everything. They use their RAS to assist them in focusing their attention on achieving what they desire, while being honest and authentic and making choices that follow their 'good' gut feeling (gut-brain axis) and not ignoring their 'not good' gut feeling. The eternal warrior smiles because they know how to use the Law of Creation, and how to listen, feel, think, be, say, do and have, so that they can create and manifest their dreams into reality, and as such are always in alignment, synergy, authenticity and synergism, Being their optimal self and living their life purposefully. The eternal warrior smiles because they know that the only rule, which is more of a serving suggestion (e.g. you decide whether to take it or leave it), is to do what is right by them, for them, and to be themselves, for the betterment of the universe because they are aware of the four wins, irrespective of the dogmas around them. They smile because they know they can ask, answer and receive what they desire from the universe using the Law of Creation.

CHAPTER 14

Being unreasonable

This means doing while *Being*. It also involves establishing honest and authentic relationships and rule breaking, but why do you need to consider 'how' to change the way you make friends? I encourage you to focus on this for a minute. When you were in kindergarten and you met someone new, you knew them for about as long as it took to find out their name and you were instantly best friends! What happened to establishing best friends as you grew up into primary school, secondary school and the rest of your adult life? Did it become easier or harder? It became harder! If you walk up to an adult and say 'Hi, my name is [insert your name here], would you like to be best friends?', you would not usually get the same response as you did in kindergarten.

Many adults actually report finding it difficult to make new friends. I have certainly observed this within Western culture, and it doesn't work for me as an individual. The solution I have found is to travel as often as I can! Why? Interestingly, I've found that, when I'm travelling, I increase the odds of re-creating the opportunity to make friends, just as we did in kindergarten.

When you travel, you meet all kinds of people, and guess what, everybody lets down their guard more (not less). Now, I don't mean they become instant best friends as happened in kindergarten, nor am I talking about the person who approaches you trying to sell you something, like mobile phones and watches, from under their coat, and then runs and hides whenever the police go down the road! It's the everyday meetings that you have when you are travelling, like standing in queues or meeting at restaurants in unfamiliar territory. You meet new people and end up exchanging details so that you meet up again later that day or later on in your travels or stay in contact after the trip has ended. In contrast, when you are at home, you are in your comfort zone. If someone starts talking to you — well, let's face it, you are nice, but usually you can't wait to get out of the conversation. But when you are not in your comfort zone, something changes, and this reflects what I have observed. Nothing exciting ever happens in a comfort zone!

I decided to test this observation (as I have done with everything I am sharing and encouraging you to follow), so I tried initiating some conversations at random locations within my comfort zone of where I lived, like cafes, bars or standing in line. Most times (approximately 90%), the conversations went for about thirty seconds before the other person started looking at the ceiling or the carpet and avoiding me completely when I asked them to exchange contact details to stay in touch. The other 10 per cent were an interesting mix, where some people lied to me and gave me phone numbers that they didn't respond to, some met up and went out with me at a later date, but that was the last I saw of them, and some (1% of that 10%) are still friends to this day. Now, if you believe that it might be just me obtaining these results, you would be right. So I decided to enlist some friends to repeat this experiment and — surprise, surprise — they met with similar results, with the big exception being the girls talking to the guys. The guys were always happy to exchange contact details and meet up with the girl later for some reason! Please feel free to replicate this experiment and contact me with your results!

Now compare this to travelling outside your comfort zone, for example, travelling overseas where you don't know anyone, but the surroundings are also unfamiliar to you — the outcome was completely different. What do I mean? When I was travelling overseas, I had the experience aboard a train where at first, I didn't know anyone, but by the time the train reached the destination, I had met some people who were also on their way to the same hostel I was travelling to. After striking up a conversation, we ended up spending the next two weeks sharing rooms and doing everything together just like kindergarten best friends! This included meeting up with them in two separate countries and staying together again. The point that I am sharing with you here is that my overseas experiences were completely different to doing the same random chats with people in and around my comfort zone. Which experience do you believe it would be better to have? Of course, you could state the obvious before answering this question, that is, you could say here that I was in two different situations that brought about different outcomes because of where I was, and that's correct. It was where I was, but it wasn't just about the location! It's about how *you* see yourself within those locations. This is where I encourage you to consider getting unreasonable!

Getting unreasonable

This should sound very familiar to you now! What I encourage you to do now is get unreasonable with your friends, your family, your partner, well, anyone! I don't mean getting unreasonable about any old thing. I encourage you to focus on being unreasonable with your relationship. When I first started writing this book, someone had asked me what was the best friendship I ever had? When I stopped to consider it, I found that I had many good friendships, but no great ones. So, I decided to ask what would make a *great* relationship? This was part of what I called the 'unreasonable period', because to sit around and ask yourself these tough questions and answer them while being honest and authentic with yourself, and accepting that most, if not all, of your relationships are average, is very unreasonable. It takes a certain type of courage, that I know you will find on your journey to find the answer. When I finally had my answer to that question, I had to put this into action, so I went to each of my friends and outlaid my plan for a new *great* relationship.

In the process of finding the answer to what makes a *great* relationship, I had to firstly challenge society's dogma and ask the following questions:

- Who defined what makes a relationship anyway?
- Then who defined what makes a relationship good or even great?
- And for those in society who did define it, what do they know about my life or me for that matter?

Here are the answers that I came up with to these questions:
- I don't know.
- I don't know.
- Nothing.

My answers to these questions therefore made the choice simple for me, as it will for you. I was the person best suited to define what I wanted from the relationships around me. This meant that I also needed to challenge my current values about relationships and change them, as they were obviously not working for me. So, I made choices, firstly to follow the 'Three steps to change my station', make the choice to feel good and follow my gut-brain axis and make the choice of *Being* the eternal warrior and listening to my innate wisdom, as advocated by the Law of Creation. I redefined my values about relationships and then I went to my friends to share this with them. When I told them that a restructure was going to occur for our relationship, most of them were excited about this idea. No one had ever done this before! That is, they liked the concept and were enthusiastic about being part of something new, but as the process went on, I noticed they lost interest and became what I describe as 'drifters' (being the eternal worrier).

I will share with you the outcomes that I believed I wanted from my relationships (my new relationship values), which have now become known as the eight tenets of a *rea*lationship for *Being* the eternal warrior. Like *Being* and the Law of Creation, I had to redefine relationship to *rea*lationship, which means *Being* an eternal warrior for yourself and your partner. For example, a *rea*lationship allows you to be who you really are, no masks, *Being* honest, and in alignment, synergy, authenticity and synergism with yourself within your environment, where you are *Being* your optimal self, living your life of purpose. This automatically immerses you in healthy bio-electric signals and cues and a healthy biofield, which all leads to the ongoing healthy expression of your bio-electric code and genes and you receiving the healthy transmission of you.

The eight tenets of a *rea*lationship
1. Absolute integrity
2. Absolute love (with partners, friends, family, everyone)
3. Absolute honesty and authenticity (no bull, no lies, all the time)
4. Absolute like
5. Absolute respect
6. Absolute trust
7. Absolute communication
8. Absolute commitment (goal and relationship), not investment

Yes, I am using the word 'absolute' a lot, and it's used to make the point that there is no middle ground with this — it is all or nothing. If you cannot say in this relationship, 'I have absolute integrity, love, honesty and authenticity, like, respect trust, communication and commitment', then it's not a relationship you should be in because it is not real (hence realationship). It's that simple. So how did this new regime of relationships work? Well, a lot of my 'friends' just kind of fell away, maybe because I was being unreasonable? Or maybe because they feared the word 'absolute'?

Irrespective of the reason, some ran away and some got really scared, and that was fine, because I accepted that was where they were at in their life, and where they were had little if anything to do with me because it isn't about me.

In short, in my time of *Being* 'unreasonable' and working all this out, you may jump to the conclusion that I became a very lonely man if most friends dropped away. Let me now clarify here the use of the word 'lonely'. In the concept of creating change with the values I held with *Being* in a *rea*lationship, I was not feeling lonely! It was quite the opposite. I was feeling inspired in creating my new reality. However, in the process of creating this change, very few people called and even fewer visited me. I recall the record was six weeks without any of the 320 'friends' in my address book making contact with me after implementing my unreasonable absolute definition of a *rea*lationship. I realise that this is what you would be referring to when you thought that I had become a lonely person, but I did not say *all* friends dropped away. What I soon discovered with my new and improved values for a *rea*lationship was that the people I thought were friends, those that came around and drank beers (my beers) with me were not truly friends, as they were the first to disappear when I implemented my new definition of a *rea*lationship. This then raised the question for me whether any of those 320 people that I considered friends were really friends in the first place.

For those few friends that did visit me after I implemented my new values and definition of a *rea*lationship, their response often went one of two ways. One was to get excited and go for the changes (the least taken option), and the other was to tell me that wanting a change in the friendship meant that I wanted them to change, that it was not their problem but my problem, and that I needed to sort it out for myself. So, they self-excluded themselves from my friendship. The initial response I received was totally unexpected, but please, do not let this discourage you, as you will read below. From my personal experience, I can confidently make you aware that some people will join you, but the majority will not — and would you want friends who also share the same values in a *rea*lationship, surrounding yourself with others who are also *Be*ing eternal warriors, or would you prefer to spend the rest of your life surrounded by the same eternal worriers? For me, it was a no brainer and by now I am certain for you it is too!

As you progress on your journey of redefining you, when you are ready, you will choose to redefine your relationship*s to rea*lationships. To be forewarned is to be forearmed, so I will share with you the three excuses that you may hear from people (based on my friends) who will not join you as you make the choice to redefine your relationships. To make it easier for you, I have also included my response to them, which may assist you when the time comes for you to create *rea*lationships:

1. 'It's your issue.' My response: 'Yes, this is true. Wanting a deeper more honest and authentic, more beautiful relationship is definitely my issue.'
2. 'It's not me, it's you.' My response: 'Yes, it is, see my above response.'
3. 'I'm happy with the way things are.' My response: 'Great! I suppose one happy person in the relationship is better than none!'

Initially, I didn't just give up on the friends who did not want to join me with my new definition of *real*ationship. I went out of my way to explain why I was redefining relationship to *real*ationship. On reflection, maybe I should have been asking why someone would be fighting so vehemently to preserve a relationship that wasn't working, or try to simplify it (as in, well, it's enough for me), when for a 'tiny' change they could have a huge payoff. Creating a *real*ationship with someone would be similar to knowing you will win lotto for sure and all you have to do is pay your $13 to win the $27 million prize. You may consider explaining the change in your values to your friends as going on a journey with you, a journey you would be honoured if they would join you on, because the people you are asking are special and amazing (they must be, or you would not be asking them to accompany you). What have they got to lose for coming on this journey with you? Nothing! In fact, you both have everything to gain from an absolute *real*ationship. If, however, your friend does not come on this journey with you, then they were possibly not a *real* friend. What I discovered was that, for those who don't try, there *are* other people out there looking for this exact higher connection with people like you who are adopting the values of a *real*ationship! So, if you are not actively listening and using the Law of Creation, you will not find these *real*ationships, but if you are making the choice of *Being* the eternal warrior, you are opening yourself to the possibility for absolute eternal *real*ationships. This is what occurred for me!

Although I only had two people who initially resonated with my new values of a *real*ationship, these friends were inspired and wanted to join me in this newfound *real*ationship journey. To this day, these *real*ationships continue, in addition to now having new *real* friends created by *Being* the eternal warrior and implementing the Law of Creation. As previously explained, although many friends self-excluded themselves from the opportunity of creating a *real*ationship and I initially fought to maintain those relationships, when people are not prepared to change or at least be open to the possibility of change, I made the decision to stick to my plan and cease expending energy there. I refocused on those who shared my new values and beliefs around *real*ationships, and on creating and manifesting new people into my life. In hindsight, I probably needed to lose these people as friends — as the old saying goes, it is better to bend than break!

The reality here is that once a person in a relationship redefines what it is to be in that relationship, they can no longer exist on the same relationship ground that they did before. If you believe you can hold on to the same old tenets of a relationship when the other person has changed the game, you are fooling yourself. The fact is, irrespective of who changes the tenets of the relationship, once something like this occurs, it is irreversible. The truth here is that, in any relationship, if the person has just made that change today, the chances are that they have been considering it for a while (as I did). If their partner or one or more of their friends don't make the change with them (as I experienced), then they are all at risk of losing friendships. If, however, the partner or friends accept the new paradigm of the relationship (as two of my friends did), then a new relationship dynamic begins, although the loss of the 'old' friendship still needs to be processed as the new relationship forges forward.

The reality now is that you only have two options — grow with your friends or live without them. This is where you could go with your gut feeling, as it is rarely wrong! A question that you could consider here is why would you ride in a rust-bucket if you could ride in a brand-new Ferrari? If my car analogy doesn't do it for you, then to assist you in understanding the process of redefining relationships, I would like to briefly explain how I began. Firstly, I looked at what I wanted in a relationship. I had to define what a relationship would look like to me using the common names that already exist in terms of relationships. I have listed them in order from what I consider to be least important to most important. Here is what I came up with (if you come up with more, please add them to this list!):

- *acquaintance*: person you can at least say hi to and have the noncommittal chat to about the weather
- *friend*: greater than an acquaintance, you both know something slightly personal about each other, and can chat quietly for at least five minutes about topics greater than the weather without any awkwardness
- *mate*: someone who knows many things about you and vice versa, but they don't know all of your secrets yet
- *pal*: as Billy the Kid said in *Young Guns*, a pal will do anything for you, without question or thought of reward. They do it because they love you and want the best for you
- *spouse:* never questions you as a person and accepts you unconditionally, they are all love
- *family:* all of the above, and they will do whatever you ask and whatever you need in order to see you succeed. They don't have to be related by blood to qualify here either.

From these definitions, the next step was to then come up with a list of absolutes of what I valued in my new definition of a relationship and proceed to apply it. I can hear you ask why I would want to put myself through this in the first place, based on what happened with the majority of my friends. It doesn't sound pleasant, does it? Well, this is what *Being* honest, authentic and unreasonable is all about! Let me share with you *the benefits* of persevering and following my convictions, not living in fear (of not having any friends) or being too lazy to change. Despite the perceived difficulties, I now have friends who are *'pals'*. The paradox here can be that you are all on the same page with what you mutually want from your relationship with each other but were fearful of asking for it in the first place! I will share with you a story as an example of what occurs with my newly found friends based on my definition of a *real*ationship. I will talk about the first friend who became my 'pal' as per my new definition (I will refer to her as PP).

When I first mentioned the bare bones of this idea to PP, she immediately saw the benefits of what we would be trying to do, and knew some of the problems she would have explaining how it worked to other people in her world and to her partner. Despite these possible problems, we pushed on. There were misunderstandings along the way, after all, I don't know of anyone who had attempted this before. As this was uncharted territory for both of us, it could have been easy to worry about the outcomes, but, as I have been explaining throughout this book, you are looking for the eternal warrior within (*Being*), and the amazing thing that was created and manifested from this relationship was truly unpredicted.

Recall that, because the *real*ationship is based on absolute love, trust, honesty and authenticity, PP and I always hear each other out, even when it is painful to hear or say. We talk about everything that we feel, think, experience, and well, everything — no holds barred! Why? Because we based our friendship on the eight tenets, that is, it's based on liking each other (if you don't like each other, why would you love, trust and respect each other?), it's based on respect (we listen to each other and actually hear what is being said, we are there for each other at the drop of hat, and if we can't be, the other knows it's not about them), and it's based on trust (there is little either of us could do, aside from violating the tenets of our *real*ationship, that would break, shake or affect our trust in and for each other and vice versa). Sound good? Heck yeah, it does! Consider what I have now created and manifested into my life. No matter where I am or what I am experiencing, there is someone in the world who will ring me or text me just to say 'I love you', and the best part? There is no awkwardness or misunderstanding about the 'L word'. I get to say it with all my heart openly and honestly to someone I like, love, trust and respect: 'I love you too'. It really is a liberating experience, and the only reason you don't have it now, or at least, not to the extent that I am talking about, is because you subscribe to someone else's definition of what you have in a relationship, or even what a relationship should be!

Why we all fell for it, I don't know. I, however, chose to challenge societal dogma and change my definition of relationship, and I give thanks every day for the depth and beauty I have in my redefined relationships. I encourage you to find yours, as I have, by using everything I have shared with you in this book. *Irrespective of who the person is, a real*ationship needs to be *real.* If you have a relationship that is not 'real', the chances are it's not real because you and your acquaintance, friend, mate, pal, spouse or family have not spent the time to define your relationship, and then all you have is 'ationship' because you are not relating to each other, nor being real. Get some new ideas and new definitions of what to expect from an unreasonable relationship. Recall the eight tenets of a realationship as outlined above and use them as a guide, which I encourage you to borrow.

Love gets unreasonable (your new understanding of how to love)

Love and its energies. What do I mean by this? Diane Ackerman, in *A natural history of love*, pointed out that thirteen per cent of cultures don't even have a word for 'love', so how, then, do they express it?[1] Being a healer, I often hear that I have a healing touch. Now, if you consider that statement, a healer has a healer's touch, so by association, a lover must have a lover's touch! This makes sense, as when your special someone does touch you, you know beyond doubt that they mean it, don't you? They could tell you a thousand times they love you, or you 'mean the earth' to them, but it's not until they actually touch you, such as taking your hand and staring you right in the eye saying those words, that their point will really sink in and hit home. You now know that 'love' is a healthy bio-electric signal and cues, which reinforces a healthy biofield. This creates a nourishing environment for growth of your whole system, including your personal growth and the healthy functioning of your organs, endocrines and body parts, by being immersed in the energies of love, which contributes to making the choice of *Being* the eternal warrior of your life where you are living optimally and purposefully.

Fear, on the other hand, is a bio-electric signal and cue that is hard-wired into us to keep us alive, and it does the opposite to love. It is not until you get stuck in the emotion of fear that it becomes an unhealthy bio-electric signal and cue, which then causes you to become separate or isolated from others and your environment. The consequence of this reactive response for protection from the environment is that it cuts you off from a nourishing and nurturing environment offered by love energies, reinforcing your unhealthy bio-electric signals and cues and an unhealthy biofield and so on.

Cutting yourself off from the nourishing and nurturing environment offered by love energies cuts you off from life. This has been observed with infants for whom, without the healthy bio-electric signals and cues of 'love' and 'the loving touch', every growth parameter is reduced by 30–40 per cent or more, including their size, height and physiology. Why? Because they are not being immersed in healthy bio-electric signals and cues generated by 'love' and 'the loving touch', which is equivalent to losing nourishment and nurturing! The love and support necessary to feel the healthy bio-electric signals and cues associated with feeling protected and safe are absent, and without this, they are trying to protect themselves and self-generate their own healthy bio-electric signals and cues, which only expends energy and impacts on growth. They have not yet been taught the skill of consciously generating their own healthy bio-electric signals and cues.

This not only affects infants but every living person and thing on this planet, including you. In the perceived absence of 'love' is 'fear', and the resultant perceived 'fear' will impact on, and inevitably shut off, your system. How can and does this occur? I have discussed this in terms of bio-electric signals and cues. Fear is a bio-electric signal and cue that, when perceived as unhealthy (such as being stuck in fear for a prolonged period of time), will become an unhealthy bio-electric signal and cue, which creates an unhealthy biofield and the unhealthy expression of the bio-electric code and genes, resulting in receiving the unhealthy transmission of you. This then has an impact on your anatomy and physiology, for example, on your hypothalamic-pituitary-adrenal axis (HPA-axis), which is often referred to as your master switch. Essentially, your perceptions of your environment will impact on your master switch, so if your perception is dominated by fear that results in unhealthy bio-electric signals and cues, this will activate your HPA-axis!

Let's consider stress as an example. Why? Because stress is something that you cannot see but is instead perceived by your brain (recall my discussion of perception). Bearing this in mind, you will perceive stress differently from other people. For example, if you focus on a loud noise (such a loud motorbike riding past a café where you are sitting) and you perceive this as a scary noise (something to fear), then by default it is a stress for you. You automatically self-generate an unhealthy bio-electric signal and cue to this noise, recalling from our past discussion that everything has its own unique frequency fingerprint. What does this mean? Well, whenever you see, feel, smell, hear, taste or even think about this noise, the unhealthy bio-electric signals and cues for it are still present, and are exacerbated whenever we hear or recall this noise. This then automatically activates your HPA-axis and your body goes into its hard-wired natural protection mode response (fight, flight, or freeze), as if you are about to face a life or death situation — which you are not, it's only a noise you are perceiving as fearful, but your physiological responses don't know any better.

Now this is okay if, as previously mentioned, the perceived noise was a matter of life or death. You would be one hundred per cent justified, and it would be necessary for you to engage in protection mode, otherwise death could result! Once the threat is gone, your HPA-axis will automatically 'lift its foot off the accelerator' and your body returns to a normal state of growth (the opposite of protection mode). However, what occurs when the noise from the motorbike is not a direct threat to life, yet whenever we think about it, we experience spikes of stress? Well, you continue to be immersed in unhealthy bio-electric signals and cues related to this noise, which become amplified each time you think about it, and as the HPA-axis cannot differentiate whether the threat is real or not, your perception of the noise is enough to maintain unhealthy bio-electric signals and cues, which initiates the protection mode in a non-life or death scenario.

What does this mean for you? You now are aware that protection mode overrides growth mode, and as such, when the HPA-axis is activated due to a perceived fear (a non-life or death event), instead of being in the growing and developing mode, you will find yourself in constant protection mode. Unlike a life or death event, which very quickly resolves itself, your body continues to be stimulated into self-generating unhealthy bio-electric signals and cues, which keeps it being in protection mode based on the perceived stress! This scenario does not allow for health, wellbeing, growth and development. How, then, can you create change here when you perceive the threat as being real, when it is in fact not presenting to you as the life or death situation?

One possible way to create change, which I recommend highly to you, comes from the energy of love, which you are better able to transfer through touch than with words.

What do I mean by this? Well, recall from above what love and the loving touch mean to infants. You could say to the infant 'I love you' one million times, but this will not convey the meaning of love unless you actually touch them with love. With infants, words alone do not convey the message of love, as they have not yet learned the word 'love' and have no idea what it means as yet! Mind you, many adults do not know what the word means either, and confuse love with sex, nor do they understand what constitutes a loving touch. It is not about placing your hands on someone's genitals, albeit the loving touch between you and your partner may involve touching on or near the genitals! The power of touch reminds me of a story that I will use to explain touch and its effects.

I vividly remember driving in a car with a group of friends, one being my female roommate. When she playfully slapped the inside of my leg, the mood in the car immediately changed! I could not articulate the change that happened, but there was a definite change in mood. What just occurred? What questions were being raised by the other friends in the car who saw what just occurred? I will point out here that I don't have any issues around personal space. It does not bother me how close people get, and I like being touched by girls on the inside of my leg, but in the appropriate setting! Not everyone, however, shares the same belief, and that was evident in the car that day, where people's perceptions ran wild based on this touch to my inner thigh!

In addition to this experience, here are some other things that I have noticed with regards to touch. When engaged in talking to someone, I have been known to lightly touch the person on the elbow or forearm as a gentle reminder of my engagement with them (recall here chapter 11 and listening). This touch reinforces to the other person that I have been kind enough to stand there and listen to them, and that I would like them to engage with me and not the corners of the room where they may be distractedly looking. Interestingly, in these situations where I have used touch in conversations, I have observed two distinct effects: the first is kind of funny, that is, if you know what is happening. The person who has been drifting off usually gets a small fright, and quickly excuses themselves from the conversation. The other response, and my favoured one, is that the person I am talking with suddenly realises that I was listening to them, that is, *really* listening and not just waiting for my turn to speak, and they get a whole new passion for the conversation that we are having.

To me, this is an amazing phenomenon — that with this small gesture called touch, you can make someone either flee or focus! The power of touch is often underestimated. It is, however, well documented that, without touch (either the loving touch or physical touch), as previously discussed, infants under-develop, and it is suggested that babies without this contact die within twenty-four hours after birth. A study at Princeton University found that babies and kids who are touched a lot, until twelve years old, are much more able to be intimate and loving in a *real*ationship. They found these people are more able to snuggle, cuddle, hug, touch and hold hands. The people who didn't receive that amount of touch as a child are very uncomfortable and struggle to make that kind of connection with people later on in their life.[2]

Another study that I will share with you, which demonstrates the power of touch and supports my theory of touching an elbow or forearm in a conversation, involves researchers putting money in the change box of a public telephone. When people used the phone to make a call, inevitably, many of them would check the receiver at the bottom to see if there was any change left, and of course, there was as the researchers always left $1.35. After the person used the phone and pocketed the money, the researchers sent a person to ask them if they had found any money in the change box, as they had left their change behind. The research documented that 97 per cent of the people who pocketed the change would answer no! Then in the same experiment setup, the researchers changed the design slightly. The research person who asked if they found any change would also reach out and touch the person on the shoulder or the arm. In this scenario, the researchers reported that 95 per cent of people said, 'Yes, I found money in there', and they offered it to the research person.[3] How amazing is that? The power of touch!

Love and cell states (i.e. protection or growth)

The cellular biologist, Bruce Lipton, demonstrated in his research that cells grow and develop with the healthy bio-electric signals and cues associated with 'love' and do the opposite with prolonged 'fear' (unhealthy bio-electric signal and cue).[4] From this, you may infer that every cell in your body, when immersed in healthy bio-electric signals and cues, will create a healthy biofield and the healthy expression of our bio-electric code and allow for the healthy growth, development and strength of our cells, such as immune system cells.

As previously discussed, by creating choice, *Being* conscious, honest, and living in alignment, synergy, authenticity and synergism allows you to create healthy bio-electric signals and cues, which can be self-sustaining. Healthy bio-electric signals and cues may be received through love and the loving touch, such as receiving a hug, provided it is perceived in that way, thereby reinforcing and enhancing your own healthy bio-electric signals and cues, so that you can be open to *Being* your optimal self and living your life of purpose, based on how you choose to see your life. This means that the love you choose to feel, and the love you receive from the loving touch, provides you with ways to communicate love, not only for yourself, but with other people, and in so doing, you can influence your cell health and your fellow human being without misunderstandings or fears of rejection! This, in addition to what I have presented to you above, demonstrates the importance of the healthy bio-electric signals and cues associated with the unique frequency fingerprint of love and touch.

Love – the word

Love, as a word, has different meanings and is interpreted in many ways — sometimes in ways that create fear and conflict, thereby creating unhealthy bio-electric signals and cues. When I was living in China, I learned that there are actual rules that govern what and to whom you can say things to in relation to, not only the 'love' word, but many different words. The table below gives you a brief idea of how you would use words to address different people in Chinese.

Chinese words/phrase	English translation	To whom you would use these words	Frequency or how often used
Wo ai ni	I love you	husband to wife or wife to husband	Rarely
Wo xi huan ni	I like you	boyfriend girlfriend	Sometimes
Depends on which part of China you come from (e.g. northern China): Ge men er	You're a friend	boy to boy or boy to girl or girl to boy or girl to girl	Sometimes

Although the above table is not an exhaustive list, and it was only compiled based on my experience in China, what it demonstrates is that people, even husbands and wives, are not using 'love' as much as they could, and based on the energies of love, the people I surveyed are denying themselves all the benefits that go with it. This is an interesting observation, considering that, according to Rose Quong in *Chinese characters: their wit and wisdom*, the character for love in Chinese translates to 'that which gives breath (i.e. spirit) to the heart, with graceful motion', yet it's not applied in everyday life based on the people I surveyed.

Chinese is not the only culture that demonstrates how *love* has different meanings and how it can be misunderstood in conversation. Our Western culture also creates misunderstandings with the word love, and I will share with you another one of my personal experiences to demonstrate this point. When I was in China, I went travelling on my own and mistakenly left my passport back in my flat. When I turned up to the hostel in a different Chinese province to where I was based, I was informed that without a valid passport, I couldn't book in to the hostel. This was not a problem, except that it was about 11.30 pm! I texted my roommate, but couldn't get in contact, so in desperation, I tried one of my other classmates, who did receive the text. In short, this person obligingly ran around town to find my roommate, who eventually got a fax of the passport through to me. The faxed passport was not accepted, but before I knew that outcome, in that moment I was, needless to say, extremely happy because I assumed it meant I didn't have to sleep on the street, so I texted her, 'Thank you, love you so much right now'. Now, my words apparently were too much for the girl to accept! Based on her perceptions of love and what that meant, she panicked to the point where she had to ask my roommate (who knew me a little better on account of us living together) if I meant anything by it. Thankfully, my roommate put her fears to rest. Although use of the word 'love' in this situation carried with it a healthy bio-electric signal and cue, it was perceived, based on this classmate's filters and what she made it mean, as an unhealthy signal and cue!

Although thirteen per cent of cultures reportedly have no word for love as mentioned above, my culture does, but unfortunately, it's been misused and misunderstood, but, hey, what's in a word anyway? As the above story demonstrated, a lot, depending on who is using the word and to whom! Another personal experience where using the love word was misinterpreted was when I met a most charming and captivating girl at university. We went and saw a movie together, had a late dinner, and stayed up all night talking, then went to our respective classes and met up that afternoon in the computer room to do some work before heading out again. Now during the interactions and conversations, this girl did something that I perceived as being incredibly cute and endearing, and from my mouth came, 'That's so cute, I love you for that'. Well, it was as if I'd said, 'I am a vampire and I want to suck your blood'. That was almost the end of our friendship and budding romantic realationship right there!

She went rigid and said, 'Oh my god, what did you say?' I then spent the next thirty minutes or so explaining that I knew I couldn't 'love' her in the short time that we had known each other. I highlighted that she was interpreting the word 'love' in a very different way, and that she shouldn't panic because I was not an axe murderer (as they are apparently the only people who fall in love that quick, at least, according to her!). Another misunderstanding in using the word 'love'! Maybe those cultures without the word know something that our culture doesn't!

As I have shared with you, misunderstandings do arise when with using the word 'love'. I assume that people may misunderstand the word as only belonging in one intimate realationship, but if you don't accept someone else's definition of a realationship, why, then, should you accept when, where and how you should be able to use the love word? Or when, where and how you can display your affection for a fellow human being? Well, answering this question proved challenging, and since I preach flexibility, I figured that I would compromise. If the Eskimos can have sixteen different words for snow, why can't we have more than one word for love, or at the very least different words associated with love to describe the situation you are in. After all, the Chinese do, as discussed above, but they are a society, albeit a Chinese one, and didn't I advocate the need to question society? And that's what I am doing now.

Our Western society has a very limiting view around love. Why do you believe this is the case? Let's get your mind working then (remember, yours is as good as mine and vice versa and together — if you are emitting healthy bio-electric signals and cues, you resonate this) so that you can start to evolve the word 'love' and not be limited by its use. In my endeavour to answer this question about love, this is what I came up with, but please feel free to add more if you wish.

I playfully suggest that to tell someone you just met that you love them, you can use a word called 'lemma' — 'I lemma you'. I created the word lemma by dropping 'ove' and adding the name of the person to the 'L' from love, hence lemma, which I have defined as the act of loving someone you just met, understanding full well that you do not know everything about them, nor are you truly 'in love' (and that you are not an axe murderer!). To tell a friend of the opposite sex you love them but you are after a platonic *real*ationship, the word you use is 'lill' — 'I lill you'. Lill is the act of loving a friend where neither of you have any illusions — yes, you are friends, and that is it. You are the closest of friends and will redefine what closeness and intimacy between friends is while still honouring the classic code of platonic *real*ationships. And of course, you have had the sex conversation (since we are being honest). To tell someone you love them while they are taking you to the cleaners behind your back, the word is 'lassandra' — 'I lassandra you'. To tell an ex-partner you love them, the word is 'letra'. 'I letra you'. Letra is the act of loving an ex, understanding full well that you have both moved on, that you are not trying to win back their affections or curry favour — you are just glad that they are still in your life and you honour the tenets of a *real*ationship spelled out in this book. To tell a friend of the same sex you love them: girls, you're fine — females in Western culture generally do not have an issue with this; guys in Western culture seem to exhibit the tendency of telling their male friends they 'love them' when they get drunk! These are all playful terms that I have shared with you to show you that you can create your 'love vocabulary' and I encourage you to do so. Every person who I have shared these words and definitions with has enjoyed a laugh and been entertained but has also understood the point of the conversation. Now being serious, there are four fantastic definitions of states of love coming from the Greek language that I discovered in my research.

Greek words for love (classic definitions)

In Greek, the word *love* is meant to cover many states. Here are four of these states:

1. Eros — physical love — is the attraction between two people that drives them physically together.

2. Pia — familial love — is the love you feel for family members (parents, your children, your extended family/clan). Pia is the 'blood is thicker than water' love that binds people together.
3. Philos — brotherly love — is love that extends past the family to members of a larger group that sees themselves as having common bonds (in a war situation, for example, this is the love that drives soldiers to risk their lives for their comrades).
4. Agape — total acceptance of all beings — includes accepting and loving the prostitutes, the murderers, the rapists, the torturers and so on. Agape doesn't see any difference between people. It sees the 'I am' in all. Agape doesn't expect anything in return. It is all.

An interesting point to make here is that most relationship advice is centred on communication. Would it not stand to reason that, knowing the above conditions, communication would be easier and so frequent that there would never be room for misunderstanding? Experts also state that for good health, you should have a good stable relationship, again I believe that is achievable because communication is key to a relationship and if you have all eight tenets of a *real*ationship met, it would flow easily. As communication is truly key to successful relationships, how long do you believe it takes for people to work out that you are 'living in your head'? The answer is not very long, so why then do people stay in dead relationships?

Possibly because you are too lazy to change it, or fear being single, or hate being wrong (in your choice of partner) or you want a return on the investment — on the love, time, money and energy you feel you put into the relationship. For example, what is the reaction of someone who feels short-changed after a relationship has ended? You know it, you've seen it, and it's what gives people in divorce such a bad name — that senseless, ill-advised and childish behaviour that we all detest, where they try to take everything and deliberately attempt to cause as much damage (financially, in the family, socially and so on) as they can while failing to honour the words they spoke to create the vows of their wedding. So why do it? Because they get to feel vindicated that they were right.

From my clinical and life experiences, it is hard to have a good, stable relationship without the eight tenets above being met. It is made even more challenging if you don't know what a good, stable relationship is in the first place. You just have to look at the divorce rate statistics and look at your friends and how many relationships they may have gone through to find the right partner! Take a look around you at the number of people who are in their forties and fifties (nowadays even their twenties and thirties) and still single and living alone because they were not successful in establishing a lifelong *real*ationship.

This is why I advocate to you that you need to define and be clear as to what you constitute to 'be in a *real*ationship' with someone means, whether that is between you and your partner, a friend, a work colleague or a family member.

Doing this will improve communication between you and the person because you will be clear as to where you are both coming from and where you are going in the relationship, where you are *Being* the eternal warrior within your environment (the relationship) so that both of you reinforce and strengthen each other's healthy biofield and the subsequent healthy expression of your bio-electric code and so on. This provides the relationship with the best possible chance of achieving the purpose of the *real*ationship.

What do you want to accomplish by being part of this *real*ationship?

If you were going into a business relationship, the chances are, if you were smart about it, you would write a business plan, you would study the market, do up profit-and-loss sheets, and look at the overall feasibility of the project. Going into a personal relationship should be exactly the same. You need to establish a goal to start working towards — rather than just a direction, you need a vector. A vector is something containing the information about where you are going, the direction and the velocity (speed). If you have these things in place, then checking in to see if the relationship is working will be a simple process. Yes, it may sound unusual to do this, but recall, you are challenging current societal dogmas on relationships (e.g. 'They are cute, I will date them') and creating rules so that you and your partner can achieve the best possible outcome for both of you and all your relationships. Recall that I would like you to have the most amazing and abundantly loving relationship because that will create healthy bio-electric signals and cues, which will enrich the environment, of which I am a part.

Considering this, and because this section of the book is a 'want to' section, I encourage you to go crazy, that is, use the table below to list all the 'wants' you want from your *real*ationships and from your life together. If you are, for example, reading this book with your partner, you can list your 'wants' and your partner's 'wants' separately, and a list of 'wants' that you both share and have in common. It does not matter if you don't obtain all of your wants (yours, theirs and together), the key thing here is initiating the process of having a goal, after all, the only truly poor are those without dreams.

Table 14.1 Wants in life – rank out of 10

My wants	My partners wants	Our wants

What are you actually going to accomplish?

When listing out your 'wants' or 'goals', they can be anything from saying 'I love you' daily to having a million dollars in the bank in five years. The good news is that they are goals, so they must be specific and attainable (i.e. no point aiming for a million dollars in five years if you live on one income of $50,000 per annum). If you would like to specifically set a crazy, nonsensical, pie-in-the-sky goal that seems unattainable (like that example), you need to refer to my book, *Real health: The system that needs an overhaul*, because it can guide you on the 'how to' component of achieving goals. I encourage you, however, to make your wants and goals malleable, flexible and completely changeable (provided both parties agree with the changes if the 'want' is a shared one). This section is the more down-to-earth and realistic component of the dreams section. It is also where you prioritise how committed you are to each project and goal. The more committed you are to a project (e.g. the higher its priority), the sooner you will achieve it. For example, you may be prepared to wait until after you have purchased a house for the Caribbean cruise.

How are you going to communicate this to your partner?

Effective and clear communication is usually an issue in every relationship, and is vitally important, as discussed above. When communication does not work, you often blame the other person for not delivering their message well, and hold them responsible for communication breakdown. But communication is, in fact, a function of what is heard rather than what is being said. What are you choosing to hear or not hear from your partner? Do you have filters (recall the 18 filters)?

Having said this, when figuring out how to effectively communicate with another person (e.g. your partner), I recommend you purchase How *to effectively communicate with [insert spouse's/partner's name here]*. I believe that this would provide a better explanation on how to effectively communicate with them. Cannot find this book? Well, if you have not already written it yourself, the chances are your partner has not gotten around to writing out the best ways to communicate with them either. Until your partner sits down and writes *How to effectively communicate with [insert spouse's/partner's name here]* for you to have, read and use, I encourage you to complete this exercise — write a manual entitled *How to effectively communicate with [insert your name here]*. First, I would ask that you sit down and apply the Law of Creation, where you actively listen, feel and think about it, and then eventually write the manual. It should contain all the things you do want to talk about, don't want to talk about, sensitive topics, personal information, desires and goals for life, embarrassing information and so on. We are all unique, so too is the way we communicate.

Be generous

In writing your manual, and in life, be generous. That is, give people more than they expect and do it cheerfully. It is a sure winner, and who better to do this for than your family, partner or friends. You should also do it for strangers too, as they are friends that we haven't met yet!

Don't be right!

I once asked a client who continually argued with his wife what they argued about? He told me: 'About everything, all the little things, random facts, that kind of stuff.' I then asked him if he corrected her and why he had to correct her, and he replied that he didn't really know — it was just their 'pattern'. I asked him what this 'pattern' normally led to, and he replied that normally he would end up out in the shed working on 'something' and his wife would end up baking or watching her shows. I pointed out to him that their pattern (him being right all the time) seemed to make him and his wife spend lots of time alone, to which he agreed. In discussing this with him, he could understand that being right (his payoff) cost him love (his cost). He wanted to create change, so a solution we came up with was to change his need to always be right.

Being able to 'not have to be right' became his focus, either by agreeing to disagree, accepting the other person's point of view as valid (even if it was wrong in his eyes) or outright agreeing, which was achieved by saying to the other person, 'Yes, you are right'. Using these words usually ends any argument immediately as there is nothing to argue about anymore!

The point being made here is that giving up the 'need to be right' really means to surrender the 'need to make someone else wrong'! Instead, you need to identify what value is being violated and assess its current priority in your life (find the real reason or undercurrent). Then you need to offer a solution (recall from chapter 8 that life is problems and living is solving them).

A final word on relationships: be committed to *real*ationships, not invested

The difference between the words 'committed' and 'invested' and the states that they cause in relationships is truly amazing. If you have invested yourself, your time, your energy and your love into the relationship, then you have set yourself up for a potential disaster, a time bomb, if you will. An investment is something you make when you have an excess of something (e.g. money) and expect a payoff later on — either when you have a 'deficiency' or are just ready to, using the example of money, 'cash out'. To be invested in your relationship implies the exact same meaning. It assumes that you are waiting for a 'lump sum' payout of some kind. Investments usually mean you put something in once and then wait, without really being involved or participating.

Being committed in your *real*ationship, however, is a much healthier option. Why? Because being committed means you are constantly involved and participating in something, rather than leaving it to build on its own and waiting for a payout later. You know when people commit to something, they tend to work on it, whereas things that people are not committed to inevitably fail. Having two people commit to a *real*ationship is a 'test of fire', where no one needs to be blamed if it does not succeed, which is rarely the case. Blaming someone if it fails only implies that someone was not committed enough. Being committed to a *real*ationship means there is no blame, no victim mentality, and you are still responsible and in charge of your life (i.e. Being the eternal warrior). Picture in your mind the difference in performance of an athletic sprinter who is committed to winning gold at the Olympics as opposed to one who is invested in the gold. If they raced, who do you believe would win?

Real and false self

There is a real you (a healthy bio-electric signal and cue) and a false you (an unhealthy bio-electric signal and cue, which we previously discussed as masks). The real you is the one you usually show to your partner, where you are able to be honest and authentic, particularly when you get to know your partner better. Being real means that you are not scared to be yourself, you speak without the need for protection, the 'warts and all' you. The *false* you (masks) are the ones you show off at first meetings so that you are accepted and not rejected. You want to come across as being usually fun, witty, intelligent and well-mannered, or whatever mask you wear to impress and belong with those you are meeting.

When it comes to long-term relationships, I recommend not confusing the two, and attempting as soon as possible to show the real you to your partner. If you are going to spend time, any length of time (like a lifetime), with this person, you had better get rid of the false self, the masks, the act, now rather than later because it inevitably falters. If you enter a relationship wearing masks and create these changes early, your partner may believe that you lied or, at best, falsely advertised yourself, but it's necessary to be real, honest and authentic. This is where you make the choice of *Being* the eternal warrior, *Being* conscious, responsible, flexible and knowing your values of a *real*ationship. If you can achieve this with your partner, you should also practise this with your friends and family. Most people see through the false us/masks anyway, and the further that our real self is away from our false self/masks translates to increased stress, and no one wants or needs more stress in their life.

Words and actions

Say what you mean (clear communication) and do what you say (be honest and authentic). Always live up to your word because when all else falls away, you can still have your word. If you have been honest and authentic in keeping your word, then people will still trust in you.

Integrity

Integrity is following through on everything in the above section.

The take-home message — your transformation from eternal *worrier* to eternal *warrior*

The *eternal worrier smiles* because they are reasonable and accept relationships as they are and exist mostly within their comfort zone. They are reasonable about everything and their relationships are not *real*ationships that obey the eight tenets of *real*ationships. They smile because they have drama in their life when they fall in and out of love, because they have not defined what love means to them. They smile because they are ignorant to their own and their partner's wants and are able to avoid responsibility because of this.

The eternal worrier smiles because they and their partners have no idea of how important communication truly is in relationships. They are invested in their relationships instead of being committed, and they smile because they break their word and have no understanding of how breaking their integrity and not being honest and authentic costs them who they are, or that they lose others' trust by doing so. As they have not defined love, they do not understand the higher forms of love (e.g. agape) and will therefore suffer what is given to them and blame others for their misfortune in love. They find the need to be right but cost themselves the love they truly want.

The *eternal warrior smiles* because they take the actions to make themselves unreasonable while being outside of their comfort zone (where all change and growth occur). They are unreasonable about everything, and their relationships are all *real*ationships that obey the eight tenets of *real*ationships. They smile because they define what love means to them, they choose to express it in all ways, especially touch, because they know it stimulates growth and strengthens immunity. They are consistently moving toward agape.

The eternal warrior smiles because they know their own and their partner's wants and are authentic, where both people are *Being* in alignment, synergy, authenticity and synergism, *Being* their optimal selves within their environment so that they reinforce and strengthen their and their partner's healthy biofield and the subsequent healthy expression of our bio-electric code and gene, and receive the healthy transmission of themselves. They smile because they and their partner have written *How to effectively communicate with [insert spouse's/partner's name here]* for each other to demonstrate that they are generous and are committed to the *real*ationship (not invested in it). The eternal warrior smiles because they honour their word and live with integrity, revealing their real self as frequently as possible until it is a natural way of being. As they are loving and can express love based on their definition of it, they can relinquish the need to be right, and when their values are being violated, they prefer to find a solution to resolve it. They keep their word, they maintain honesty and authenticity, others trust them, and they create their own healthy bio-electric signals and cues, a healthy biofield and the healthy expression of their bio-electric code and genes.

CHAPTER 15

Living and not living: identifying and implementing

Living and not living

If it's not feeling, it is dead. You need to feel to be alive. If it's not moving, it is dead. You need to move to be alive. If it doesn't make sound, it is dead. You need to make sound to be alive (even breathing makes sound).

If you are alive (not just taking up space and oxygen), then you should be experiencing emotions (this is feeling), not faking them. You should be living a life 'on the move' (moving), not talking about one or existing in your comfort zone. Others should know that you are around and that you have something to offer because they can hear you at the appropriate time (making noise). If not, you are classified as being 'dead', so to speak. You may not be physically dead, but it is still a potential waste of a life. So, what are you doing? Dare to let yourself and others know that you are alive. Feel, even if it is uncomfortable or unpleasant or different. This is where you can use the pro·m·emo essences or UEFT to assist you to feel the emotions of living. Get out and about, do something, interact with others and experience them and life. Remember that all growth occurs when you are out of your comfort zone. The benefits are endless.

Identify

What do I mean? Firstly, identifying is one of your main goals in life. I have left the discussion of this topic until now in the book because, now that you know all the things we have previously discussed, understanding this stage will be relatively easy. So, let's learn to identify with yourself, as it may be one of the best *real*ationships you will ever start. Once you have mastered identifying with yourself, you can learn to identify with others. One of the many jobs I had while supporting myself through university was in customer service. I was extremely good at my job, simply because I could relate to the customers' problems. The customer service job I had was in complaints. Do you know why most people get annoyed, frustrated and angry, which causes them to complain? Because, as an eternal worrier, they believe that their identity has been compromised. Recall from chapter 12 that expectations and values influence our identity and how we feel within ourselves.

For example, you decide that you are going to pay $10 for a high-quality coffee rather than a $1 cup of coffee. There is now an expectation of high quality from that $10 cup of coffee, and if you feel that it's not the way you wanted it because it does not match the value you perceived, the chances are that you will complain! Why? Because your expectation of a high-quality coffee was unmet and the value of the money that you worked hard to earn was diminished, so your identity was compromised.

We complain when our identity is compromised based on our expectations and values (usually when they are not met). We know the reason to complain has to be powerful because for us to complain, we need to overcome two things:

- It's not nice to complain — most people do not complain because they enjoy it.
- You know when you do complain, the snotty-nosed jerk opposite you couldn't really care if you did or did not get what you wanted. What makes it worse is that they then turn to you and says something like 'I really feel for you' or 'I understand where you're coming from', and the insincerity is overwhelming! Worse still is when they defend the company and the company has actually made an error that they are attempting to cover up. No wonder people in today's society hate the absence of service we are currently dealing with, and in every customer service poll, people indicate a rising frustration at the lack of good customer service.

Do you know why I was good at my customer service job and what made my bosses (and the people complaining) agape me so much? Simple! I treated everyone who came to me in the way that I would want to be treated — that is, I *listened* to them. I made the effort to actually understand their problem, rephrased it to make sure I had heard and understood their complaint right, and then took personal responsibility for it and dealt with the person directly. Identifying with them and their complaint allows for a better understanding of the person and their situation. If you can identify with people, most common misunderstandings can easily be avoided. So, identify — with yourself, others and situations. Identifying who you are, your boundaries, your expectations, your wants, your feelings, your beliefs and everything that you are is so vitally crucial to your life. Without knowing who you are, how can you have a great life, let alone create healthy bio-electric signals and cues that, as you now realise, create the foundations for the healthy expression of you? To identify what is going on relies on all the other topics covered in this book. For example, how could you identify what is occurring for you without being conscious? You can't! This is where you need to continue making the choice to redefine you and your *real*ationships and making the choice of *Being* the eternal warrior.

Implement

There is no point knowing all of this great stuff if you don't use it. How much of it you decide to implement in your life is completely up to you. No one can force you to use it, but I hope that you do use it. Anything that you learn or read about is only theory, the magic happens when you put theory into practice! This is what is referred to as wisdom — there is a difference between 'knowing the path' and 'walking the path'.

The take-home message — your transformation from eternal *worrier* to eternal *warrior*

The *eternal worrier smiles* because they become numb to their life. They end up like this because feeling their emotions makes them feel uneasy or weak. They therefore distrust their natural 'gut feeling' and often find their life in folly because they do not listen to themselves. The eternal worrier smiles because they are stagnant, that is, they do not move, and their processing of life (mental and emotional) is restricted due to their physical body being restricted and stagnant. They smile because they believe that making any noise is contributing to other people's lives, rather than making quality noise (e.g. having an inspiring conversation with a friend). The eternal worrier smiles because they are able to be ignorant to what is occurring in their life (feelings, thoughts, actions and so on) and are able to blame others when something in their life is not working. They must suffer when things are not working, because they cannot identify it to change it into something that does work for them. They smile because they avoid responsibility of implementing anything that will improve their life.

The *eternal warrior smiles* because they know to feel their life. They live in harmony with their emotions and trust their 'gut feeling'. They smile because they move, and movement assists with the processing of emotions (movement is the natural state of the body). They smile because, when they make noise, they are being themselves and contributing to life. The eternal warrior smiles because they are able to identify what is occurring in their life (feelings, thoughts, actions and so on) and are able to know themselves, and when something is not working, they quickly identify it and change it into something that does work for them. They smile because they implement all that will make their world better!

CHAPTER 16

Hints and tips to pave the way to Being an eternal warrior

Realise how much time you have

William Dear made a film called *The school of life*, where he brilliantly brings to light the question, 'How much time do we have?' From this movie, the answer is, 'Not a lot'. This is without a doubt one of my favourite films and I recommend it highly. I bring this up here because, from this point on, this very second, on this very day, you should start realising how valuable and how precious every minute, every second truly is. You may have heard the quote from Marc Levy:

If you want to know the value of one year, just ask a student who failed a course.

If you want to know the value of one month, ask a mother who gave birth to a premature baby.

If you want to know the value of one hour, ask the lovers waiting to meet.

If you want to know the value of one minute, ask the person who just missed the bus.

If you want to know the value of one second, ask the person who just escaped death in a car accident.

And if you want to know the value of one-hundredth of a second, ask the athlete who won a silver medal in the Olympics.[1]

Now, I agree with you that this is a cliché, but it is also true. There is no point harping on it; you just have to accept that you don't have a lot of time here and that is all there is to it. So, start listening, feeling, then thinking.

An interesting exercise I use to remind myself of what is important is to picture myself locked in a room, knowing full well that in three and half minutes I would die and all I have is my mobile phone. Who would I call and what would I say? I ask you to enter into the spirit of this and play this game. You don't have to call anyone, but run though what you would say in your own mind. Before you begin, I want to bring to your attention the following fact — time doesn't exist! Did you know this? The thing (time) which runs your life doesn't actually exist! Humans made it up. Time is a man-made tool, albeit a useful one, but still just a concept or tool. So, if you realise that time doesn't exist, does that make you feel a little differently about things? If not, let's continue with the above exercise. Recall all the people you would have called in that three and half minutes and what you were intending to say to them. Then look at the reasons why you don't actually say these things to them every chance you have!

I will assume that one of the things that you would want to say to the person you called is 'I love you', as would most people. Although the loving touch is more powerful, as previously discussed, it still begs the question why it is that people, including you, don't say 'I love you', or at least say it often enough? Well, there are many reasons, and some that I commonly hear in clinical practice are:

- The time wasn't appropriate.
- I assume they know I love them anyway.
- I will eventually get around to it sometime.
- I will, when the time is right.
- People may believe I'm strange for saying it all the time.

Let's now look at these statements about why people don't say 'I love you', or in fact any of the other important things in your life against your old truth about time. Let's start with saying 'I love you' or anything of importance — when would that not be appropriate? I was in disbelief when that was offered up as an excuse. Come on, really? Who doesn't like to hear they are loved, and how could that possibly be inappropriate? And you know what is said about assume? It makes an 'ass' out of 'u' and 'me'! Be the warrior, not an ass (worrier)!

The next statement starts with 'I will' and should really end with 'never happen' because 'sometime' never comes. This could also be considered procrastination, and procrastination can be considered a form of laziness, which we have discussed in depth. The same is true for the third statement, because the time is rarely, if ever, 'right'. Don't procrastinate or be lazy.

And the final statement, when investigated, becomes, 'I would rather be considered "normal" (an eternal worrier) and have my partner or friend *not* know that I care about them'. However, when *Being* an eternal warrior, saying 'I love you' **would** be 'normal', and it would be authentic and honest. I would rather be considered 'strange' and have my partner or friend know that I care about them. Also, if you recall the *message from water* from chapter 11, both of you have just shared something beautiful that aids in your health and wellbeing, all for the small price of possibly being perceived as strange. These excuses are all unhealthy bio-electric signals and cues that you, *Being* an eternal warrior, would not choose to use.

Now, if you accept that each and every second you have here on this great rock, we call earth is precious, why would you want to spend any more time here in the 'feeling bad' hole discussed in chapter 13? You wouldn't! The second you realise you are in it and have spent any amount of time in it, you should be scrambling for any way out that you can find.

As a very interesting side note here: what about statements such as 'I need some time alone' or 'me time'? Firstly, time doesn't exist, and secondly, you could not be separate or alone if you tried. I will very briefly explain that now. We are all intimately connected by energy. Quantum physics is explaining this concisely now via a theory called 'entanglement'. If you would like to know more (but without the scientific jargon), please pick up my book on consciousness, *The golden ring*. The point that I am making here is that all these excuses regarding time lead to the same outcome — unhealthy bio-electric signals and cues. Love and touch, honesty and authenticity, *Being* conscious (aware), listening to your gut feeling, following the feel 'good' and avoiding the feel 'not good' signals are all pathways to creating healthy bio-electric signals and cues, a healthy biofield and the healthy expression of the bio-electric code and genes, which ultimately leads to a change in the 'you' program because you are open to receiving the healthy transmission of you so that you can live life optimally and with purpose. In addition to this, the following list of recommendations will also contribute to generating healthy bio-electric signals and cues.

Get up the same time every morning

Ideally, you should live your life in accordance with the four seasons. The Chinese actually had this worked out a few thousand years ago. Read on and see if this doesn't make complete sense to you. In spring time, you should retire early and rise early, in summer time you retire late and rise early, in autumn time you retire and rise with sun, and in winter time you retire early and rise with sun. These principles are from the ancient Chinese medical text called *The yellow emperor's classic of internal medicine*, and while they make perfect sense for you and your health, you may have a hard time convincing your boss that showing up to work two hours later than your starting time because you are listening to ancient Chinese wisdom is a good idea. Would it get you off the hook? Possibly not (which is a shame), so instead, make it easy on your body with the next best thing — a pre-programmed time that it knows is wake-up time.

Now, if I had a dollar for every time someone told me they wake up tired and lethargic, and then proceeded to tell me about their sleeping pattern — getting to bed at erratic hours all nights of the week, trying to do a thousand things every day and getting nowhere, and trying to sleep in for that ever elusive five minutes more every morning - well, I would be living in the Bahamas (I hear that it's warm and a tax haven!). Here is a little secret — those 'extra' five minutes don't exist because time doesn't exist! It does not matter how much more time you try to 'steal', you're going to be tired. There are two ways to deal with it. One: in an ideal world, you would sleep for as long as you needed so you woke refreshed and ready to go. This, however, may not work with the commitments you have in your life. Two: *Being* an eternal warrior, you make the choice to get up at the same time each morning, then if you're tired that night, you go to bed earlier, and eventually your body will reprogram itself. The only way to prove this wrong is to try it for yourself. If you try it (honestly try it), you will find it works. If you are one of those people who has convinced themselves that they need fifteen hours of sleep, or some other number higher than eight, let me share with you that you don't. This is, however, what is in your head — you do need that many hours of sleep and you don't wish to change it. Well then, go to bed early enough to allow your body to have your desired amount of time to sleep. Easy, but not much of a life; however, the payoff is at least when you are awake, you have energy to do, feel and be alive.

Here is another little hint about sleeping. Get to bed early and get up early. If you go to bed late, still get up early anyway. You can prove to yourself that you can reprogram your body to do whatever you want, and if you do it enough, you will be jumping out of bed bursting with energy. If you want to magnify the experience, get out of bed and go immediately into exercising (well, get dressed first), or doing a program specifically designed to boost your energy levels like 409 Degrees – *Just hold it*. But a word of warning: if you get used to this, you will feel great, you will boost your metabolism and burn fat more effectively. The gym buddy I was talking about earlier in the book, we would get up at 5.00am and go straight to the gym together, then grab coffees or smoothies before starting our day at university. When we were sitting in the lecture room, we were literally bouncing out of our chairs with natural energy! We could not help but notice the faces and body positions of the other students around us who were not. Everyone else walked in, head down, shoulders slumped, looking at the floor, and in their eyes, they had that characteristic 'I just woke up' look. Trust me, you *will* start to notice the positive changes and feel great about them too.

Now, I don't mean to make it sound like every morning for me at university was that easy. On the contrary, that was my Honours year, and if you've been through an Honours year, you know what a back-breaking, soul-destroying year it can be at times. Added to this was the fact that I had to work night shift basically every night to make ends meet, so you can imagine my sleeping patterns (or lack thereof — classic self-supporting student lifestyle — work, university, work, university, spend money to eat, worry about money, work, university, sleep). Some mornings, I couldn't be bothered even thinking of the gym, let alone going! Which is when my gym buddy rocked up to my doorstep and said (in a very Lleyton Hewitt way), 'Come on!' Because I knew they were right and had made the effort to get up and be my support, so I went. Other days, it was my buddy who I'd prop up (two-way support), and on the rare occasion that neither of us could be bothered, bacon, eggs, tomato and mushrooms, and a long chat, was the backup plan, because it was felt we had both earned it. Now, because my gym buddy and I were both committed, this type of breakfast was eaten twice in a whole year. Some mornings, however, I recall being light-headed and feeling ill while trying to exercise. This is where you need to use your mind and listen to your gut feeling, which was saying to me: 'Stop', so I'd stop! Whatever I was doing, whether it was lifting heavy weights, speed ball, stretches or cardio, I listened and stopped doing that and tried something less demanding!

By doing this, you have already won because you are up early, have moved and breathed, and can enjoy the start of the day (like I did with my friend).

Chunking down or chunking up

If it (life, my recommendations or your stressors) all sounds all too much, then I recommend 'chunking down'. If, however, the opposite is true and it is not enough to excite you and get you passionately involved, then I recommend 'chunking up'. Let's use weight loss as an example to demonstrate what I mean. If you want to lose ten kilos but can't seem to find the inspiration to get up early, roll out of bed, do fifty crunches, sixty push-ups and a five-kilometre run, then that's fine. Recognise that this does not work for you, and instead, chunk it down. Rather than trying to do all of this at once, chunking down could be waking up early and focusing on breathing. That is, all you do is practise getting into the habit of waking up early and practising your breathing (e.g. any one of the breathing methods previously described). But you don't have to get out of bed to do it, and you don't have do anything else, just wake up and breathe! When you are ready, you can make the decision to chunk up a little, that is, once you are inspired to wake early and breathe on a regular basis, then chunking up could be deciding to get dressed in your sports gear, breathing and performing a seven-minute session of 409 Degrees – *Just hold it*. Once you do this on a regular basis, you may notice an increase in your energy, and then feel inspired to chunk up again and do some exercise, as discussed below. Either way, you still need to be able to work within your parameters, but the key point here is that you still need to change something.

Exercise

There is no substitute for it. If there was a pill available that gave you all the benefits without the need to do exercise, I still would not take that pill. Why? Because it is the doing part of exercise that feels good. And let's face it, if you don't exercise, you get out of shape, if you are out of shape, your health suffers big time, and it only gets harder to get back into shape. So the question you need to ask yourself is not 'Why you are out of shape?' but rather 'How much of a challenge do you want to get back into shape again?' I say 'get back into shape *again*' because at some point, even if it was in primary school, you were fit and healthy. There is a plethora of information out there about the positive effects of exercise, such as decreasing the risk of cardiovascular disease, decreasing the effects of diabetes, improving mood, and generally improving whatever condition it is you may have. There are, however, two key reasons why I believe you would want to exercise, which are mentioned in books, but rarely elaborated upon:

1. **Exercise releases endorphins**: if you don't know what these are, they are chemicals in your body that make you feel good — no, not good, I mean gooood! People spend thousands of dollars a year buying smack, crack, grass, booze or some other illicit substance to feel this good, and all you have to do is exercise (getting sweaty is just a bonus)! For a small monthly fee, you even get a place where you can go and get your high! These days there are numerous programs that you can purchase, like 409 Degrees – *Just hold it*, that you can do in the comfort of your own home. In all seriousness, if you get hooked on feeling good, whether you achieve it with 409 Degrees in your home, or at a gym, you should know that people make these specialised routines where they

give you access to all the gear you need to get this high! All you need to do is show up, walk in (with no shame or guilt because this addiction is gooooooood), supply the energy, and you get your high. I do not know any other addiction that has buildings specifically built for it such as gyms (yes, yes, pubs and clubs, but read on), where, when you go there, you are not judged, you benefit from it mentally, physically and emotionally, and you feel good. Not enough for you? There really is no judgement in gyms. You may feel paranoid that you are the only 'out of shape' one, but you are not, and don't forget that those 'in shape' people probably once started from where you are now. But more important than this, it's your choice what you choose to feel, as your coach I have explained throughout this book! Remember that only you can change your feelings, so make the choice, follow your gut, feel good and *Be* the eternal warrior. Still not enough? Okay.

2. **Exercise is fun:** let's face it, if you can get past the stage of 'It hurts' and 'It's too hard' and 'I can't do it' (because you can, we all can, accept it, stop wasting that energy on this energy-draining denial and direct it toward exercise), then it becomes fun. If you can last six weeks, you become addicted to it. That is, you now feel something is missing in your life if you don't do some form of exercise these days, and you feel alive and exuberant, strong and confident after you have. I want to point out here that there is also a difference between pain and good hurt. If you hang around a gym long enough, you will hear catch phrases like 'feel the burn' or 'good pain'. I remember driving one day with my gym buddy and his fiancée, and her telling me to stop pushing her man so hard because he was always sore. I was concerned at first because I thought my friend had been exercising with an injury (a great way to decrease the fun factor and not very clever). I turned to him immediately and asked what had happened, and he replied, 'Don't worry about it, it's good hurt.' To which I sighed a sigh of relief and his fiancée went crazy, informing us that no pain was good! I could now waste your time and my time and a chapter of this book trying to explain what 'good hurt' is, but you will never know unless you get off your bum and get out there performing 409 Degrees, running, get into the gym or anything — ride a bike, walk, jog, swim — anything! Then you will know.

Recall that it is your choice how you see things, and by following your gut feeling of feeling good, you create healthy bio-electric signals and cues, which are reinforced when you see things, such as exercise, as being fun. Not only do you influence your healthy bio-electric signals and cues with the subsequent healthy expression of you, you are more likely to continue doing things you see as fun to do, as opposed to those that you perceive as not fun. The key word here is 'perceive', as discussed previously. So, if running was never your thing and you don't enjoy running, well, don't run — try yoga, tai chi, rock climbing, 409 Degrees, *anything*. The point is to do something different and exercise so that you are moving your body in any way you can. If you want the energy to exercise first, check out my revolutionary healthcare and exercise program 409 Degrees — *Just hold it*, which is designed to stimulate your natural energy levels back to optimal levels by combining the wisdom of Chinese medicine and exercise physiology principles.

Here is the cautionary note with any exercise you choose to do: start small (chunking down) and then work big (chunk up). It is always best to start with 'chunking down' first. If you can't run five kilometres to begin with, then walk half a kilometre. Then as your fitness level increases, each and every time you exercise you can build it up (chunk up) bit by bit. It's like that ad that said, 'It won't happen overnight, but it will happen'. All you have to do is to do it!

Other key reasons why I believe we all would want to exercise — improved health at a glance. Exercise:

- increases efficiency of heart and lungs
- reduces cholesterol levels
- increases muscle strength
- reduces blood pressure
- reduces risk of major illnesses such as diabetes, heart disease and obesity
- improves appearance
- increases stamina and energy
- enhances social life
- improves sense of wellbeing.

These are just a few added benefits to your health that may be achieved from exercising, in addition to the increased endorphins and perceiving exercise as fun, as discussed above. The research supports the healthy benefits of exercising, so it makes sense to incorporate this into your life if you have not already done so. If you would like to read more about the benefits of exercise and embark on an inspiring lifestyle change, I recommend my 409 Degrees – *Just hold it* program, which I created when I made a choice to improve my physical and energetic health.

Drinking and diet (food and drink)

Drinking

By drinking, I am referring to alcohol. If you must drink alcohol for any reason, do it moderately, as recommended by the new national standards for drinking alcohol as proposed by the Australian Government (more detail at http://www.alcohol.gov.au/internet/alcohol/publishing.nsf/content/guide-adult). If you enjoy drinking, have you considered what would happen to your weekend (specifically Friday and Saturday nights) if you couldn't drink? What else could you do? Who could you do it with? Drinking alcohol has become so ingrained in Western cultures that it borders on being a pathological addiction. Binge drinking is done mindlessly, possibly because that's what everyone else does (your need to belong) — this is what you perceive in the circle of friends that you associate with. If you have this belief, then binge drinking becomes the expected thing, where you think you need to do it to be accepted, to feel as if you are part of some group, to belong. This behaviour continues until you make the choice to change your perceptions of binge drinking and the people you associate with who support this behaviour, or the side effects override the perceived benefits (cost becomes greater than your perceived payoff). You know, or at least are aware of, the negative effects associated with binge drinking on brain function, the mind, the liver and your life. The perceived benefits to engage in binge drinking, however, often outweigh the reality of the side effects that occur. This is another example of where perceptions (the reasons to binge drink) do not match the RUN (the documented side effects of excessive alcohol consumption). If this is an issue for you, you now know the tools you can use to create the necessary changes in your life. If you require further support you could call the National Alcohol and Other Drug Hotline for free and confidential advice about alcohol and other drugs on 1800 250 015. Other support services include beyond blue 1300 224 636, family drug support 1300 368 186, family relationship advice line 1800 050 321, life line 131 114, or suicide call back service 1300 659 467.

Diet

The origin of the word 'diet' refers to the types of food that you eat, not the modern-day misinterpretation of avoiding some kinds of food or restricting calories. All types of food are okay as long as they are not an allergic substance for you and are not indulged in excessively. Importantly, to qualify as 'food' there must be some life force in the food product. What do I mean by this? For example, an apple picked directly off the tree has maximum life force compared to an apple that has been picked, stored in cold storage for two weeks, shipped on a truck for two days, stored in the supermarket cool room for a week, and then picked by you from the supermarket shelf — this apple now has very little life force, although it still has some. However, a product that is completely processed and is no longer recognisable as its natural form has no life force at all. For example, with breakfast cereals, manufactures have to add back some minerals (not all, as it would possibly be too expensive and reduce the company's profits) to their now devitalised product, which had initially existed in its original vital form! Real corn picked fresh does not look like brand X corn flakes that come out of a box, which will have less life force than real corn! I encourage you to take the time to read what's listed as the nutritional content on the packet of a common breakfast cereal that contains, for example, wheat, and then compare this to whole wheat. You will be surprised what's missing in the breakfast cereal! This, of course, is true of all processed foods.

The second issue around diet for you may be that you do not actually know when you are hungry. Do you recall what it is to be hungry? You may eat because it is time to eat and not because you actually have an appetite. If this is you, then play with your body and reconnect with the type and quantity of food your body really wants, and remember, nothing tastes as good as a strong, fit and healthy body feels. This is where you need to go with your gut feeling and really listen to the 'not good' feeling, which you tend to ignore when it comes to overeating food.

Communication

Above all else in this world, learn how to communicate, as discussed with creating *relationships* and your *How to effectively communicate with [insert spouse's/partner's name here]* that you wrote in chapter 14 (if you haven't written this yet, I encourage you to do so). As I have stated previously, communication is not a function of what is being said, it is a function of what is being received. You spend a lot of time trying to find different ways to say things, but the only thing we really need to ever say is 'Do you understand me?' Any time you hear silence from someone, dare to ask if they understand you correctly, as it saves hurt feelings, misunderstandings, and bad times later, all of which are unhealthy bio-electric signals and cues that can be avoided by asking this question. Better still, if you were already *Being* the eternal warrior, at your optimal self and living your life's purpose, receiving information would occur seamlessly, and you would without hesitation repeat the message to the person communicating that message so that you can clarify with them what they had wanted you to hear.

Keys to successful communication include freeing up time (time is still an illusion, but a necessary one) and space to speak openly, honestly, and authentically with people. Can you recall the number of times that you have truly sat down and tried to speak from the heart about a topic, only to be interrupted by something, whether it's time to pick up your children or a phone call, or having to finish dinner — or maybe you didn't actually get to that point to begin with? These are all distractions to effective communication. So, the first thing to consider for effective communication is to *always clear the space* for communication to occur, and make certain there are no distractions for you or the other person.

Secondly, it is essential to leave judgements, dishonesty and lies at the door. It is impossible to hear what someone is trying to tell you or communicate to you if you are judging it as it is coming out of their mouth. Likewise, it is impossible to hear if we believe that whatever is being communicated is not honest or authentic. Remember to 'get yourself out of the way' and hear what is going on for them. Listen as intently as you can. Recall that communicating is a function of what is received.

Thirdly, listen to what is really being said. If you are being the eternal worrier, this is harder than the previous two points because you are being asked to actively listen to what is being said, and not just waiting for your chance to speak or defend yourself! This is not a problem, provided you have made your choice to be an eternal warrior, and I hope that you are now in the process of converting the information contained within this book into wisdom (action). By implementing some of the new techniques, modalities and ideas from this book, it will be easy. Also, you can apply all other ROAs to ease your passage from being the eternal worrier to *Being* an eternal warrior.

Fourthly, reframe what is being said so that you are completely sure that what you have understood was what was being said.

Fifthly, use examples to illustrate your communication — the more specific and more detailed the better. This has to be done from a place of non-judgement and love.

Otherwise, it can come across as blame.

Finally, don't be an *already-always-listening person*. This is a person who knows what the other person is going to say, even before they have said it, and if you listen from this place, it is a sure way of not hearing anything, making it extra hard for others, such as your partner or friends, to reach you because they may be saying something totally different to what you thought they were going to say, or the exact same thing you thought they were going to say, but with a different feel, or anything in between these two options. If you are an *already-always-listening person*, you will miss this communication.

Rest (mentally and physically)

A change is as good as a holiday, and your mind and body know this. Every single one of us has the ability to 'push on through'. The question that needs to be asked here is, is it appropriate? Follow your gut feeling — does pushing through feel 'good' or 'not good'? When you need to dig deep, you need to dig deep, and when you need to rest, you need to rest. Your gut feeling is a good guide to assist you through these times. All aspects of your life require rest, and it is your sole responsibility to get it. No one else will rest up for you. You have to acknowledge that you require down time, and then you need to give yourself permission to enjoy that down time or do something you enjoy. What is the point of living your entire life if you cannot rest up one day? Work hard and rest when appropriate. This will make you better able to go harder or dig deeper the next time you need to. Rest is the reset button for the BodyMind complex (as I refer to it in FlameTree), and we need to push it occasionally.

Sunlight

Sunlight is essential for you. There has never been a report that has said 'sunlight is bad'. All of the reports that are painted with that brush start with 'excess' or 'too much', or the real issue, 'sunburn'. Now sunburn is bad, and there is a multitude of evidence out there now that categorically proves being burned is bad for your health. However, small doses of sunlight (without the burning) are essential for you! Exposure of your skin (the largest organ of your body) to sunlight aids your body in producing vitamin D, which is essential in the prevention of rickets (which results from decreased sunlight exposure) and various other diseases, including certain cancers. Exposure to sun seems to also be a natural requirement of the body for harmonising moods and feelings. The advent of seasonal affective disorders (SADs) seems the very validation of the link between sunlight and moods. People report more depression and sadness in the winter months, and these same people report increased feelings of wellbeing in the months with greater sunlight. People are treating SADs with full spectrum light bulbs (bulbs that emit the full light spectrum found in natural light), and the results from such treatments reinforce that people feel better when they are exposed to the full range of natural light. The point here is that small amounts of sunlight, without getting burned, are essential for good health and good life.

Stable *real*ationship with your true partner

'Playing the field' is a waste of time and energy! Remember, if two people are committed to a *real*ationship and not invested in it, it will always work. The stable part of the *real*ationship, however, translates to a little bit of work if you are not accustomed to it. The two people in the *real*ationship must have similar values and must be committed to working on the *real*ationship, the communication in the relationship, and the velocity (speed and direction) of the *real*ationship as previously discussed. Having a true partner in life is to have true love that will never shift, and will offer true support for you to be able to say and do anything you need or want and to feel free of judgements or fear. Judgement and fear are the antithesis of a stable relationship.

Education

You really can never have enough. Education is a great power, and with great power comes great responsibility, including the power to contribute to making a change in the world. A hero changes the world for the better and education allows you to do this, so education is a hero's journey. The information contained within this book is an educational resource for you that, when applied (wisdom), may assist you to create the changes in your life so that you too can contribute to making change in the world by *Being* the eternal warrior, with healthy bio-electric signals and cues that create the possibility to live your life optimally and purposefully.

The take-home message — your transformation from eternal *worrier* to eternal *warrior*

The *eternal worrier smiles* because they believe many things can be done tomorrow, as they have the belief that they will always have time to do it later. They are in fact clueless to what they would do if they actually had limited time, because they believe they always have a lot of time. The eternal worrier smiles because they are not aware of the priorities in their life. By not being aware of their priorities, they are not prepared to look 'strange' or challenge the status quo by saying what needs to be said the moment it needs to be said. They smile because many things that should be said in their lives go unsaid, and people around them remain unsure of their place or meaning to that worrier.

The eternal worrier smiles because they take time out or believe they need time alone, and as such believe they are separate from everyone else, ignoring their intimate connection to everything else. They smile because they allow their body to dictate their sleep and life cycle, and because of that they do not have a routine. Their day is haphazard and unplanned. They become overwhelmed by simple problems and are not aware of the concept of chunking them up or down, based on assessing their situation. Even if they are aware of this, they choose not to implement these concepts. The eternal worrier lets their body fall away by not exercising, because they believe exercise is either too hard or they do not have the time to do it, although they think they have unlimited time to do things tomorrow! They ignore their body and eat when they think they are hungry. They smile because they give their body any type of food, usually in excess, which makes them feel good or comforts them temporarily, only to have to repeat eating these things again so that they keep that feeling. They smile because they drink alcohol in excess so that they feel good, or to fit into their group.

The eternal worrier lives to eat, not eats to live. The eternal worrier smiles because, when someone else does not understand their communication, it means the other person was wrong. They waste much of their life blaming others for getting it wrong or misunderstanding them, rather than working at ensuring people are on the same page as them. They do not know the value of effective communication, and as such, fail to clear the space, have many judgements, and listen passively. They smile because they do not reframe scenarios to understand what is being said, fail to use examples to illustrate their point, and usually fall victim to being *already-always-listening*, and therefore miss out on valuable communication, but they still get to blame others! The eternal worrier smiles because they think that it is okay to tell white lies and push themselves to extremes without appropriate rest, that sunburn is good because you 'tan up' after a burn, and they allow unstable relationships to be created that generate drama in their lives, which puts them in the position to blame other people for not achieving their best.

The eternal worrier smiles because they are prepared to accept any type of relationship where values may not align and the other person might be invested in an outcome (e.g. sleeping with them to get another 'notch on their belt'). They fail to see the value in education, and do not have to try and improve themselves. Therefore, they continue to blame others and their environment for where they end up in their life. They are unaware that their actions are creating and reinforcing unhealthy bio-electric signals and cues that can become self-sustaining through their unhealthy biofield, which allows for the ongoing unhealthy expression of their bio-electric code, not allowing them to reach their optimal self or live their authentic life of purpose.

The *eternal warrior smiles* because they know the answer to the question 'How much time do we have?' is 'Not a lot!' But they also know that time is a man-made illusion, and as such they smile because they know exactly what they would do if they had limited to no time. They are aware of the priorities in their life and realise that time does not exist. This means they are prepared to look strange or challenge the status quo by saying what needs to be said the moment it needs to be said. They smile because they realise there is no such thing as time out or time alone, as we are all intimately connected.

The eternal warrior smiles because they get up at the same time every morning and have a routine that works to maximise their day. They approach problems by chunking them up or down depending on the situation. They exercise because they feel good, look good, and have increased stamina, improved energy levels, a better social life and an improved sense of wellbeing. They smile because they listen to their innate wisdom and eat when they are hungry and give their body the types of foods it needs in moderation. They drink alcohol moderately (if at all) and eat to live, not live to eat.

The eternal warrior smiles because they know that communication is a function of what is received. They smile because effective communication saves time and decreases misunderstandings, and they know that by asking simple questions like 'Do you understand me?', they eliminate the chances of being misunderstood. To assist with effective communication, the eternal warrior clears the space, leaves judgements at the door and actively listens. They smile because they reframe scenarios to understand what is being said, use examples to illustrate their point and never fall victim to being *already-always-listening*.

The eternal warrior smiles because they know when it is appropriate to rest, that sunlight is good and sunburn is not, that stable *real*ationships are essential to happiness and should be based on similar values, where both people are committed and not invested. They smile because they know the value of education and they know how to apply it within their life. They know that this collectively creates and reinforces their healthy bio-electric signals and cues, which can become self-sustaining through their healthy biofield and allow for the ongoing healthy expression of their bio-electric code and genes, thereby allowing them to reach their optimal self and live their authentic life of purpose.

CHAPTER 17

Be the blue stool

If a blue stool could speak, what would it tell you? I believe, if it was a healthy, non-complicated stool, it would tell you something like, 'I am a blue stool, that is all I am and I am okay with that!' Now the important part here is that a blue stool can think it's a red stool, but it's not. The blue stool can think it's a blue bird, but it's not, or it might think it's a red bird, but it's not. The blue stool will always be a blue stool. Even if someone paints it red, underneath it's still a blue stool. It was made to be a blue stool, and no amount of lying about what it is will change that.

The point I am making here is that the stool's journey is to learn and accept, and more importantly, be honest and authentic with itself, that it is a blue stool. Any other course of action will only result in unhealthy bio-electric signals and cues, which, if the blue stool does not become aware of it, through resonance, will only attract further unhealthy bio-electric signals and cues, which results in an unhealthy biofield. Unless the blue stool becomes aware and creates change immediately, an unhealthy biofield becomes self-sustaining, and results in the unhealthy expression of its bio-electric code and genes, which keeps the blue stool in its misguided place and prevents it from receiving the healthy transmission for a blue stool.

Along the way, the blue stool must learn not to be what others want it to be, and that lying to itself will not change its unhealthy biofield, nor the outcome of what it is or the outcome of its journey through its life. Said another way, if someone wants a red armchair in their lounge and the blue stool pretends to be that armchair (because it hates to see people go without, or because it always wanted to be a red chair, or because the person means a lot to them and they just want them to be happy, or whatever reason the blue stool uses to justify to itself for trying to be something that it's not), the blue stool would still be a blue stool! When the blue stool died, on its death bed, the blue stool would die a blue stool (not a red armchair or anything else it tried to be), and if the blue stool had a moment of clarity just before it died, it would realise that it had not lived its life optimally or purposefully as it could have, because somewhere deep down, the blue stool knew that it was not a red armchair or any other thing it tried to be.

In other words, it doesn't matter what others think you should be, what or who you pretend to be to appease or make others happy, or even whether you get lost on your path. You will always find yourself again, that is, you will become what you were made or destined to be, based on the Uni-code or universal plan, as previously discussed.

You need to be aware of the 'you' programming and change it, but this can only come through *Being* conscious (aware). Now that I have made you aware of this fact, how much pressure does it take off your life? Do you understand my point here with the blue stool analogy? You can't stuff it up! You may stuff up along the way in your attempt to understand yourself and your life, but eventually your path, lessons and journey will reveal themselves to you. All that you have to do is to accept who you are when you learn what that is! Like the blue stool learning to accept that it is a blue stool, be like the blue stool, my friend, and learn to accept yourself.

The take-home message — your transformation from eternal *worrier* to eternal *warrior*

The *eternal worrier smiles* because they think that a blue stool can pretend to be a red armchair.

The *eternal warrior smiles* because they accept that a blue stool is a blue stool and they make a conscious choice of observing the blue stool *Being* an optimal blue stool, and living purposefully as a blue stool, emitting only healthy bio-electric signals and cues and raising its own frequency, as well as that of their environment and via resonance assisting them to achieve the same.

CONCLUSION

From being an eternal worrier to Being an eternal warrior

To transform from being an eternal worrier into Being an eternal warrior, you need to:

- practise the four elements of the awakening process
- live by Being in alignment, synergy, authenticity and synergism
- use the four elements of the Law of Creation (resonance, coherence, consonance and respect) and the other elements of actively listening and feeling, thinking, Being, saying, doing and having (creating and manifesting)
- consciously be aware of what you are feeling and thinking and therefore transmitting
- live unfiltered
- pave the way to your world by following the actions in chapter 16
- never blame or justify — anytime you complain (an unhealthy bio-electric signal and cue), you attract to yourself exactly what you are complaining about
- never compare yourself to others — every one of us has our own journey and we cannot take anyone else's journey for them; everything has its own unique frequency fingerprint, including you
- accept, understand and be excited that you create your life— yes, *you*
- play to win — remember there are no rules, except the ones you make
- commit, commit, commit to devoting yourself unreservedly to anything that you want to be successful
- persist, persist, persist, and never let anyone else make you question your goals or aspirations
- actively be the warrior and take action

- feel big, and as one door closes, look for another door or window opening (look for opportunities)
- admire and associate with those you wish to be like
- do what works for you and be unreasonable
- act in spite of fear (fear is the flip side of excitement, that is, if a frown is a smile upside down, fear is excitement looked at the wrong way). Use technologies such as ROAs to make this easier
- get out of your comfort zone and learn to grow — your comfort zone may be comfortable, but it is boring
- walk the path — there is a difference between 'knowing the path' and 'walking the path'. Knowing all the academic information in this book and expecting it to change your life will not work. Walking the path requires action, patience, faith, trust, practice and commitment
- use (if needed) the three step check in, the three steps to change your station, or the three steps to effectively communicate your needs
- use any of the ROAs
- walk the walk, if you talk the talk. That is, who listens to an obese doctor who says lose weight? No one! Be authentic. Be you. Be eternal. Be the warrior.

If you want results, and I am sure that you do as you have made it this far through the book (unless you jumped straight to the conclusion, in which case I recommend you go back to the beginning so that you can understand the next sentence!), you have to actually start participating in your life. You need to create and manifest the change from being the eternal worrier to *Being* the eternal warrior so that you create, transmit and receive healthy bio-electric signals and cues, which results in a healthy self-sustaining biofield and the subsequent expression of your bio-electric code and genes so that you are able to be the optimal expression of who you are *Being*, and living your life in alignment, synergy, authenticity and synergism, and purposefully living life. This is exactly what this book is about — seamlessly incorporating knowledge into your lifestyle to create changes in your beliefs, which can be interpreted as healthy bio-electric signals and cues. Knowledge is power, but knowledge applied is wisdom!

The take-home message — your transformation from eternal *worrier* to eternal *warrior*

The *eternal worrier smiles* because they do not have to do anything to change their lives and they blame others and not themselves for the outcomes that are created or manifested in their life. As such, they are immersed in unhealthy bio-electric signals and cues, with the consequences from creating, reinforcing, transmitting and receiving these unhealthy bio-electric signals and cues.

The *eternal warrior smiles* because they now have many answers and solutions to problems that they encounter in life. They smile because they are excited and inspired about making all the changes in their life that are suggested in this book after using the four elements of the awakening process. They also smile because they can actively listen & feel, think, *Be*, say, do, feel while incorporating information from the four elements of *Being*, the four elements of the Law of Creation and the unfiltered five senses and have (create and manifest) a life of power, abundance, inner peace and love for them while they are living to their fullest potential in every way. When they need to, they can implement the three step check in, the three steps to change your station and the three steps for effective communication or any of the ROAs. As such, they choose to immerse themselves in healthy bio-electric signals and cues, with the consequences from creating, reinforcing, transmitting and receiving these healthy bio-electric signals and cues to live optimally and purposefully. Dare to be the *eternal warrior and achieve the eternal warrior's smile!*

References

About the author
1. Socrates – Apology of Socrates. (All the words we attribute to Socrates actually come from Plato).

2. Plato – Plato's Aesthetics.

3. Plato, *Seventh Letter.*

Introduction
1. Tracey, B 2005. *Something for nothing*, Nelson Current.

2. Stein, DJ, Newman, TK, Savitz J and Ramesar, R 2006. Warriors versus worriers: The role of COMT gene variants, cited by *5Get access*, vol. 11 no. 10 pp. 745–748.

Chapter 1
1. https://www.quora.com/Do-babies-experience-fear-What-makes-us-fear.

2. Feynman, R 1988. *The making of a scientist*, p. 16.

3. Pearce, JC 2016. Honoring the innate potential, *Pathways to Family Wellness*, Issue 51, Fall.

4. Rand, A 1957, *Atlas shrugged*, Random House, p. 1012.

Chapter 3
1. Ropeik, D 2004. The consequences of fear. *EMBO Reports*, vol. 5 (Suppl 1): S56–S60. doi: 10.1038/sj.embor.7400228

2. Maciocia, G 1995. *The foundations of Chinese medicine*, Churchill Livingston, p. 132.

3. Ivey, AC 1933, The effect of worry on digestion, *The Scientific Monthly*, vol. XXVII no. 3 pp. 266–69.

4. Kubzansky, LD, Kawachi, I, Spiro, A, Weiss, ST, Vokonas, PS and Sparrow, D 1997. Is worrying bad for your heart? A prospective study of worry and coronary heart disease in the normative aging study, *Circulation.*, vol. 95 no. 4

5. Maciocia, op cit.

6. Duke University Medical Center 2004. Anger, hostility and depressive symptoms linked to high C-reactive protein levels, *ScienceDaily*.

7. Victorian State Government. Better Health Channel. https://www.betterhealth.vic.gov.au/health/healthyliving/anger-how-it-affects-people

8. Maciocia, op cit.

9. Buckley, T, Sunari, D, Marshall, A, Bartrop, R, McKinley, S and Tofler, G 2012. Physiological correlates of bereavement and the impact of bereavement interventions. *Dialogues in Clinical Neuroscience*, vol. 14 no. 2 pp. 129–139.

10. State Administration for Traditional Chinese Medicine 1995. *Advanced textbook on traditional Chinese medicine and pharmacology Vol 1*, New Word Press Beijing, China.

11. Schwartz, GE, Weinberger, DA and Singer, JA 1981. Cardiovascular differentiation of happiness, sadness, anger, and fear following imagery and exercise. *Psychosom Med*, vol. 43 no. 4 pp. 343-64.

12. Kuczynski, John-Michael 2012. *Empiricism and the foundations of psychology*, John Benjamins Publishing, p. 261.

13. Maciocia, op cit.

14. State Administration for Traditional Chinese Medicine, op cit.

15. Melamed, S, Shirom, A, Toker, S, Berliner, S and Shapira, I 2004. Association of fear of terror with low-grade inflammation among apparently healthy employed adults, *Psychosomatic Medicine*, vol. 66 no. 4 pp. 484–491.

Chapter 4
1. Lipton, B 2005, *The biology of belief*, Hay House.

2. Ibid

3. Ibid

4. Cairns, J, Overbaugh, J and Miller, S 1988. The origin of mutants, Nature, vol. 335 no. 6186 pp. 142–5.

5. https://ase.tufts.edu/biology/labs/levin/research/spatial.htm

6. https://www.ebi.ac.uk/research/goldman/dna-storage; https://www.nature.com/news/how-dna-could-store-all-the-world-s-

data-1.20496; Extance, A 2016, How DNA could store all the world's data, *Nature*, 31 August, Corrected 2 September.

7. Cairns, op cit.

8. Ćosić, I, Chien, M and Behrenbruch, C 1998, Shared frequency components between Schumann resonances, EEG spectra and acupuncture meridian transfer function, *Acupuncture & Electro-Therapeutics Research*, vol. 23, no. 1

9. Ibid

10. Liboff, A 2004. Toward an electromagnetic paradigm for biology and medicine, *The Journal of Alternative and Complementary Medicine*, vol. 10 no. 1 pp. 41–47.

11. WHO. Extremely low frequency fields. Environmental Health Criteria Monograph No. 238, http://www.who.int/peh-emf/publications/elf_ehc/en/; cited from Singh, S and Kapoor, N 2014. Health implications of electromagnetic fields, mechanisms of action, and research needs, *Advances in Biology,* vol. 2014.

12. Bellieni, CV, Pinto, I, Bogi, A, Zoppetti, N, Andreuccetti, D and Buonocore, G 2012. Exposure to electromagnetic fields from laptop use of 'laptop' computers, *Archives of Environmental & Occupational Health*, vol. 67 no. 1.

13. Tseng, AS & Levin, M 2013. Cracking the bioelectric code: Probing endogenous ionic controls of pattern formation, *Communicative & Integrated Biology*, vol. 6 no. 1

14. Folcher, M et al 2014. Mind-controlled transgene expression by a wireless-powered optogenetic designer cell implant, *Nature Communications*, vol. 5 no. 11

15. Ibid.

16. Ibid.

17. Ornish, D et al 2013. Effect of comprehensive lifestyle changes on telomerase activity and telomere length in men with biopsy-proven low-risk prostate cancer: 5-year follow-up of a descriptive pilot study, *Lancet Oncology*, vol. 14 no. 11 pp. 1112–1120.

18. Carlson, LE et al 2014, Mindfulness-based cancer recovery and supportive-expressive therapy maintain telomere length relative to controls in distressed breast cancer survivors, *Cancer*, vol. 121 no.3 pp. 476-84.

19. Kelsey, SC 2011, *Qualification and quantification of telomeric elongation due to electromagnetic resonance exposure*, Department of Biomedical Sciences, Missouri State University.

Chapter 5
1. Epictetus (c 135 AD), *The Enchiridion*.

2. Ropeik, D, op cit.

3. Mohrhoff, UJ 2008. Sri Aurobindo International Centre of Education. Evolution of consciousness according to Jean Gebser, *ANTIMATTERS*, 2 (3).

4. Ibid.

5. Ibid.

6. Berkeley, G 1713. *Three dialogues between Hylas and Philonous*, Broadview Press.

7. Lanza, R with Berman, B 2009. *Biocentrism: How life and consciousness are the keys to understanding the true nature of the universe*, Benbella Books, Dallas, TX.

Chapter 6
1. https://onlinelibrary.wiley.com/doi/abs/10.1002/qua.560020505

2. Tuszynski, JA and Kurzynski, M 2003. *Introduction to molecular biophysics*, CRC Press, p. 145.

3. Benzoic, JL et al. 1988. *Ann. Rev. Cell Biol*, vol. 4 pp. 405–428; Lefkowitz, RJ et al. 1980 *Curr. Top. Cell. Regul*, vol. 17 pp. 205–230.

4. Lefkowitz, op cit.

5. Xu, Z et al 2007. Effects of enriched environment on morphine-induced reward in mice, *Experimental Neurology*, vol. 204 no. 2 pp. 714–9.

6. Feinstein, D and Eden, D 2008. Six pillars of energy medicine: clinical strengths of a complementary paradigm, *Alternative Therapies in Health and Medicine*; Jan/Feb, 14, 1.

Chapter 7
1. *Sylvia, C and Noval, W 1997. A change of heart: A memoir*.

2. *Mail Online*, 9 April 2008.

3. Miguel, N TEDMED 2012,
    https://www.ted.com/talks/miguel_nicolelis_a_monkey_that_controls_a
    _robot_with_its_thoughts_no_really

4. International Congress: 'Science Information, Spirit', St Petersburg 2001.

5. Prendergast, L et al 2011. **Premitotic Assembly of Human CENPs -T and -W
    Switches Centromeric Chromatin to a Mitotic State.** *PLoS Biology*, vol. 9 no.
    6, https://www.ncbi.nlm.nih.gov/pmc/articles/PMC3114758/

6. Ćosić, op cit.

7. Lanza, op cit.

8. Lipton, op cit.

Chapter 8
1. Doidge, N 2018, *The power of thought, updates in brain plasticity*, Conference
    hand out, Melbourne, pp. 21–22.
2. Ibid.

3. Ćosić, op cit.

4. Tuszynski, op cit.

5. Ibid.

6. Garland, EL et al 2010. Upward spirals of positive emotions counter
    downward spirals of negativity: Insights from the broaden-and-build
    theory and affective neuroscience on the treatment of emotion dysfunctions
    and deficits in psychopathology. *Clinical Psychology Review*, vol. 30 pp. 849–
    864.

7. McClare, CW 1974. Resonance in bio-energetics, *Annals of the New York
    Academy of Science*, vol. 227 pp. 74-97.

8. Garland, op cit.

9. Clavell, J 1975. *Shogun: Volume 1*,
    https://hardlywritten.wordpress.com/2011/01/27/shogun/.

Chapter 9
1. Lipton, op cit.

Chapter 10

1.   de Chardin, T 1965. *The phenomenon of man*, revised english translation, Harper and Row.

Chapter 11
1.   Emoto, M 2010. *The Message from Water*, Hay House.

Chapter 12
1.   Cryan, JF and O'Mahony, SM 2011. The microbiome-gut-brain axis: from bowel to behavior. *Neurogastroenterology & Motility*, vol. 23 pp. 187–192.

Chapter 13

1.   Shaw, GB 1903. Maxims for revolutionists, stated in *Man and Superman*.

2.   Csikszentmihalyi, M 2008, *Flow: The psychology of optimal experience.* HarperCollins Publishers Inc

Chapter 14

1.   Ackerman, D 1994. *A natural history of love.* Vintage.

2.   Moullin, S, Waldfogel, J and Washbrook, E 2014. *Baby bonds: Parenting, attachment and a secure base for children*, Research for The Sutton Trust.

3.   Kleinke, CL 1977. Compliance to requests made by gazing and touching experimenters in field settings, *Journal of Experimental Social Psychology*, vol. 13 no. 2 pp. 218-223

4.   Lipton, op cit.

5.   Quong, R 1968. *Chinese Characters: Their Wit and Wisdom*, Cobble Hill Press.

Chapter 16
1.   Levy, M. *Et si c'était vrai..., Vous revoir, édition complète 2 en 1.* Versilio.

Rhett Ogston

SHAWLINE
PUBLISHING
GROUP

www.shawlinepublishing.com.au